CELEBRITY AND ENTERTAINMENT OBSESSION

CELEBRITY AND ENTERTAINMENT OBSESSION

Understanding Our Addiction

Michael S. Levy

ROWMAN & LITTLEFIELD
Lanham • Boulder • New York • London

Published by Rowman & Littlefield
A wholly owned subsidary of The Rowman & Littlefield Publishing Group, Inc.
4501 Forbes Boulevard, Suite 200, Lanham, Maryland 20706
www.rowman.com

Unit A, Whitacre Mews, 26-34 Stannary Street, London SE11 4AB

British Library Cataloguing in Publication Information Available

Library of Congress Cataloging-in-Publication Data

Levy, Michael S., 1953–
Celebrity and entertainment obsession : understanding our addiction / Michael S. Levy.
pages cm
Includes bibliographical references and index.
ISBN 978-1-4422-4312-5 (cloth : alk. paper) — ISBN 978-1-4422-4313-2 (electronic)
Celebrities. 2. Fans (Persons)—Psychology. 3. Fame—Psychological aspects. I. Title.
HM621.L488 2015
305.5'2—dc23
2015006197

∞ ™ The paper used in this publication meets the minimum requirements of American National Standard for Information Sciences Permanence of Paper for Printed Library Materials, ANSI/NISO Z39.48-1992.

Printed in the United States of America

CONTENTS

INTRODUCTION

The hero was distinguished by his achievement; the celebrity by his image or trademark. The hero created himself; the celebrity is created by the media. The hero was a big man; the celebrity is a big name. —Daniel Boorstin

When the century started, famous people were still required, as of old, to do something first and then get famous for it later. As the century progressed, people who became famous for what they did got more famous just for being famous. —Clive James

Celebrity-worship and hero-worship should not be confused. Yet we confuse them every day, and by doing so we come dangerously close to depriving ourselves of all real models. We lose sight of the men and women who do not simply seem great because they are famous but are famous because they are great. We come closer and closer to degrading all fame into notoriety. —Daniel Boorstin

In America, we are never denied the opportunity to amuse ourselves. —Neil Postman

As a psychologist, I am fascinated by people—how we think, what we do, what interests us, and what drives us to act in certain ways regardless of how outlandish our actions may be. What first attracted me to the field of psychology was the realization that how we think and what motivates our behavior is what drives the world. People can behave very strangely: a 40-year-old teacher who sends nude photos of herself to one of her students, the married man who carries on affairs with other women while thinking his wife will never find out and then gets caught and pleads for her mercy, or the person who commits murder over some disparaging comment. I can go on and on—the things we do never cease to amaze me.

While those are individual actions that many people engage in, there are more general motifs that define us as a species, such as our level of aggression, our need for power, our love of drugs and the need to alter our consciousness, our relentless pursuit of wealth, our unquestioning belief in God and adherence to religious ideology, and our overpowering sexual feelings.

Among our peculiarities is another fascinating idiosyncrasy that concerns why we as a society are obsessed, captivated by, and enamored with people who work in the entertainment field—movies and television in particular. Also included are singers, musicians, people on reality television, and sports figures—people who we have made into *celebrities*. While all celebrities are famous, not all famous people are celebrities. Being a celebrity entails not only being well known but also in others' having great interest in them. Celebrities are attention-grabbers. We are infatuated both with being entertained and with the people who entertain us.

This obsession even extends to many people who appear in the media and who are famous solely for being famous or simply known for their well-knownness.[1] While we know very little about these individuals (except what we read), we are nonetheless fascinated by them, and they become direct objects of our attention. The media—major newspapers, tabloids, magazines, television news stations, late-night entertainment, celebrity television shows, or the Internet—all focus on celebrity comings and goings—the clothes they wear, who they're dating, the babies they birth, where they dine, with whom they're having an affair, whom they're marrying or divorcing, their legal problems, their drug or alcohol problems, and any other piece of information that can be ascertained. Even celebrity photographs can generate huge sums of money. *Forbes* put together a list of the most expensive photos during the past 10 years, and some generated over $4 million.[2] Celebrities also advertise and market a variety of products, as their appeal is so enormous, and many have successfully launched their own line of merchandise—clothing, cosmetics, and jewelry.

It is baffling to consider why certain people, only because of their chosen profession, are excessively revered—and even adored—and this adoration sometimes has very little to do with significant talent. And even when there is talent, the adoration that is bestowed on them is over and beyond their level of talent and what they offer to us and to the world at large. Acting, in particular, while it is a skill, is not a talent necessarily that takes years to hone.

In 2010, Gabourey Sidibe, an actress with limited experience, appeared in the film *Precious*, for which she won a Golden Globe award, as did Meryl Streep, for her role in *Julie and Julia*, who is a seasoned actress with years and years of experience. Haing Ngor, who had no acting experience, won an Oscar in 1984 for the best supporting actor for his role in *The Killing Fields*. Anna Paquin also won an Oscar in 1993 for the best supporting actress for her role in *The Piano* despite having no prior acting experience. Another Oscar winner with no prior acting experience, Harold Russell, won the best supporting actor in 1947 for his role in the film *The Best Years of Our Lives*. Given Ms. Sidibe's, Mr. Ngor's, Ms. Paquin's, and Mr. Russell's limited acting experience, can acting be that incredibly difficult? Katharine Hepburn aptly illustrates this point: "The most minor gifts and not a very high class way to earn a living. After all, Shirley Temple could do it at the age of four." Our celebrity captivation seems out of proportion.

While outstanding talent exists among some of our most revered actors and actresses, not everyone in the industry merits the same recognition. Community theater generates some excellent talent, but few receive major recognition and do not have celebrity status. So it can't be acting per se that is the critical variable. Even if acting were an arduous undertaking, it's unthinkable that individuals who work in the entertainment field and become known would get recognition and adoration over and beyond that of a competent brain surgeon who saves people's lives. Only the entertainment field instantaneously propels people to celebrity status. Conversely, the pathologist who has worked for years toward the advancement of cancer treatment and finally makes an important discovery will never achieve the celebrity status of the actor. Nor will an architect's new building design lead to celebrity-hood. Even the lawyer who frees an innocent person previously convicted and imprisoned for first-degree murder will not garner the same attention granted movie actors. Except for a brief news story covered in the media, fame is nonexistent unless the person he or she was defending had celebrity status. Nor will the chief executive officer (CEO) of a nonprofit organization make it on the celebrity circuit, even if he or she spent 20 years building a company that helps thousands of people expand services and revenue 100-fold.

Among today's celebrities are people involved in the sporting industry. Although many athletes possess great skill, the recognition they receive is significantly greater than what people who excel in other occupations obtain. Their fans parade around in jerseys with the names of their favorite athletes, but nobody wears a jersey promoting the name of a talented doctor, car mechanic, architect, or CEO.

During the past 100 years, our focus has shifted regarding *who* merits celebrity status. In the past, while there are exceptions, such as kings and queens and other royalty, those individuals who achieved celebrity status actually accomplished something of significance and *gradually* achieved celebrity status. Some examples include the following: Thomas Edison, Albert Einstein, Abraham Lincoln, George Washington, Dr. Martin Luther King Jr., and Mahatma Gandhi, to name just a handful. This kind of fame and celebrity status evolved over time; as their achievements expanded and as more and more people began to hear about them, their status as celebrities grew and developed.

A change began to occur during the course of the twentieth century with the instant achievement of celebrity status. No longer were celebrities men or women of great accomplishment who had given the world something to be proud of and to celebrate, but now it was people involved in the world of light entertainment, even including people who transmit news to us over television, or newscasters. The interest in political figures, inventors, writers of serious literature, fine arts, dance, and theater took the backstage.

The shift in who we are enamored with can be seen in the following: from 1901 to 1914 in the *Saturday Evening Post* and *Collier's*, 74 percent of the people who were written about were in politics, business, and the professions. Feature stories included the president of the United States, a governor, the secretary of state, J. P. Morgan, a banker, an aviation pioneer, a scientist, the secretary of the treasury, the inventor of the torpedo, a black educator, a writer, an opera singer, and a poet. But from 1922 to 1941, the percentage of serious coverage shrank to less than 50 percent when the world of entertainment began to take center stage. During the 1940s, the largest group consisted of individuals like Jack Johnson (the boxer), actors, actresses, nightclub entertainer Adelaide Moffett, and the gorilla Toto.[3]

This change can also be seen in simply asking people whom they most admire. Beginning about 75 years ago, the Gallup Poll began conducting a survey that asked people which man they most admire. Sixty years ago, the results of a Gallup Poll about whom people most admire listed such luminaries as Albert Einstein, Thomas Dewey, Winston Churchill, President Dwight D. Eisenhower, and Douglas MacArthur. Move forward 15 years to 1963, and we have the following: Albert Schweitzer, Adlai Stevenson, Charles de Gaulle, President John F. Kennedy, and Pope Paul VI. Not one entertainer, sports star, or media personality made the list. But fast-forward to 2000–2009, and we have stars like Bono, Glenn Beck, Tiger Woods, Denzel Washington, and Michael Jordan. While male politicians have always been high on the list, male entertainers are surging ahead.

Although women have risen in political stature during the twenty-first century, during the first 10 years of the Gallup Poll, recognition was given only to the wives of politicians, European queens, and the more popular entertainers of the day: Kate Smith, Ethel Barrymore,

June Allyson, Marian Anderson, Helen Hayes, and Dinah Shore. Between 1999 and 2009, while some politicians and wives of politicians made the list, that same celebrity list was expanded to include Oprah Winfrey, Elin Nordegren Woods, Ellen DeGeneres, Angelina Jolie, Martha Stewart, Jennifer Lopez, Julia Roberts, Madonna, and Rosie O'Donnell. One year earlier, I must mention another woman who made the most-admired-women list: Monica Lewinsky.[4]

Our obsession with those who entertain us is epitomized by the results of a survey given to fifth- through eighth-grade girls in 2004. Jake Halpern talks about this survey in his book *Fame Junkies*.[5] One of the questions asked these girls, "When you grow up, which of the following jobs would you most like to have?" They were given five options, and the results of the survey follow:

- 9.5 percent: chief of a major corporation, such as General Motors
- 9.8 percent: Navy SEAL
- 13.6 percent: U.S. senator
- 23.7 percent: president of a major university, such as Harvard or Yale
- 43.4 percent: personal assistant to a famous singer or movie star

Our interest lies in people who entertain us as opposed to people involved in other occupations who may also be worthy of our interest and attention.

On television news programs, we often hear as much, if not more, about the lives of high-profile celebrities than about other more important issues of the day—war, the proliferation of nuclear technology, or our economy—as opposed to concentrating on something meaningful that could have far-reaching benefits to society. I remember a number of years ago that there were two big stories that took center stage: the passing of health care reform in the United States and the return of Tiger Woods to golf following his struggles. I was and still am not sure what story was bigger or which story people were most interested in.

I believe that our obsession with entertainers is something to be concerned about since we will have missed opportunities to learn from others who could provide valuable ideals and standards to our young. I am also concerned that in our celebrity-obsessed world, a motivating factor for many people is to *become known* and achieve *celebrity status*, even for a brief time, as opposed to concentrating on something more meaningful that could have far-reaching benefits to society. A celebrity-obsessed society has a short-lived focus, and instant recognition is becoming the norm. With the growth and development of social media, venues like YouTube, Facebook, Instagram, and reality television offer people the opportunity for personal recognition on a large scene, and to become known and identified by others is now a major motif in our society. But the question remains: is our obsession with celebrities and our wish to become one the best use of our time? I am also concerned that too much time is being spent on entertaining ourselves, as perhaps we could be doing more worthwhile things with our time.

Our captivation with being entertained and with those who work in the entertainment field, as well as with others who simply are famous for being famous, is an amazing phenomenon, powerful, and omnipresent presence in society. My decision for writing this book is to shed light on *why we as a society are obsessed with such people and with being entertained.* A secondary goal is to wake people up so they can view themselves through a different lens and with a changed perspective.

Since our obsession with figures in the entertainment field and others who appear in the media is multidetermined and has resulted from a coming together of many forces and variables, to understand this phenomenon, we need to appreciate a variety of coalescing factors. First, let's review some of the common universal traits we all possess since without such attributes, this phenomenon could never have been forged into existence. Second, we must appreciate our current social climate that influences us while shaping the inherited qualities we all possess. Most important, we need to appreciate the impact that mass media has on our existence and sense of being. Mass media envelops and surrounds us and is a major force in our lives. The coming together of these elements to create this phenomenon is what I refer to as the *perfect storm*.

Following this conceptualization, *Celebrity and Entertainment Obsession* is divided into three parts. Part I focuses on people and the common characteristics we all share that are relevant to understanding our obsession with today's celebrities. While many universal traits can be listed, I have focused on the ones I believe are most critical to understanding this phenomenon. Some of these features are so basic and well known that we take them for granted. Nonetheless, they are essential and key to understanding our celebrity fascination, and without them, our very intrigue would be nonexistent.

Part II shifts the attention from people to our social climate and the forces in our current environment external to us that impact and have an effect on our existence and life experience. Over time, there have been numerous modifications in our surroundings, and in fact, our social environment is constantly changing. In this part, I have focused on the changes that I think are particularly relevant to our preoccupation with being entertained and with celebrities, and, as you will see, one big influence on all of us is mass communication and the media, which permeate our sense of being.

Part III ties everything together in an effort to make sense of this social spectacle. You will learn how and why our society is obsessed and preoccupied with the entertainment field and that our brains have been *hijacked* in much the same way as the human brain can be seized and hijacked by drugs. Finally, some thoughts are presented about what we can do to free our brains from captivation.

When reading this book, there are times when others may be offended by some of the things I write. This is not my intention, and I apologize in advance if anyone is put off by any of my remarks. I have occasionally mentioned certain people to illustrate particular points. If I had been writing this book at another point in time, whether this was a few weeks, months, or years ago or several weeks, months, or years from now, other individuals would have been mentioned. Who our current celebrities are changes rapidly, and the people I mention just happened to be in the spotlight and in the news when I was writing this book. Again, it is not my intention to insult anyone. I have just written what I observe. These observations are solely my own and do not express the views of my publisher.

Celebrity and Entertainment Obsession contains personal observations, but explaining any cultural phenomenon is no small task. Our fascination with celebrities invades all aspects of our culture, and to fully explain this wonder is to elucidate a giant slice of life. But it remains a challenge because research on this subject is relatively new, and we have few proven facts to drawn on. The perspectives offered in this book reflect my personal thinking and supportive evidence when available. It is my hope that you, the reader, will be inspired to learn more about this topic.

Part I

The Human Species

I

ENTERTAINMENT AND NOVELTY

Most people are willing to pay more to be amused than to be educated. —Robert C. Savage

Boredom is the root of all evil. —Søren Kierkegaard

An important attribute relevant to our obsession with celebrities is our desire and need to be entertained. To get outside of ourselves and to be immersed in something that is stimulating to us is central to our species. To be bathed in newness and interesting diversions is important for happiness and life contentment. Anyone who has ever been around a very young child knows that babies love to be entertained. We work hard to make a baby smile by making silly faces and doing crazy things, and once the mission is accomplished, we repeat our actions to achieve the same effect. I did this with my daughter when she was young—and not only for the personal thrill of getting her to laugh and be entertained but also because she wanted to do it repeatedly. We used to act out Cinderella time and time again. I was the prince who would search all over the kingdom to find the foot that would perfectly fit the glass slipper. I would place the slipper on every doll's foot or stuffed animal my daughter possessed until, finally, I would find her sitting with her foot held out waiting for me to go over to her and place the slipper on her foot to see if it would fit. And sure enough, when I placed it on her foot and we pretended that it fit perfectly, the rush and delight that she felt was unparalleled. And as soon as we were finished, she would immediately say, "Do it again!" In fact, I once got a Father's Day card from her (though bought by my wife) that wished me a Happy Father's Day, and inside it stated, "For all the times you did it one more time."

So we see that very young children love to be entertained but are largely dependent on adults to stimulate and entertain them. They are also frequently delighted to do the same thing repeatedly. As children grow and develop, entertainment continues to be extremely important, but unlike the very young, they become more independent and learn to amuse themselves by playing games, interacting with their peers, reading books, or getting engaged in other recreational activities that interest them. With older children, too, the amusement obtained from a previously entertaining activity can often quickly wear off, and they require more and more amusement in order not to be bored. Who hasn't been around children who go to their parenting figure and lament that they are bored or that there is nothing to do? And then the parent may try to interest his or her child in something, only to hear that "I already did that," "That's no fun," "That's boring," or something to that effect.

Adolescents, too, need to be amused, and unless they are stimulated and occupied, problems with boredom can cause even bigger concerns. It is essential that adolescents get involved in extracurricular activities, whether this is participating in sports, dance, clubs, or other academic pursuits. Those who just hang out and have nothing to do will create their own entertainment, and sometimes this can be dangerous. Whether we are talking drug use, sexual acting out, petty crime, or hazing games, kids having a lot of downtime can be unsafe. If boredom sets in, they will find ways to cope with this, and in some of the cases, the choices are destructive.

Even adults generally don't do well with boredom, and we all need to be involved in activities that provide us with entertainment and pleasure. For a greater part of my career, I have worked with people who struggle with alcohol and drug addiction as well as those who struggle with gambling. When first stopping the addiction, a big issue for people in early recovery is what to do with their time and how to handle boredom. Their addiction has taken so much of their waking life that when they are no longer gambling or using drugs or alcohol, it can feel like they have nothing to do, and they do not know what to do with their time. Research I conducted concerned a reason-for-relapse survey that was administered to about 350 people who struggled with alcohol and drug use.[1] In the survey, there were about 30 possible reasons for relapse, and people were instructed to circle all of the reasons that were relevant to a past relapse or return to alcohol or drug use. Reasons included things like feeling angry, being bored, feeling anxious, having too much money, having relationship problems, or stopping treatment. They were then asked to list the three most important reasons for relapse based on their experiences, and of all of the reasons, in the top five was boredom. While depression and anxiety are painful feelings that can also lead to a return to drug use, boredom can be an equally challenging emotion, though often it is underappreciated. In treatment, individuals are encouraged to find substitute avenues and to develop other sources of leisure and pleasurable, fulfilling activities in which to invest their time. Providers know how important it is for those in early recovery not to feel bored.

Other researchers have found that having no outside stimulation and having nothing to do but think is not a pleasant experience for many people. In a series of experiments, using both college students and members of their community who were recruited from a church and farmer's market, participants were instructed to spend time entertaining themselves for a period of 6 to 15 minutes with no other stimulation, such as cell phones, writing implements, or listening to music. They were also instructed to stay awake and to remain seated. In general, participants did not enjoy the experience, and about half reported enjoyment that was at or below the midpoint of the scale they used to measure this. It was also found that about one-third of the college students "cheated" by using their cell phones, listening to music, or getting up out of their seats.

While having nothing to do but think was found to be unpleasant, the researchers wondered whether people would prefer to engage in an unpleasant activity rather than simply being involved in no activity. To study this, participants were instructed to entertain themselves with their own thoughts for 15 minutes, and during this time, they were given the option of administering an electric shock to themselves that they had previously received and rated as being an aversive experience. Despite having stated that they would not want to receive such a shock again, 67 percent of the men and 25 percent of the women chose to give themselves this electric shock. It appears that having nothing to do was so troubling for many people that they elected to give themselves an electric shock.[2]

If you have any doubt that we hate to be bored and that we need to be entertained, it will be hard to maintain this skepticism in light of the entertainment machine that exists today. No matter where you turn, events to seduce, entertain, delight, and capture us are ever present. The sheer number of television shows, movies, concerts, and shows is astounding. I recently was glancing at a newspaper that informed readers of what movies were planned to be released over the summer. I counted about 90 movies over about three months that were scheduled for release, which is about one movie every day. And shortly thereafter, after the summer was over, I again read an article that outlined upcoming movie releases, and it was the same: almost one movie every single day.

When television was in its infancy, only a few stations existed. Now, thanks to cable television, there are more than 100 available stations. In addition, there are also an unlimited number of movies that can be rented, downloaded, or bought as well as a multitude of television series that can be purchased. There is the technology where your favorite shows can be watched if you missed them, or they can be recorded in case you want to view them at a different time. There are also DVDs of previous sporting events, whether this is baseball, football, boxing, or basketball, that can be purchased. Even though the person knows the outcome of the game or contest, watching it over and over again continues to provide entertainment. The A. C. Nielsen Company reported that the average American watches about 153 hours of television each month, or about 1,800 hours each year, which is over two months of nonstop television watching per year. If a person lives to about 65 years old, that person will have spent close to 10 years glued to the tube.[3] Casinos have also entered the entertainment business. They are no longer just for gambling; they also offer a variety of other forms of entertainment. So do cruise ships, providing entertainment besides traveling the globe.

The power and unbridled passion with which we seek entertainment has become unprecedented in recent years. Have you ever tried to purchase tickets online to a hot concert only to find all seats already sold out even though you had tried to place your order the second they went on sale? This is because tickets frequently are sold beforehand, so when tickets go on sale to the general public, most have already been sold. The cost of tickets is another issue. Try to get tickets to a Red Sox–Yankees game at Fenway Park. The markup is absurd, but there are people willing to pay the price. And this doesn't even include tickets to the playoffs, World Series, or Super Bowl, which can be in the thousands of dollars. When it comes to being entertained, we seem to have no limits.

In 2013, *USA Today* reported that the average overall compensation package for college football coaches at over 120 major programs was a little over $1.8 million, with a range of $250,000 to over $7 million and a median salary of about $1.5 million.[4] In comparison, presidents of public research universities earned a median compensation of slightly over $440,000, which is about a quarter of what football coaches made.[5] While this could be understood if the sports programs brought money into the school, it was reported that of 228 athletic departments of NCAA Division 1 public schools, only 23 generated enough revenue in 2012 to cover their expenses, and of those, 16 received some kind of subsidy.[6] Only our passion for entertainment allows these coaches to make that kind of money, as it is believed that being featured in the news and winning will bring recognition to the school and, in turn, prospective students.

What is also apparent is that the effort required to obtain some kind of entertainment and to get away from our typical consciousness and ordinary way of being in the world varies from being quite easy to being rather demanding and requiring more energy and determination. At one end of the continuum is simply being in the presence of an entertainer and passively taking in the experience to get our requirement for entertainment met. Seeing a dance troupe perform a ballet, a theater group put on a show, or a sporting event or watching television or a movie are ways that we can meet our necessity for entertainment that demand little effort. These kinds of experiences give us a quick fix without having to expend too much effort. In the same vein, the use of alcohol or other drugs, as well as gambling and eating, also falls into this category: some kind of entertainment is achieved, and our consciousness is altered without having to work too hard or consume too much energy.

As we move to less inactive mechanisms to achieve our need for diversion, there are other activities that require somewhat more effort, such as reading a book, going to a museum, or having some friends over for a party. Instead of being a completely passive recipient, at least some modicum of exertion is needed to receive the enjoyment. Finally, there are other activities that necessitate even greater work, such as learning to play a musical instrument or dance, meditating, drawing or painting, growing a flower or vegetable garden, writing a poem, or exercising—even authoring a book. Whether we are the passive recipient of some form of entertainment or learn to entertain ourselves, being amused sustains us and is a necessity.

SEEKING NOVELTY

Closely related to our need for entertainment is our inherited voyeurism and tendency to be drawn to novelty, which can be detected even in infants. For example, it has been demonstrated that, initially, infants have a preference for familiar objects. However, after extended exposure and the opportunity to assimilate the object, their attention shifts to more novel objects.[7] Our tendency to be drawn to the "less typical" and to be sensitive to changes in our environment is genetically built in to our hardware, as it is in most other animals. The "orienting reflex," as first described by Ivan Sechenov in 1863, is a reflex that reacts to and is sensitive to sudden changes, novelty, and sounds in our environment.[8] A fresh noise will incite a cat or dog to perk up its ears and will captivate its attention. An odd smell or unfamiliar person will do the same. This attunement to the environment is a critical attribute of most species and enables them to survive. It will help prevent victimization, and it can also help the battle for survival, as attention to the environment can lead the way to sources of food, water, and shelter.

Similarly, we need to be exquisitely attuned to events that surround us to prepare us for whatever is in store. In some cases, this could be a matter of life or death. For example, being informed that there is some kind of disaster approaching helps people prepare for the event. We want to know if someone has escaped from prison, what areas are safe for travel, or what airlines are safe and have the best security features. It is also important to know about people—in particular, whom we can trust and whom we can count on as opposed to whom we need to be on the lookout for—so that if they come into our lives, we will be ready. To some extent, our voyeurism and being attuned to our surroundings is critical for our survival. Without this, our chances of staying alive would be diminished, as we would be prey to any outside influence or event.

Not only are we drawn to change and novelty, but, deprived of outside stimulation, the human brain can atrophy and will not develop the way it should. For example, babies placed in orphanages and denied optimal stimulation suffered from deficient language skills and other cognitive functions. The length of time the child stayed in the orphanage was directly associated with the amount of impairment and the number of domains that were affected. While some "catch-up" may be possible, often the impairment continues and cannot be ameliorated.[9]

A familiar example to most everyone that demonstrates our attunement to novelty and our inability not to look at the strange and unusual is when we are driving down the road and suddenly there is a traffic backup. Not until you approach the scene do you discover that the reason for the backup is an automobile accident that might even be on the other side of the road. Everyone on your side of the road has slowed down to look at the wreckage. J. D. Salinger referred to such people as "rubberneckers," or those who twist their necks to take in the action.[10] Television traffic reporters have often referred to this phenomenon as the "curiosity factor"—when the other side of the road is jammed up due to an accident on the other side. In fact, to combat the congestion that can occur due to rubbernecking, in the United Kingdom, officials put up a green mesh around automobile accidents to prevent people from peering at the disaster. While they imagined that this might help to some extent, they found that the congestion cleared up immediately.[11]

By nature, we are all transfixed by disaster. Whether it is a fire, a flood, a tsunami, a tornado, a building being demolished, a plane crash, an earthquake, or a train wreck, we love to see these kinds of things. The media focuses on such events, and photographers devote their lives to documenting these events to satisfy our insatiable need. Coverage of such events can be so consuming that psychologists encourage people not to stay so glued to the television, as viewing such trauma can lead to vicarious traumatization.[12] Nonetheless, we inherently desire to know about these things, and we are captivated by and drawn to them.

I had the opportunity to volunteer to help the victims of Hurricane Katrina shortly after it ravaged New Orleans and the coasts of Mississippi, Louisiana, and Alabama. The devastation was overwhelming, and I must admit that there were times when I and others simply could not stop ourselves from looking around and taking everything in. Almost like voyeurs, we could not stop looking. We simply could not close our eyes to the devastation but felt compelled to see more and more of what had taken place.

Before traveling, in order not to appear to be a voyeur, I made the decision not to even bring my camera because I was going there to help and not to gape. However, when there, as others did bring their cameras and took pictures as we worked, I ended up buying a camera to capture firsthand what I was seeing. Although I felt a little guilty, I felt compelled to purchase a camera and clicked away.

There is even a magazine completely devoted to our being voyeurs: *Found Magazine*. The magazine's website (www.foundmagazine.com) answers the question of what this all about: "We collect found stuff: love letters, birthday cards, kids' homework, to-do lists, ticket stubs, poetry on napkins, doodles—anything that gives a glimpse into someone else's life. Anything goes." And if that isn't enough, you can also buy Davy Rothbart's book—*Found: The Best Lost, Tossed, and Forgotten Items*. As noted by *Publishers Weekly* on Amazon's website, "At times, reading the notes and letters feels uncomfortably voyeuristic, and inevitably, readers are left wanting more, wishing for more details about these lives beyond what the sketchy fragments provide."

In summary, our need and love of entertainment and our requirement to be stimulated by events outside of ourselves, including our attraction to novelty, is a major human motif. We thrive on entertainment, whether we create it ourselves or it is provided by others. On some level, we are all voyeurs, being drawn to newness, novelty in our environment, and the strange and unusual. We hate to be bored, and, as you will see, these attributes are very relevant to our obsession with celebrities.

2

THE IRRESISTIBILITY OF BEAUTY

Beauty is a greater recommendation than any letter of introduction.
—Aristotle

It is amazing how complete the delusion is that beauty is goodness.
—Leo Tolstoy

Another trait that is relevant in trying to make sense of our obsession with celebrities is our love of physical attractiveness. I almost can't think of a bigger motif in our society than our fondness for beauty, and this includes our love, interest, and obsession with being and wanting to look beautiful and our captivation and infatuation with people who are pretty. We are inundated with images of beauty and ways to become more attractive, and we are drawn to people who are good looking. As has been noted by Nancy Etcoff in her book *Survival of the Prettiest*, "throughout human history, people have scarred, painted, pierced, padded, stiffened, plucked, and buffed their bodies in the name of beauty."[1]

Go to your local drugstore or food store, and you will see aisles and aisles of products that offer other ways to improve our physical appearance and body image. There are hair products to thicken, straighten, or curl our hair and to make our hair shinier or less frizzy as well as agents to change the color of our hair or take the gray out. There are products to take lines out of our face, to change the color of our lips, and to make

our lips shinier and fuller. There is merchandise to thicken our eye-
lashes, to thin out our eyebrows, to remove facial hair that we don't
want, and to take out unflattering spots as well as products too numerous to name that will change the color of our eyelids, fingernails, and
toenails. The shelves are full of antiaging creams as well as teeth whit-
eners, and outside of drugstores, electrolysis and waxing are available
for hair removal. There are contact lenses for those who don't want to
wear glasses and contact lenses to change the color of your eyes for
those who don't even need to correct their vision. If you want or need to
wear glasses or just want to wear glasses to create that certain look,
glasses have now become a fashion statement, and there are thousands
of frames to choose from to give you the right image.

Our obsession with body image can also be seen in the dollars we
spend on dieting. The ABC News Staff reported that about $20 billion
each year are spent on diet books, diet drugs, and weight loss surgeries.
And it isn't just women: it is estimated that of this amount, men account
for 15 percent of this overall cost.[2] The different types of diets that are
promoted and marketed are almost endless. To name just some: the
Atkins Diet, the South Beach Diet, Jenny Craig, Nutrisystem, low-carb
diets, low-fat diets, Japanese Women Don't Get Old or Fat, the Sonoma
Diet, WeightWatchers, DietWatch, SparkPeople, the Best Life Diet,
the Food Doctor Diet, Medifast, Burn the Fat, Feed the Muscle, the 5
Factor Diet, the Abs Diet, Denise Austin, Change One, Slim in 6, the
Mediterranean Diet, Anne Collins, the Zone Diet, and the Mayo Clinic
Diet. There are even diets geared just for kids, such as Trim Kids and
SlimKids. Finally, if you want to lose weight in less than three days,
there is always the Hollywood 48 Hour Miracle Diet. While health
reasons to diet, as well as wanting to feel better, are relevant, the main
reason is the desire to look better.

The fashion industry also capitalizes on our obsession with being
beautiful. Each year, new clothes are placed on the market to enable us
to look our best so that we can catch another's eye. Like any other
product that is offered, this is tied to capitalism with the goal of earning
money. However, this industry succeeds because we are obsessed with

beauty and trying to look our best. Fashion can be used to help us look thinner, younger, sexier, and taller as well as make a woman's breasts appear bigger.

Our obsession with beauty can also be seen in the number of magazines devoted to helping a person improve his or her looks. Whether it is how to lose weight, to tone and trim the body, to improve the look of our skin, or to look good as you age, there is a magazine to help. In addition, many magazines, while not exclusively focused specifically on helping you look more beautiful (and desirable), often contain many articles that focus on this or other fashion tips, and those are a big part of the magazines' appeal. Some include *Complete Woman*, *Glamour*, *Self*, *Shape*, *Elle*,*Shorthair*, *Oxygen*, *Allure*, *Muscle and Fitness Hers*, *Lucky Hairstyle Guide*, *Redbook*, *Harper's Bazaar*, *Lucky*, *Marie Claire*, *Vogue*, and *Cosmopolitan*.

Our preoccupation and obsession with beauty begins early. There are magazines that focus on teens and tweens (10- to 12-year-olds), and much of the content in these magazines focuses on helping them look their best. Some of these include *CosmoGirl!*, *Seventeen*, *Sassy*, *Teen*, *YM*, *Teen Vogue*, and *Elle Girl*. While not all of the content in these magazines focuses on looks, an analysis of the content of *Teen*, *YM*, *Seventeen*, and *Sassy* in 1997 found that the largest percentage of articles were on appearance (37 percent), followed by dating (35 percent) and fashion (32 percent). Only a handful of articles appeared on topics such as alcohol, drugs, and smoking (3 percent), sexually transmitted diseases (3 percent), and contraception (2 percent). A few more articles were on self-confidence (16 percent), family (15 percent), career (12 percent), school (12 percent), and becoming independent (5 percent). Far and away, appearance and fashion, along with dating, dominate the content, showing the importance of these subjects.[3]

While it says a lot that magazines now focus on tweens and teens, the focus on beauty can be even younger. *Toddlers and Tiaras*, a TLC reality television program, is a show in which toddlers are dressed up, made up, and primed to be models. They learn to strut, their hair is fixed up, and their nails and toes are polished so that they have that perfect look. Obviously, it is the children's parents who are involved in this, but, nonetheless, this shows how powerful our obsession with being beautiful is.

Here are some amazing statistics:

- Forty-three percent of six- to nine-year-olds use lipstick or lip gloss.
- Thirty-eight percent use hairstyling products.
- Twelve percent use other cosmetics.
- Forty-two percent of first to third graders want to be thinner.
- Eighty-one percent of 10-year-olds are afraid of getting fat.
- Eight- to 12-year-olds in this country already spend more than $40 million a month on beauty products.
- Teens spend $100 million on beauty products. [4]

If this isn't enough, surgical and nonsurgical cosmetic procedures are a booming business. According to the American Society for Aesthetic Plastic Surgery, a little over 11.4 million surgical and nonsurgical cosmetic procedures were performed in the United States in 2013, and Americans spent about $12 billion on cosmetic procedures. Since 1997, cosmetic procedures have increased by about 471 percent for women and by 273 percent among men, with increases of 371 percent in abdominoplasty (tummy tuck), 210 percent in breast augmentation, and 106 percent in liposuction. The most popular surgical procedures in 2013 were liposuction, breast augmentation, blepharoplasty (eyelid surgery), abdominoplasty, and rhinoplasty (nose reshaping). The top nonsurgical procedures were botulinum (botox), hyaluronic acid injectables, hair removal, and microdermabrasion and photorejuvenation, both used to improve the look of a person's skin. To give you an idea of the extent of this business, here are the top cosmetic surgeries for women and men in 2013:

- Women: breast augmentation (313,327), liposuction (312,176), abdominoplasty (151,200), breast lift (137,233), and blepharoplasty (133,185)

- Men: liposuction (61,736), blepharoplasty (28,204), rhinoplasty (26,825), male breast reduction (22,638), and otoplasty, or ear surgery (16,905)[5]

Miss Plastic Surgery has even come to the world beginning in 2009. While we have long had Miss America, Miss Universe, and Mr. Universe, contestants for this pageant, which took place in Hungary, had to prove that they had actually had plastic surgery to qualify and be allowed into the competition. Botox or collagen injections just do not suffice. Contestants displayed breast augmentations, nose surgeries, and face-lifts, and one person was the proud owner of surgically adjusted toes.[6] Similar contests have taken place in England, and contestants must have undergone plastic surgery, and they must also want more, as the prize is additional plastic surgery.[7] I guess Billy Crystal from *Saturday Night Live* was right: "It doesn't matter how you feel. What matters is how you look . . . and you look mahvelous!"

WE ARE ALSO ATTRACTED TO AND GIVE PREFERENCE TO OTHERS WHO ARE BEAUTIFUL

Not only are we obsessed with looking our best, but we are also enamored with others who are beautiful. The pretty person gets our heads to turn and receives all of our attention. To be born beautiful is such a blessing. When a child is born, the greatest compliment that can be given is "She is such a beautiful baby!" Beautiful babies will get the most attention.

A recent study clearly demonstrated this. Men and women were asked to look at baby pictures, some of which had normal faces; others had abnormal features. Using key presses, the participants could alter the amount of time they spent viewing the pictures. It was found that women participants worked harder to shorten the time they spent viewing the baby faces with abnormal features compared to viewing normal baby faces, and the theory is that "babyishness," or cuteness, is linked to nurturing feelings and behavior in women.[8] Another study took videos of mothers and infants shortly after birth and then three months later. It was revealed that mothers of the more attractive babies spent more time holding them close, staring into their eyes, and talking with them than did the mothers of the less attractive babies. In addition, their attention to their babies seemed to be more intense and stronger than was the attention of the mothers of the less attractive babies.[9] In a similar fashion, even young babies are attracted to and attend to facial attractiveness,[10] and it has been observed that very young babies who are only days old tend to stare longer at faces deemed beautiful by adults than those not believed to be as attractive.[11] It is programmed into our makeup.

Children who are attractive are also at an advantage and get better treatment. In one study, about 500 11- to 12-year-old boys and 500 11- to 12-year-old girls were assessed in terms of their overall attractiveness by their teachers with reasonable agreement. It was found that the teachers' ratings of student attractiveness were significantly correlated with their assessment of the students' sociability, popularity, academic brightness, confidence, and qualities of leadership.[12] In another study, photographs of attractive and unattractive boys and girls were attached to identical psychological reports and given to teachers for them to assess their judgments of future school performance. Teachers systematically rated attractive children more favorably than the unattractive children and held higher expectations for them in terms of future academic and social development.[13]

Having good looks in adulthood continues to be beneficial and important. The reality is that the handsome and pretty are at an advantage for many things. While brains are important, looks trump that by a long shot. We can see this in everyday life, where the handsome man or the pretty girl gets the date of their dreams, whereas the less attractive are not nearly as fortunate. It has been shown that the attractive girls in high school are more likely to get married than are less attractive girls.[14] More attractive girls also tend to marry men with more income and education than they have.[15]

Attractive people may also have an advantage in getting others to help them. In one study, a female who was either attractive or unattractive asked 30 males on a large college campus for directions, and it was shown that the males offered more help to the attractive females. This study also had females considered to be attractive or unattractive ask 40 men to mail a letter for them. Again, the attractive females received more assistance.[16] In another study, 442 males and 162 females in public phone booths found a completed graduate school application form along with a photograph of the applicant and an addressed, stamped envelope. The picture was used to convey information about the applicant. It was found that delivery of the application occurred more often for the attractive applicants than for the unattractive ones.[17] In another experiment, male college students were shown pictures of very attractive woman and others who weren't as attractive, and they were asked to choose the person they would be most likely do the following for them: loan money, move furniture, donate a kidney, give blood, swim one mile to rescue her, save her from a burning building, and jump on a terrorist hand grenade. In all cases, except loaning money, they were more likely to help the more beautiful women.[18]

There are also supermodels, or those pretty women who are hired to sell clothes, perfume, cars, jewelry, or whatever else manufacturers want to sell. Our obsession with pretty people is epitomized by the money they make simply by modeling and having their picture taken. Gisele Bündchen, for example, earned about $47 million in the year preceding June 2014 according to *Forbes* magazine.[19] Can it really be a good investment to spend that kind of money, and do companies really sell more products because of the specific pretty face that is shown advertising their product? I can't imagine it is worth the exorbitant sums of money they spend, but I guess I must be wrong. Consumers are so obsessed with beauty that it appears that having a beautiful person advertise a product helps increase sales—or at least companies believe that it does.

Attractiveness and body image are also important for men but in somewhat different ways than for women. Rather than facial attractiveness, for men, height, and bigness count, as does muscle. Malcolm Gladwell polled about half of the Fortune 500 companies and found that the average height of chief executive officers (CEOs) was just slightly under six feet, which is about three inches taller than the height of the average male in the United States. He also noted that about 3.9 percent of men in the United States are six feet two inches or taller, whereas among Fortune 500 CEOs, 30 percent of them are this height.[20] It has also been noted that during the 1900s, in every presidential election, the taller man has won, except once.[21] And here is another interesting finding: looking at over 800 male graduates of a master's in business administration program in the mid-1980s, it was found that men who were six feet tall earned about 10 percent more than did men who were five feet five inches.[22] In another comprehensive analysis of how earning power is related to height, looking at over 8,500 people, it was found that tall individuals have advantages in a number of important aspects of their careers and organizational lives.[23] Regarding a muscular build, there is a preference for men with V-shaped torsos, which is why bodybuilding is such a huge business.[24] Many men (and even women) resort to using steroids to pump up their muscles and to develop a desirable physique despite the evidence of the negative health benefits of using steroids for this purpose.

WHY IS BEAUTY SO IMPORTANT?

Doing everything we can to enhance our attractiveness and being attracted to others who are beautiful has long been a central motif in society. While we have always been obsessed with looks, the focus on attractiveness, body image, and our external appearances may be even greater now than in the past, and the reasons for this will be reviewed in chapter 8. Regardless, evolutionary theory suggests that physical appearance is important, as this is relevant to our ability to survive, meaning our need to copulate and reproduce. It has been suggested that deeply embedded in our biology, which we really aren't conscious of, attractiveness, especially a female's physical attributes, is equated with youth. In turn, a youthful appearance among women is equated with the ability to reproduce, as younger women are able to have babies, whereas older women cannot. As a result, men are particularly attentive to the physical qualities that women possess, as this means that the woman is of childbearing age and is a potential partner to have sex with and to make a baby. An older women who is past her childbearing years cannot reproduce, which may be why men are attracted to younger (and perceived to be more attractive) women. Physical attractiveness may also be equated with being free from diseases and parasites, which can also make a woman appear to be desirable in terms of reproductive potential.

On the other hand, it isn't as important for a woman that her partner and target of attention be particularly attractive (and young). First, men can reproduce later in life, so being young (and good looking) isn't as critical. In addition, more than facial attractiveness, bigness and strength are important, as bigness, muscles, and power can offer the woman and her offspring protection, which is critical for her for survival. It can even be argued that today, an older man may even be a better catch in terms of survival value. A man on in his years may be in a better position to care for the mother and the mother of his child, as an older man typically has more means (money) to give to his family and to support them. Pure physical power isn't as important as it used to be, though that is still a turn-on for women. In society today, power comes in other ways, such as a man's financial situation and overall status.[25]

These points were demonstrated in a study that showed pictures of men and women who ranged in terms of attractiveness and who were described as training to be a waiter, a teacher, or a doctor. When people looked at the pictures, they were asked if they would be interested in having cup of coffee with, dating, having sex with, or marrying the person. It was found that women were most interested in the most attractive men with the most money, or those training to be a doctor. Next, the women were most interested in the average-looking or the unattractive men training to be a doctor, who received the same ratings as very attractive teachers. For men, though, no matter what the women were training to be, it was found that unattractive women were simply not preferred.[26] In another study that demonstrates the importance of financial power as opposed to pure attractiveness of men in attracting a partner, women were shown pictures of four men. Some women saw two of the men in a Burger King uniform, and the other two men wearing a shirt, tie, and blazer along with a Rolex watch, and the other women saw the same men, but what they were wearing was reversed—the men in the Burger King uniform were now wearing the shirt, tie, and blazer along with a Rolex watch, and the other two men who were dressed in the business attire were now in the Burger King uniform. It was found that the women were unwilling to consider dating, having sex with, or marrying any of the men in the Burger King uniform but were willing to consider these options when the men were dressed in the business attire.[27] Again, a male's physical attractiveness may be less important for women, as women look for other things, such as the ability of the man to care for her and her offspring. This idea helps explain a woman's greater fascination with a man's financial situation, overall power, and success in the world as opposed to an exclusive focus on his looks, although physical appearance is not completely irrelevant.

The bottom line is that we are absolutely obsessed with the looks of others and looking and being beautiful ourselves. It truly is a gigantic motif in our current lives and very relevant to our obsession with celebrities.

3

SOCIABILITY

Man is a social animal. —Baruch Spinoza

One is a member of a country, a profession, a civilization, a religion.
One is not just a man. —Antoine de Saint-Exupéry

It is clear that we are a social species and that we need and like to have contact with others. Like other animals, we need to have sexual relations with others to ensure the survival of our species, and this demands at least some social contact. However, apart from that, we have a powerful motive to be around, interact with, and establish connections with others. Granted, there are some people who tend to live like hermits and most of the time do not desire contact with others. In general, however, we are animals that congregate together, and we have developed sophisticated ways of communicating with each other.

When studying all cultures, it is clear that human beings form and live together in groups. Whether it is the clan, the tribe, the family, the village, the town, the city, the state, or the country, we are social creatures that flock together. There are also an infinite number of organizations, clubs, religions, political affiliations, and alumni groups that people partner with, join, or become members of and that hold us together.

In fact, we are always interested in participating and being involved in some social gathering or activity. Examples are numerous and include parades, national celebrations, festivals, birthday parties, drinking at a local bar or tavern, attending a dance or family get-together, or people watching. Others like to vacation with their families or friends or take a cruise with others whom they don't know but whom they would like to get to know. If people spend an evening alone watching a sporting event on television and you ask them what they did that evening, it might be reported that they didn't do anything other than watch television. On the other hand, if they spent the evening with some friends doing the same thing, they would likely report that they got together with some friends and had a great time. Most people enjoy and need to have social relationships in their lives to feel satisfied and fulfilled.

Facebook, the biggest social media website in the world, demonstrates our desire and need to be connected to others. What originally began as a way for college students to stay connected to their friends, Facebook has now entered mainstream America, and even businesses are using Facebook to enhance their connection to its buyers, customers, and the public. For those who do not know, a person joins Facebook, and suddenly the person can potentially be connected to thousands of other people, be they people they know, people they want to get to know, friends of friends, friends of friends of friends, distant relatives, people you went to high school with whom you haven't spoken in years, college classmates who have been forgotten, and people you used to live near. You can post all kinds of personal information on your wall and even let people know what you are thinking about that day or what you are doing at the moment. Twitter and LinkedIn are other venues that foster connections with others.

Certainly, if we weren't a social species and didn't like to be connected with others, Facebook would never have grown so exponentially or even come into existence. As will be noted in chapter 7, because our current society has led to increased isolation, Facebook has further grown in importance, as it allows people to stay connected to each other despite some societal forces that keep us apart. It helps counter the isolation that our current society breeds.

Our need to be in social contact with other members of our species begins in infancy. Unlike some other animals, when we are born and throughout infancy, we are completely dependent on a parenting figure for survival. An infant can't do much for itself. An infant can cry for help, but if help doesn't come, the infant will certainly perish. Particularly with us, our need to be close to another person or people lasts for a long time. Whereas many animals are off on their own immediately or perhaps days, weeks, or months after birth, we can be dependent on our parents for a long time. For some, this dependency lasts until they graduate from college and for some even longer. So our need to be in contact with and connected to other people cuts right to our essence.

Short of an absolute lack of caregiving, even separations from and losses of a parenting figure can lead to tremendous psychological consequences. A good attachment to a parenting figure is essential for reasonable mental health, and the primary consequence of a poor adjustment to life is a disruption of this critical relationship. John Bowlby, a psychologist, based his life work on our need for attachment. Without a baby's solid attachment to a parenting figure, development would be hampered and severely damaged.[1]

Harry Harlow, a scientist who conducted many studies with monkeys, our close relatives, demonstrated the importance of attachment with baby rhesus monkeys. He conducted an experiment in which there was a wire monkey with milk and a cloth-covered, soft monkey without milk. Infant monkeys were removed from their mothers and placed in a cage with these two fake surrogate monkey parents. What he found was that the baby monkeys would go to the wire monkey to feed, but as soon as they were finished eating, they would leave the wire monkey and cling to the cloth-covered soft monkey.[2] Like us, monkeys have a need to be close to others, including the warm touch. Harlow also conducted numerous studies on depriving rhesus monkeys of social contact with other monkeys, including some experiments in which young monkeys were deprived of maternal contact, and found that social isolation could have disastrous consequences on their social development, peer relations, and overall emotional functioning.[3,4] Again, monkeys, too, just like us, need to have social contact and relationships.

From an evolutionary point of view, it makes sense that we are social. To survive, even as adults, we need other people. Being part of a social group increases our chances for survival, as we have others to depend on and who can help us. For example, there may be some things that I do well that you don't and vice versa. This exchange of functionality is beneficial and can increase the chances of survival of both parties. Many years ago, living together in groups was critically important for existence. There is strength in numbers, and a group of people living together afforded the members protection against intruders. Working together also enhanced their ability to feed themselves, allowing them to hunt larger, more powerful animals, as there was no way one person could accomplish what a group could do. Even today, this same principle operates: we need a variety of commodities to survive, whether this is food, heat, electricity, housing, or transportation, to name just a few essential supplies. As no one person could possibly supply all of these wares, having relationships with many people who can provide these various products allows us to subsist and carry on.

GOSSIP

Another example of how attuned and connected we are to each other is our obsession and fascination with gossip. No matter where we live, there is always some gossip about someone. Donna is having an affair with Jimmy, Bob is dating Julie, Bill recently lost his job because of embezzling, or Margaret made a fool of herself last night. The world is full of gossip.

The history and function of gossip and a definition of gossip will always be complex and controversial. One definition of gossip is that it is "a rumor or report of an intimate nature, or chatty talk," and a gossip is "a person who habitually reveals sensational or personal facts about others."[5] Another definition of a gossip is that "senders of gossip either believe that they are transmitting truthful information or they know that they are they are intentionally spreading lies."[6] Whatever the exact definition, originally the word "gossip" came from "godsibs." Gossip was simply the activity that a person engaged in with one's "godsibs," or a person's peer group, equivalent to one's godparents. Gossip was talking to other people who were in one's close inner circle. The word "gossip" also referred to companions in childbirth and became a word for women friends in general. While the term now has a derogatory meaning, it didn't start out that way.[7]

As gossip is so prevalent in society, many ideas regarding the function and purpose of gossip exist.[8],[9] For example, it can be seen as a way for people to be socially connected to each other and can clearly have evolutionary value, as it can help us remain safe. Through gossip, we can keep track of what is going on in our social networks and even discover what is going on behind our backs and what we may not be aware of. Gossip enables us to tell our friends what we know, and some of this information may benefit them. "Joey got stung in the face by a jellyfish when he went swimming, and you should have seen what his face looked like!" communicates that others should be careful when they go swimming. Gossip can also serve the purpose of telling people to whom we are close whom they need to watch out for to avoid exploitation. For example, we can warn our friends to "watch out for Martha . . . she is a backstabber" or "Be careful around Luke! He stole some money from Peter, and he could do the same to you!" So gossip can have a teaching purpose and help other people in our social network.

Spreading false and negative information about a person can also help enhance the person's own status and reputation at the expense of another's. Saying "What a fool Bill is—I would never do something like that" conveys the fact that the person spreading the gossip has better judgment than Bill. Gossiping about others and sharing their misfortune can also enhance a person's self-esteem. Knowing that Bobby experienced some misfortune can help others feel good about their own lives, as they have not experienced that kind of misery.

Gossip can also be used to teach social norms. "You should have seen the dress she was wearing. It was so beautiful!" tells others the type of dress to wear. On the other hand, "You should have seen her new hairstyle. It looked so silly" conveys how not to wear one's hair. Gossip can also help transmit information about another person's reputation and status and in turn provides insight into the type of relationship we should or should not have with the person. Whether the information conveys something the person did that was admirable or, conversely, really stupid, this information lets others know whether they should avoid the person or instead whether it would behoove them to develop a relationship with the individual and to keep the person in their social network.

Gossip can also increase our own self-esteem, as through gossip we can tell others something that we know and are privy to. This can help solidify a person's social network and enhance his or her own standing in it. It is like we are saying, "I know something you don't know, which shows you how socially connected I am. And now you know, so you are now in the club." In this regard, some researchers found that after the murder of an undergraduate at Ohio State University, those who had some inside information about this tragedy were quickly granted higher social status.[10] Whatever the purposes of gossip, it reflects what a socially connected species we are.

As has been noted by Phyllis McGinley, an American poet and author, "Gossip isn't scandal and it's not merely malicious. It's chatter about the human race by lovers of the same." And another quote by Barbara Walters: "Show me someone who never gossips, and I will show you someone who is not interested in people." Finally, as Robin Dunbar has stated, "Without gossip, there would be no society. In short, gossip is what makes human society as we know it possible."[11]

A NEED TO BELONG

Not only do we like social contact, but we also have a psychological and emotional requirement to want to belong to a group. Psychologist Erik Erikson developed a theory about the stages of psychosocial development, and a need to belong was central to his theory. One of the stages concerned how people either develop a sense of intimacy or face isolation. That is, as people mature, a sign of health is that they achieve the ability to be intimate with others and to develop a sense of connectedness to society. If that does not occur, they will experience a sense of isolation and aloneness, which can be very painful and disruptive and cause severe emotional distress.[12]

Abraham Maslow, another psychologist, developed a theory that concerned critical needs that all humans have, and again the need to belong was a central component.[13] In this theory, he postulated that all humans have a hierarchy of needs that must be met in a sequential way. In particular, after physiological needs are met, people can then be concerned about the need for safety and security. In turn, after this has been accomplished, the next need is one of belonging, and this can entail wanting to be married, have a family, or be part of a community, a club, or any other fraternity or group.

Our need to belong and be a part of society can be seen in the development of fads. Fads are something that a large number of people do for a brief period of time largely because it is considered to be popular. Fads can include engaging in some kind of behavior, wearing a certain type of clothing or piece of jewelry, or even eating a particular type of food. Some popular fads over the years have included goldfish swallowing, streaking, telephone booth stuffing, break dancing, and numerous diets. While engaging in these kinds of activities can be fun, a huge driver is simply the need to belong and to be a part of society.

It also been noted by some researchers that our need to belong is the most powerful motivation that we experience. And the opposite feeling—feeling ostracized—can have disastrous consequences.[14] In experiments when people are ostracized or excluded from the social group, people feel absolutely miserable.[15] Interviews with people who have been ostracized report feelings of depression and increased rates of eating and promiscuity disorders, and some have even attempted suicide.[16] Again, our need to belong to a social group is essential.

In this regard, I am sure that most of you can remember what it was like to enter adolescence and to be an adolescent. And if you can't remember that far back, if you are a parent and living through or have lived through your children's adolescent years, you will remember the importance of the peer group. As children begin to separate and individuate from their parents and enter a world apart from the orbit of their parents, teenagers' peer groups become much more important. Being part of a social group and what the group thinks of you becomes critical and even more important than what parents think. During this time, adolescents can become susceptible to peer pressure, as their peer group is of paramount importance. Younger people may even engage in activities they really do not want to do so that they are accepted, as a lack of acceptance can lead to despair, depression, and extreme loneliness.

Even as adults, a sense of social connection is crucial. Some couples stay together for years despite being absolutely miserable with each other. While there are many reasons couples stay together despite having enormous problems and being very unhappy together, a big reason is simply the need for companionship. For many, it is better to be with someone, though unhappy, than to be alone. In fact, a loss of a relationship can lead to emotional dysregulation, feelings of despair, suicide, and homicide. Even families who experience problems with each other often stay tightly connected, as their emotional bonds are so profound.

In summary, an attribute that epitomizes who we are is our sociability. We enjoy being around and congregating with others and communicating about and with each other, and we have a need to belong. In fact, without this characteristic, we could not exist. As will become apparent, this trait is important to understand our obsession with celebrities.

4

AN ADDICTIVE VULNERABILITY

Habit is the deepest law of human nature. —Thomas Carlyle

I am a psychologist who has devoted over 25 years to working with individuals who struggle with the use of alcohol and drugs. For some people, the use of drugs or alcohol has taken over their lives, and more and more time is spent using and recovering from the effects of drug and alcohol use. In addition, using alcohol and drugs has become such an important priority in their lives that other activities are neglected and relegated to the backseat. Such people are addicted to alcohol and drugs, and in this regard, addiction is defined as a "chronic, relapsing brain disease that is characterized by compulsive drug (or alcohol) seeking and use, despite harmful consequences."[1] A key element of this definition is that the behavior continues despite harmful consequences.

While we often think of addiction in regard to alcohol and drug use, there are many other habits or things we do that can become addictive-like if not an addiction. Here is just a sampling: gambling, sex, eating, not eating, exercising, surfing the Internet, watching television, playing golf, watching football, and shopping. People can get addicted to other people, too, and when the relationship ends, they can't imagine living without that person, and this can result in suicide, homicide, or even both. The point is that there are many activities that have come to be

seen as potentially being addictive, and it is clear that people can become addicted to a wide variety of activities.

WHY DO PEOPLE GET ADDICTED TO THINGS?

The question as to why people get addicted to things consists of two
related questions. First, what is responsible for addiction when it occurs, and, second, why do some people get addicted to things whereas
others do not? While there is no clear absolute answer to either of these
questions, there is much that we do know. Let's take these two questions separately.

First, regarding what may help explain addiction as a phenomenon,
most of the science about addiction focuses on people who are addicted
to drugs or alcohol, although some other public health issues, such as
gambling and obesity, have also received attention. Researchers have
been interested in what can explain addiction because if this can be
better understood, it may be possible to develop better treatment to
help people who struggle with addiction. As addiction has so much to
do with our thought processes as well as our behavior, the brain has
been an obvious target of study.

The National Institute on Drug Abuse has conducted much research
on studying the brains of people who use drugs and who are addicted to
drugs. While there is still much to learn and many different neurotrans-
mitters and neurochemical pathways are being studied to fully understand a biologically based understanding of the addictive process, a
prominent pathway concerns the neurotransmitter dopamine. Essentially, it has been found that when people take drugs, dopamine, the
main pleasure neurotransmitter in the brain, gets released. In turn,
dopamine attaches to certain receptor sites in the brain, and when this
occurs, the person experiences pleasure. Over time, due to huge
amounts of dopamine being available, the brain compensates, and those
receptor sites that dopamine attaches to get diminished. As a result, it
may be harder for a person to experience nondrug pleasure when they
are addicted to drugs and especially when they first stop using drugs. In

addition, certain parts of the brain responsible for decision making (prefrontal cortex) begin to atrophy, lessening the person's ability to reason, problem solve, and think through activities. This, in turn, may make it hard for them to exercise sound decision making, which may play a role in resisting urges to use again.[2] And one more thing: even after a long period of time not using drugs, when people who were formerly addicted to a drug are visually exposed to cues in the environment that remind them of a previously used drug, certain parts of their brains get activated, whereas among people who have not been addicted to that drug, their brains do not show the same signs of activation in those areas. It is believed that this activation may be critically relevant to our understanding of why individuals continue to engage in the addictive behavior and may suffer a relapse despite all the problems the addiction has caused them.[3] As a result, the National Institute on Drug Abuse has called drug addiction a brain disease, as the brains of those who have become addicted have become changed by compulsive drug use.

Most all pleasurable activities release dopamine, such as having sex, listening to music, eating chocolate, and laughing. It is possible that addiction to these other activities may also cause similar changes in the brain, although research in this area is lacking. However, any changes in the brain that are caused by engaging in other pleasurable activities may not be nearly as great as those caused by drug use. This is because the amount of dopamine that gets released by using drugs is far greater than the amount of dopamine that gets released through other pleasurable activities.[4, 5, 6] Furthermore, it is believed that the tremendous surge of dopamine is what is responsible for some of the changes that occur in the brain due to repeated drug use.[7] Regardless, the point is that addiction and even other compulsive behaviors likely cause changes in the brain, and this makes sense. As the brain is a plastic organ, based on learning and life experience, it gets changed. My brain is different than your brain, and your brain is different than your best friend's brain, based on your history. In summary, it is believed that changes in the brain that result from compulsive drug use are, at least in part, responsible for the nature and phenomenon of addiction.

In terms of why it is that some people get addicted to things whereas others do not, we must remember that the development of an addiction is complex. It is a multifaceted problem that often has hereditary, psychological, and environmental determinants. First, let's talk about heredity, or a person's genetic vulnerability, and how this relates to an addiction.

Regarding the use of alcohol, it has been found that children of alcoholic parents, even if adopted away at birth and raised in nonalcoholic families, have a four times higher rate of developing an alcohol problem than do children of nonalcoholic parents who were adopted away at birth and raised in alcoholic families.[8] In addition, identical twins, who share the same genes, have higher rates of both twins having an alcohol use disorder than do fraternal twins, who do not share the same genetic makeup.[9] Children of alcoholic parents, when given alcohol, demonstrate a lower response to it and experience fewer feelings of intoxication compared to children of nonalcoholic parents.[10] This, in turn, is believed to be a risk factor for developing a problem with alcohol.[11] While having a genetic vulnerability to develop an alcohol problem does not mean that that person is going to develop such a problem, it is clear that heredity is important. It has also been demonstrated that genetic vulnerabilities exist with addiction to other substances as well, whether this concerns opiates, marijuana, or cocaine.[12, 13, 14] The heritability estimate as to why people get addicted to drugs or alcohol, regardless of the specific drug, is in the range of 40 to 60 percent.[15]

In addition to heredity and genetic makeup, psychological factors can also be important. Some people may begin to drink or use drugs because it decreases social anxiety, helps them relax and fit in, enables them to cope with feelings of depression, or in some way helps them deal with some other trauma in their life. I have also seen many teenagers who smoke marijuana report that marijuana helps calm them down and diminishes their angry feelings. Others who have been subjected to severe trauma may use a particular substance to numb out and help them forget their pain. Drugs can also be used to decrease the extreme anxiety that they experience. Using substances as a way to cope with some psychological distress has been called the self-medication theory of addiction.[16] Essentially, people discover that a certain drug helps them feel better, and, in essence, they are playing doctor with, or self-medicating, themselves in an attempt to feel better. Use can eventually lead to compulsive use or addiction. Research has shown that individuals who suffer from a mental illness have increased rates of having a substance use disorder compared to individuals who do not have a mental illness.[17] While the relationship between mental illness and substance use is complex, as using substances can also lead to psychiatric problems, having a mental illness is certainly a risk factor.[18] Psychological factors can also be relevant to addiction to other things. For example, a person who doesn't feel good about him- or herself unless he or she is in a relationship can easily get addicted to another person. In summary, psychological variables are often relevant to the addictive process.

A person's cultural and social environment is also important. Both overt and latent messages people receive about drinking, heavy drinking, and drug use are relevant, as these will influence how alcohol as well as other drugs are used. With alcohol, for example, a person may grow up in an environment where most everyone drinks heavily, and this will play a role in the person's drinking. This, in turn, can lead to heavier drinking and eventually an alcohol problem. The same is true with drug use. If a person grows up in an environment where many people in his or her peer group use drugs, the chances of using drugs and developing a problem will be increased. On the other hand, if a person grows up in a society where heavy drinking or drug use is frowned on or drug use is minimal, the chances of developing a problem with drugs and alcohol will be less. While this will not guarantee that the person will not develop a problem, it can influence alcohol and drug use and help counter a genetic predisposition. What people are exposed to in their environment is also relevant to other addictions. For example, a person will never get addicted to the Internet if he or she has no access to the Internet. However, if a person is lonely and perhaps has no other sources of pleasure and the Internet is available, the chance of getting addicted to the Internet will be increased.

Finally, in many cases, biological, psychological, and social factors all coalesce to give rise to an addiction. For example, with alcohol, if a person who has a biological vulnerability to develop an alcohol problem grows up in an environment where alcohol is readily available and all his or her peers drink heavily, the chances of that person developing an alcohol problem will be high. In addition, if the person struggles with depression, self-esteem, or fitting in with his or her peers, those factors can further increase the risk. On the other hand, if that same person grows up in an environment where heavy drinking is not acceptable, the chances of this genetic vulnerability leading to an alcohol problem will be greatly reduced, particularly if that person is comfortable in social situations.

In summary, an addiction to alcohol or drugs, as well as an addiction to other things, is a multifaceted and complex phenomenon and is often due to genetic, psychological, and social factors. It is also possible that what the person is exposed to in his or her social environment will also help determine what the addiction will be, whether alcohol, cocaine, heroin, a love interest, food, or the Internet.

AN ADDICTIVE VULNERABILITY

Despite there being differences in people's vulnerabilities to getting addicted, it is likely that a universal addictive vulnerability exists in all of us. We all have dopamine in our pleasure centers, and when we find things or activities that release dopamine and can stimulate our pleasure centers, we will do those activities over and over again. Simply, we will repeat over and over again those things that release dopamine and titillate our pleasure centers.

I am using the term "addiction" rather broadly. Certainly, some would state that this term is overused and that true addiction and the brain changes I described occur only with compulsive alcohol and drug use. That is, addiction to the Internet, golf, or people may not result in these same brain changes that are observed with compulsive drug use. While that may be true, studying the brain and observing what changes take place when addiction results is a new science, and we are just beginning to make sense of this phenomenon. It is certainly possible that "addiction" to other things may also result in similar brain changes, and in this regard, it has been found through brain neuroimaging that individuals who scored high on a food addiction measurement tool and who were exposed to food or the anticipation of food experienced patterns of neural activation similar to those of individuals who experienced substance dependence and who were exposed to the anticipation of drugs.[19] Other research has shown that among rats, intermittent access to sugar can lead to behaviors and neurochemical changes in the brain that are similar to the effect that drugs of abuse have on the brain, demonstrating that sugar can be addictive.[20] While it has not yet been determined whether similar changes in the brain occur with other addictions, it is likely that a vulnerability and propensity to addiction is a universal phenomenon and that addiction to a variety of things is prevalent.

The thing that fuels addiction is our desire to feel good and to zone out. No matter what the compulsive activity, the pursuit and investment in it helps people forget their ordinary reality and get into another world. It gives people a temporary break from their usual and customary way of being in the world. Numerous human activities can provide this kind of pleasure and, at least in theory, can become addictive. And when the word "addictive" is used, it means that the activity is compulsive and continues despite its causing harmful consequences to the person or to those around the individual. For example, a golfer may want to play so much golf that it begins to hurt his family life, a dancer begins to neglect other important things, a person reads to such an extent that her family begins to feel neglected, or an individual continues to exercise daily despite receiving warnings from his doctor that he needs to rest. While certain things are generally more addictive than others (drugs vs. playing golf), due in large part to the amount of dopamine that gets released (the greater surge of dopamine that is released, the greater the chances that the activity will become addicting), anything can become addicting.

If there is any doubt as to our universal vulnerability to addiction, think about this: the leading cause of preventable death in this country is death secondary to smoking or nicotine addiction, the second leading cause of preventable death is related to obesity or addiction to food, and the third leading cause of preventable death is related to alcohol consumption or addiction to drinking.[21] If this doesn't suggest that we have a vulnerability to addiction, I don't know what does. You will see how this susceptibility helps make sense of our obsession with being entertained and with celebrities.

5

OUR NEED FOR IDOLS

Every one of us is, even from his mother's womb, a master craftsman of idols. —John Calvin

Our need for idols and turning people into god-like figures is so omnipresent and evident that the decision was almost made not to even write about this attribute. However, the reality is that if we were not an idol-making and idol-worshipping species, our celebrity-obsessed society would not exist. While obvious, this characteristic is extremely pertinent, and not to discuss it would be a major oversight.

Our genetic predisposition to create and manufacture idols can be seen in what was written in the Old Testament. I remember my early religious teachings when I was educated that God was an all-powerful being that I needed to respect and worship and that I would be doomed and suffer severe ramifications if I failed to do this. I was taught the Ten Commandments, and the one commandment that is relevant to this discussion is "Thou shall have no other gods before me." That is, I should pray to this one God, and I better not think about putting anyone or anything else in front of Him, or I would be in big trouble, as I would be violating one of the Ten Commandments. When you think of it, of the Ten Commandments, I can fully appreciate edicts like "Thou shall not kill" or "Thou shall not steal" or "Thou shall not covet thy neighbor's wife." However, to have a commandment not to idolize anyone else doesn't seem quite as important as those other command-ments. However, given our tendency to worship idols, the author of the Ten Commandments must have known that this decree should be stated up front, showing how deeply embedded this inclination is within us. I also remember the story of when Moses went to get the Ten Commandments on top of Mount Sinai. For 40 days and 40 nights, Moses was away, and down below at the bottom of the mountain, the people were getting very impatient, and they gave up on him. They decided to erect an altar in the shape of a calf made out of gold, and they began to worship this idol instead of God. When Moses returned, he became enraged that the people were doing this and smashed the Ten Commandments. The point is that we have a long history of creating idols to worship.

Today, there are many examples that demonstrate our tendency to idolize some members of our species. Autobiographies and biographies, whether the person is living or dead, literally fill the shelves of bookstores, and magazines consistently publish stories of certain individuals as people want to learn about them. Television talk show hosts interview certain people who have captured our interest as other members of society want to learn more about them. We also see people who walk around with basketball, baseball, and football jerseys that represent their favorite team, and often on the back of the jersey is the name of their favorite athlete on the team. People have a need to let others know who their attachments are, who they like, and who they respect.

Our tendency to idolize certain individuals is epitomized in our desire to own the possessions of certain people, again either living or dead. Whether it is a letter a famous person wrote, an article of clothing, a signature, or a strand of hair, many people have a need to possess and own this merchandise. One doesn't really know the person, yet somehow having a possession that once was his or hers is important. In fact, it is so vital that enormous sums of money will be paid to have it. In 2009, the check for $10.50 that Neil Armstrong, the first man to walk on the moon, wrote shortly before he took off netted $27,350.[1] John Lennon's white suit that appeared on the cover of *Abbey Road* netted

$117,600,[2] the guitar played by Jimi Hendrix grossed $190,000,[3] a telephone book owned by Marilyn Monroe grossed $90,000,[4] and the gloves worn by Muhammad Ali when he fought Joe Frazier in 1971 netted $385,848.[5]

Even photographs of certain individuals can generate huge sums of money. *Forbes* put together a list of the most expensive photos (or at least the best estimate of these photos) during the past 10 years, and these were not adjusted for inflation. The top three were the following: $4.1 million that *People* magazine paid for the Shiloh Nouvel Jolie-Pitt baby photos in June 2007, Demi Moore and Ashton Kutcher's wedding photos that *OK!* magazine paid about $3 million for, and Eva Longoria and Tony Parker's wedding pictures for about $2 million paid by *OK!* magazine.[6]

We also tend to copy and want to be like those whom we idolize. This internalization of the attributes of others who are admired helps people shore up an identity and develop a self-concept. For example, a young boy may come to dress like his father, or a young girl may develop similar interests as her mother. Young children, when they want to grow up, may want to become a police officer or firefighter if those roles have status in their community. Others may dress like a person whom they idolize or may join the same organization that their mentor is a member of. A musician may buy the same guitar as someone he or she admires and may even attempt to copy certain styles of performing. I remember when Sarah Palin, John McCain's choice for vice president in 2008, entered the scene. She was virtually an unknown, but immediately when she was chosen as McCain's running mate, people wanted to copy and emulate her by buying and wearing the same brand of glasses she wore.

Our tendency to worship and idolize others can even be seen in ordinary day-to-day relationships, especially when two people meet and get romantically involved. That glow of a new relationship and the idolization of each other is one of the most powerful feelings people can experience. And, on the flip side, how often have we seen a romantic relationship end with one person, typically the man, feeling that he cannot live without his former lover and then kills her and then maybe even himself? Or perhaps a different scenario is that a lover leaves another, throwing the person into a deep depression, as the person cannot imagine living life alone and without the other person. In these situations, one person is so idolized and revered that to not be with that person causes extreme distress and despair. Other extreme examples of idolization are the unwavering obedience that members of a cult may give to their charismatic leader. Jim Jones, the leader of the People's Temple, convinced hundreds of people to commit suicide by consuming drinks laced with cyanide in Jonestown, Guyana. Charles Manson was able to persuade his followers to kill for him, and David Koresh, the leader of the Branch Davidians religious sect, was able to obtain the staunch devotion of his followers.

A PSYCHOLOGICAL PERSPECTIVE

Why do we tend to idolize and worship others, and why does owning something that another person possessed give another person such gratification? While there is no absolute answer to these questions, let me offer several ideas that can explain this.

Our tendency to place individuals on pedestals may originally stem from our extreme helplessness and dependence on our parents or whoever served as our parenting figures. When all of us are infants, we are totally helpless to defend ourselves from anything in our environment, and we are totally dependent on a parenting figure for survival. For a young child, parents or parenting figures are all-powerful and omniscient. Such figures are placed on pedestals because they are, in fact, key for our existence. In general, children tend to idolize their parents, whether they are caring or abusive, and this occurs because, regardless of the type of relationship, they are still needed for subsistence.

On a larger and grander scale, Charles Darwin postulated the theory of survival of the fittest.[7] In this theory, the fittest are able to survive, as they are able to adapt to the environment in which they live. It makes sense for members to place the strongest or fittest members of their species up on pedestals and to let them know how much they are valued, loved, and respected, as having a relationship with that member helps ensure their own survival. Years ago, developing a relationship with and being in the good graces of the best hunter, the strongest person, or the preeminent toolmaker would clearly have survival value. Today, having a special relationship with a wealthy person, politician, or other powerful individual can similarly enhance one's survival and help ensure an easier life. Whether conscious or not, essentially the person is covertly thinking and behaving in the following manner: "I think you are awesome, and I want you to know this because having a relationship with you has great value for me. In the long run, it is in my interest for us to have a relationship."

Possessing something that was owned by another noteworthy person can also give a person vicarious pleasure, as in some ways this helps convince the person that he or she, too, is special and distinctive. Ernest Becker, in his Pulitzer Prize–winning book *The Denial of Death*,[8] wrote that deep inside, we are all concerned with the fact that we are truly insignificant and no different than any other animal. We like to believe that we are special and significant, but in reality, at our core, we sense that we are just like any other animal on the planet and that when we die we are simply "food for worms."[9] To counter and deny this terrible feeling, we create a culture to convince ourselves that we are special, that we are different from other animals, and that we truly matter. We ascribe extraordinary meaning and value to cultural creations, whether these are architectural achievements, pieces of artwork and relics of the past, or items that have been owned by famous people as a way for us to believe that we are truly distinct and unique. When well-known people die, the pomp and circumstance surrounding the individual's funeral is, at least in part, designed to convince everyone that the person was special and exceptional, again helping to counter the notion that we are, quite frankly, not particularly significant or different from other animals. We also gather possessions and money to assure ourselves that we are powerful, helping to counter our inner feeling of our total insignifi-

cance and powerlessness. Related to this is our creating figures to idolize and endowing them with exceptional attributes, again to convince
ourselves that we, too, are truly extraordinary and unique. It is like we
are thinking, "Look how wonderful *so-and-so* is, who is part of the
human species. I, too, am a part of the human species, so I must be
pretty remarkable as well." This is the thought that takes place underneath the surface, although this is not necessarily conscious.

An example is the auctioning of Captain Chesley "Sully" Sullenberger's hat on eBay, along with a note from both him and his wife. For
those that do not remember, Captain Sullenberger was the pilot who
landed his disabled US Airways plane on the Hudson River in 2009.
This was truly an act of heroism and saved everyone's lives. Bidding was
going to occur over the course of one week, and near the end of the
bidding, the price had exceeded $5,500.[10] The money, mind you, was
going toward a very good cause: to two schools in California. However,
the point is, why does someone want to own this hat? Once the person
has it and it placed in some drawer or closet or maybe hung over a
fireplace, what value does it truly have? And, by the way, the hat auc-
tioned was not even the hat the captain wore when he engineered his
heroic and now famous landing. In fact, he wasn't even wearing a hat.[11]

This hat has special meaning only because we place certain people
on pedestals and attribute great worth and significance to their possessions. As a result, vicariously, it can give the person who owns it a
special feeling along with some status. It is like the person is uncon-
sciously thinking, "Look what I have and no one else has, which makes
me feel special" or "I have something that was owned by an extraordinary person, which in turn, helps me to feel exceptional, too." Whatever
the pull, a key trait that we all possess is our tendency to idolize and
place certain individuals on pedestals, and this clearly plays a role in our
obsession with celebrities.

6

SELF-ESTEEM

Of all the judgments you make in life, none is as important as the one you make about yourself. The difference between low self-esteem and high self-esteem is the difference between passivity and action, between failure and success. —Nathaniel Branden

Probably the most important requirement for effective behavior, central to the whole problem, is self-esteem. —Stanley Coopersmith

One other attribute that must be reviewed to help us understand our obsession with celebrities is our need to feel good about ourselves along with maintaining a confident sense of self and a positive self-esteem. The drive to feel good about ourselves begins in childhood, extends into adulthood, and remains a central theme throughout life. Without a positive self-regard, we are destined to experience psychological pain throughout our lives.

Beginning in childhood, we can see how important it is for young children to feel good about themselves. The young child who climbs up on a chair and exclaims, "Look at me!" does this to achieve a sense of mastery and to hear the parent say "good job!," helping to reinforce and build a positive self-concept. Children critically need their parents to be proud of their accomplishments, and they need to see the gleam in their parents' eyes. When they hear approval from their parents, it enables them to feel special and helps augment and develop a positive sense of self. If the child does not receive admiration and there is a pattern of not getting that kind of praise, this will affect the child's overall sense of well-being and impact the child's overall character and development. Receiving "good enough" parenting,[1] which consists of being the recipient of parental love and adequate and appropriate praise, is essential to the development of a positive sense of self and self-esteem.

During this time, mastery of other tasks is another way that children develop a worthy and positive sense of self. Learning to communicate, to write, to do math, and to solve other mental problems takes place, and again, success in these areas and getting positive feedback from others is essential and solidifies a healthy self-concept. As school is such an important component of the child's world during this time, how the child performs in school is particularly relevant and significant. Success leads to positive feelings about oneself, whereas failure leads to the opposite.

Throughout adolescence, youth continue to be even more preoccupied with developing a healthy self-esteem. During this time, being accepted and valued by one's peer group is critical if not one of the most important tasks adolescents face. There are also occasions when youth will do anything to get that acceptance—whether it is using drugs, stealing, doing something outrageous to get respect, or even doing something illegal. While on the surface it may appear that the behavior is irrational and not well thought out, underneath the youth is trying to create an identity and to feel good about who he or she is. During this time, adolescents may experiment with different identities, dress, and extracurricular activities in an attempt to establish a stable sense of self and an understanding of who they are. How one performs in school, how one plays on the sports field, and discovering what their interests are and what they are good at all play a key role in helping to create a positive regard about oneself.

Sexual development and creating a sexual identity is also critical during this time. Being valued and accepted by members of the opposite sex (or by members of one's own sex if one's sexual orientation is gay) becomes a major motif, and concern about one's body image becomes ubiquitous and vital. There is an increased focus on clothes, hairstyle, makeup, and general body image. Young adults continue to be involved in developing an identity and figuring out who they are and what will provide them with good feelings about themselves. Some individuals will decide on a career that interests them, and much educational achievement and striving is done to feel positive about oneself. Another may wish to open up a business, satisfying their need for fulfillment and accomplishment. Even others may decide to get married and have children, which is what they need to do to feel good about who they are.

As adults, people continue on this path and engage in activities to support and augment their self-esteem. Vocational pursuits and accomplishments persist, as does the raising of children. Getting promoted at work, making more money, or taking up and mastering some leisure activity are all ways to help us feel good about ourselves. While different people enjoy doing diverse things that provide them with stimulation and satisfaction, a component of this often is the pursuit of excellence, which helps enhance confident feelings about oneself.

In fact, many psychologists and psychiatrists have focused on the maintenance of self-esteem as a key component in their theories. Alfred Adler, a disciple of Sigmund Freud, based his individual psychology theory on the importance of maintaining a positive self-esteem and overcoming feelings of inferiority.[2] Adler maintained that the one basic ever-powerful striving behind human activity was movement from a feeling of inferiority to one of superiority in an effort to feel secure within one's self-esteem. Adler felt that it was normal to experience feelings of inferiority and that this feeling was a part of the human condition. He stated that to be human means to feel inferior, and at the same time, part of being human was to strive to overcome those feelings and to strive for perfection.

Heinz Kohut was a psychiatrist who developed a school of thought called self-psychology.[3] Kohut believed that there was a healthy narcissism, or love of oneself, that consisted of a strong and cohesive sense of self. When this was developed, people could strive forward with ambition and risk failure, enabling them to fully realize their skills, talents, and ideals. In fact, without a healthy narcissism, the person's self-esteem would be fragile and vulnerable, and this could greatly affect their overall development and ability to gain life satisfaction. Such people would be greatly dependent on others to maintain their self-esteem and could not move forward without fear. If they did venture out of their comfort zone and challenged themselves but failed, they would experience a narcissistic injury, resulting in a traumatic and destabilizing blow to their self-concept and self-esteem.

Abraham Maslow, who developed the hierarchy of needs theory that was noted in chapter 3, also believed that a critical requisite for a good life was having a positive self-esteem and that the way to obtain this, at least initially, was by procuring respect, recognition, and attention from others.[4, 5] If that could be accomplished, a person would achieve self-respect, self-confidence, and a sense of self that was less dependent on the approval of others. Without this, a person would experience low self-esteem, which he theorized was at the root of most psychological problems.

Ernest Becker suggested that the central and most important motif in the human species is our self-esteem and the need to show that our existence counts and that we are different and more special than other animals that inhabit the planet.[6] Becker argued that the need to feel good about ourselves penetrates deeper into human nature than any other element and is *the* condition in our lives. He further elaborated that culture is a symbolic hero system that is designed to enable us to achieve meaning and greatness. The hope is that the entities that we build and create will live on after us and will help give us a sense that we are truly special and that we matter. The temples, mosques, palaces, skyscrapers, and statues that we build; the children who are named after us; the books that are written; and the artwork that is created are all, on some level, designed to provide us with the myth that we count and that we truly are unique.

As has been written by John Mack and Steven Ablon of Harvard Medical School, "Political and religious beliefs and institutions are fashioned to enhance self-worth, and artistic creativity is intimately connected with the need to accomplish something which will give us value. Nothing is more important for the maintenance of well-being. Conversely, no experience is more obviously distressing, or more intimately linked to emotional disturbances of many kinds and, in psychiatry, to various types of psychopathology, than is diminished sense of worth or a low opinion of oneself."[7]

It must also be realized and understood that the solidification and maintenance of self-esteem is dependent on both one's achievements and the validation one receives from the external environment. In fact, the development and sustainment of a positive sense of self can be fully comprehended only within a social context. Beginning in childhood, the small child's successes need to be reinforced by parental approval, which in turn will help the child feel positive about him- or herself. The glow that is seen by the child in the parent's eye gets internalized, creating a sense of value and esteem. In fact, without the parent's acknowledgment and validation, a positive sense of self will not occur. Adolescents, too, need to obtain acceptance and approval from parents as well as their peers, as without this their self-esteem will suffer despite any of their achievements. This same interdependence between a person's accomplishments and the validation that is received continues throughout the life cycle into adulthood. As written by Mack and Ablon, "Just as the beginning sense of being of value grows for the infant out of the shared matrix of loving interactions with its mother, and supportive approval of its efforts to achieve mastery in early exploratory initiatives, so our sense of personal value will always to a degree depend upon relationships. It is true, of course, that a core sense of one's worth (or lack of it) may be internalized in childhood and adolescence so that self-esteem will not fluctuate wildly in adult life. . . . But at the same time, no human being's sense of his value can ever become totally independent of the valuing of other people."[8] In fact, the importance of external validation is so profound for the development of self-esteem that it has been suggested that the excessive doling of praise on children by parents—and overindulgence in general—has at least in part led to a "narcissism epidemic" where many children have an inflated sense of self without evidence of true accomplishment or achievement.[9, 10, 11]

IT DOESN'T ALWAYS HAPPEN

Unfortunately, many people struggle with their self-esteem and feeling fulfilled and satisfied with their lot in life, whether this begins in childhood, adolescence, or adulthood. This can happen when children did not receive good enough parenting, as their parents never mirrored their accomplishments, leaving a hole or void in their self-concept. Or perhaps school didn't go well, resulting in a poor self-concept, or maybe peer relationships suffered, and the person never felt accepted and a part of the group. As an adult, it is possible that jobs were lost, financial difficulties were encountered, or a person got rejected by his or her spouse. All of these events can affect a person's sense of self and impact one's view of oneself. In many cases, if a person has a solid sense of self, such events will not be too destabilizing, and he or she will recover from them. Most of us, fortunately, are adaptable and can weather these kinds of traumas. However, when the abyss is deep and especially when it began in early childhood, it can be harder to move on from such stresses and losses.

The need to feel good about oneself is so powerful that extreme measures are often developed in an effort to solidify and shore up a defective sense of self. For example, if an adolescent cannot succeed in school and, as a result, feels like a failure, an alternate way to feel good can be to stop trying completely. The adolescent may report that "school sucks," that he or she doesn't care about school, and the individual ceases to try to succeed. Failing at school in this way helps preserve one's self-esteem, as it is less damaging to self-esteem if the person no longer tries and fails than if the person is really trying to succeed and still coming up short. Another person who has never been able to fit in and suffers emotionally as a result may develop an identity and lifestyle that is purposely "antiestablishment." It is like the person is saying, "You have caused me such pain that I am showing you that I don't care about you at all. I hate everything about you and your lifestyle, and I have chosen another." This certainly can help preserve one's self-esteem and feelings about oneself.

There are also individuals who have ended up spending most of their lives in jail. Some of these individuals have in some ways come to "choose" this lifestyle as a way to feel good about who they are. For a variety of reasons, they were not able to function in society in ways that they felt good about, and by entering a life of crime, they were able to shore up an identity and develop some sense of competence. Some even pride themselves on being a criminal and the crimes they have been able to achieve. While others may not view this as a particularly worthwhile life, for them, a life in jail is still better than what they imagine life would be like for them outside of jail, where rejection and failure may be deeply feared.

Even others may live a circumscribed life, never venturing out to challenge themselves or to take a risk, whether this is going for a new job, speaking in public, or accepting or asking a person out for a date. They are terrified of failing and instead choose to stay in their comfort zone. Even though people may not be happy and do not feel particularly good about who they are, the fear of rejection or failure blocks them from going forward. On some level, they are still committed to feeling good about themselves: by not challenging themselves, as doing this could result in failure, they attempt to preserve the limited and fragile self-esteem that they have by never risking failure.

In summary, throughout life, we are always involved in efforts to maintain and sustain if not enhance our self-esteem and self-concept. Most people are able to actively engage in activities, challenge themselves, and take risks, and this can augment and enhance their self-esteem and self-concept. For them, failure can be jeopardized because even if they do not succeed, their self-esteem is solid enough to weather failure. There are some, however, who cannot challenge themselves, as they are too afraid of failing. Even if it looks like they are suffering and not living a full life, which sadly may be true, what they are doing is still better than what they imagine life would be like if they didn't follow that course. Thus, the preservation of their self-esteem is still the motive. The bottom line for all of us is that we need to feel good about ourselves, and we are always involved in efforts to preserve if not augment our self-concept and self-esteem. As we will see, this trait has particular relevance to our obsession with both entertainment and celebrities.

Part II

The Social Scene

7

ALIENATION AND ISOLATION

Loneliness seems to have become the great American disease. — John Corry

In part I, a number of key traits that we all possess were reviewed that must be appreciated if we are to understand our obsession with being entertained and with people who entertain us, the most renowned celebrities in our society. However, to fully grasp this phenomenon, we must also come to appreciate the sociocultural context in which we live, as we are all affected and influenced by the world around us. Let me now share what I believe are some of the important elements in our present social environment that have helped spawn and grow this phenomenon.

To begin, there is a trend in today's society for all of us to be more alienated and isolated than we have been in the not-too-distant past. While the population in the United States has grown tremendously during the twentieth century, from about 76 million to 300 million people, and we are exposed to more people than ever before, in general, our close social network has shrunk. This can be seen in how our living situations have shifted. At the turn of the century, households with seven or more people represented the most common kind of living situation. Fully 19 percent of all households had seven or more people living together, whereas in 2000, this has decreased to only 1.8 percent.

In addition, in 1900, nearly half, or 45 percent, of all people lived in households of five or more people, whereas in 2000, only 10 percent of people lived in this large of a household. The reason for this is that in the past, extended families often lived together, whereas today, this is much more rare. So households today are generally much smaller.

The percentage of people who live alone has also increased during this time. Back in 1900, only about 5 percent of all households contained one person. However, 100 years later, this percentage has skyrocketed to about 26 percent, or about one in four people, reflecting an increase of about 500 percent. In addition, between 1950 and 2000, married-couple households declined from more than three-fourths of all households to just over one-half.[1]

Today, it is also more common for both parents to work to make ends meet than in the past. Among other things, the price of housing is so much more expensive that, to have a reasonable life and for parents to be able to provide for their families, both parents often must work. In addition, even if one parent's income can fully support the family, it is much more common today for both parents to work, as it is more acceptable and common for women to be in the labor market. This means that after school, children generally either come home to an empty house or, at least one without a parent at home, are placed in some kind of child care, decreasing the time spent with either a father or a mother.

There has also been an increase in the number of single-parent families. In 1900, only about 4 percent of families were single-parent families, or families in which a single parent lived with his or her own children who were under the age of 18 years. However, in 2000, this percentage had more than tripled to about 14 percent.[2] Again, either children must be placed in child care or they come home to an emptier house.

WHO IS OUR NEIGHBOR?

While our close social networks have contracted, our feeling connected to our immediate social surroundings has decreased as well. It is typical for people to live in a condominium, an apartment building, or even a neighborhood where everyone owns their home and to not know whom they are living next to and who their neighbors are. While there are exceptions, in many cases, we may say a quick "hi" or engage in some small talk, but we don't really know them, and in some cases, we literally do not know them at all. Even people who live in apartment buildings often do not know the person living in the apartment right next to them. This is due to a variety of reasons, but one is simply the high mobility in this country, which has been occurring for many years. In fact, census reports show that for the past 40 years, when people are asked if they moved within the past five years, between 35 and 47 percent of the population changed their place of residence.[3] That is a lot of flux, and if you take into account that this percentage is for every five years and that often it is not the same people who move, you can see that the change in geography and whom you are living next to can change dramatically. With all of this movement, it is hard to know who our neighbors are.

This high mobility also affects our close social networks, including our relationships with family members. In the past, families would stay together for years and years, and, as mentioned above, extended families might even live together. Familial relationships were a major social support for all family members if not their most important backing and aid. Now, though, while there are instances of extended families continuing to live in and around the same community, it is common for families to disperse and to live all over the country or even in other countries. While family members may still keep in touch and feel emotionally close, they spend less time together, and their needed emotional connection and contact often comes from other sources.

Our high mobility has also affected our close friendships. Many years ago, when there was less mobility in this country, a person could stay connected to their school friends throughout their entire childhood, from elementary to middle to high school. Even when out of school, people would get a job and continue to live in the same area, and friendships would continue for life. Now, as it is so common to move, this is less likely, most friendships wither away, and maintaining friendships with school-age friends is less common. Often, early peer relationships get disrupted due to our being such a mobile society. As has previously been noted, Facebook has become a way to stay connected to others to counter our increased isolation, as it enables us to maintain these connections or to to reconnect, which is one reason why this social media website is so popular. Our increasingly isolated existence is also the reason why Internet dating sites are so numerous and why so many people use the variety of dating sites that are available. People often can't meet other people for a potential date in their day-to-day interactions, as they are less socially connected, so they instead look online. Online, it is much easier to meet people, even people who live close by but whom you would never be able to encounter without this mechanism. There are even websites to marry people who live on the other side of the world.

Many suburban environments can make it more challenging for people to meet other people. On any given day, people can go shopping in their own town or neighborhood, and it is likely that they may not encounter anyone whom they know. In many suburbs, strip malls that one drives to have replaced the nice quaint downtown area where people used to walk around, congregate, and hang out together. Everyone is a stranger, and unless one is gregarious and outgoing, it can be harder to meet others and strike up a conversation. It has been noted that the absence of sidewalks and pedestrian-oriented shopping areas can lead to greater isolation in suburban communities.[4] An analysis of two large population surveys has suggested that suburban environments may dampen social connections and lead to greater social isolation and alienation.[5] Again, while there are more and more people, ironically, connecting to and developing a close and lasting relationship with them is more difficult. To counter this, one aspect of the New Urbanism movement is "the reconfiguration of sprawling suburbs into communities of real neighborhoods and diverse districts."[6]

A car is a fantastic invention. It allows people to travel great distances and to be able to see things either that they would never see or that would take days and days if not weeks to see. As amazing as the car is, the downside is that it greatly lessens the chances of any of us meeting with and talking with each other. Instead of everybody walking to and from where they are going, which would facilitate interpersonal interaction, cars create barriers between people. We are all in our own "metal boxes," islands unto ourselves. Traveling at 20, 30, or 40 miles an hour prevents us from interacting with each other. We pass by each other but have nothing to do with each other unless, by ill fortune, we get into a car accident.

Not only does this lead us into more isolation, but driving a car can also cause us to dislike our fellow neighbors and can bring out the worst in us. When we are in our cars, it can feel like us against the world, and others in our immediate surroundings who are driving their own vehicles are the enemy. Maybe it is because driving can literally be a life-and-death situation: if the other person does something dangerous, it can mean death to the driver as well as the other friends or family members who are also in the vehicle. Other drivers also can impede whatever we are doing, a position not many of us want to be in. The thoughts that go through our heads when we drive include "What a jerk . . . doesn't he even know what a blinker is?," "What an idiot! She almost killed me!," or "Come on! The light changed . . . let's get going!" Road rage is a real phenomenon, and people have literally come to blows due to arguments that have arisen when driving. People who otherwise love and care for other people can get caught up in this. As wonderful as the automobile is, it can contribute to greater isolation and distance from our neighbors and others whom we live near.

VIOLENCE IN AMERICA

Violence in America has actually been decreasing since 1992, when violent crime peaked.[7] This includes aggravated assault, rape, robbery, murder, property crime, and larceny/theft. I would not be surprised if many people were surprised to read this. Many people are afraid to strike up a conversation with a stranger, and most parents, when their children can comprehend what a stranger is, will tell them to avoid these kinds of people like the plague. My mother used to tell me that when I was a baby, she used to leave me in a carriage near the front of the department store she used to shop in alongside the many other baby carriages containing the babies of other parents. If I woke up and started to fuss and cry, another woman would pick me up to soothe me. This was common, and it was acceptable to do. In today's society, a parent can't imagine doing that. Parents don't let their children out of their sight for one minute if not a few seconds. Someone might kidnap their child, or, at least, this is a real fear. In truth, if parents left their child alone in a department store today, they would be viewed as careless and neglectful, and they would likely get reported to the local social services department, as they would be seen as being in need of some kind of external supervision to be able to care effectively for their child or children. I also remember as a child when Halloween would arrive. My friends and I would go trick-or-treating all over the neighborhood at night when it was dark, and my parents never gave it a second thought. Now, when kids go trick-or-treating, parents keep an eye on them like hawks—and for good reason.

I believe that the reason why people believe that the United States is a very violent country is twofold. First, while violent crime has been decreasing, there is still much more violent crime now there was than 50 years ago or in the 1960s. In the 1970s through the early 1990s, violent crime increased, and while the trends are reversing, we still have a long way to go back to the level of violent crime that existed 50 years ago. Here are some statistics that demonstrate the violent society in which we live.

Among adolescents, the firearm homicide rate for children under 15 years of age living in the United States is 16 times greater than in 25 other industrialized countries combined.[8] Excluding accidents or unintentional injuries that result in death, among 15- to 19-year-olds living in the United States, the highest cause of death was homicide.[9] The United States also has an overall firearm homicide rate that is 20 times higher than the combined rates of 22 other countries that are comparable in terms of overall wealth and population.[10] In another study that looked at 835 male serious offenders in a number of juvenile correctional facilities across four states and 758 inner-city male high school students living in the same areas, it was found that 83 and 22 percent of these two samples, respectively, stated that they possessed a gun. In addition, 55 percent of those residing in detention centers reported that in the year prior to being incarcerated, they carried a gun all or most of the time, and 12 percent of the community sample reported the same.[11] Such data focus only on carrying weapons and homicide. Obviously, there are many other forms of violence, including rape, robbery, and aggravated assault. In fact, of all violent crime in the United States, murder is just a very small percentage, accounting for only 4.7 percent of all violent crimes.[12]

Very sadly, in some urban environments, children may be staying inside their homes after school because parents are too afraid to let them play outside. This is a very unfortunate state of affairs but one that may be relevant to our increasingly lonely and more isolated existence. As an aside, some researchers have found a relationship between obesity and perceived community violence. While there are many reasons that are involved in the obesity epidemic, one factor is physical inactivity. Kids are sitting on the sofa watching television, playing video games, or surfing the Internet because parents will not let them out of the house after school, as it is simply perceived to be too dangerous.[13]

Another reason we are so concerned about violent crime has to do with perception. The instantaneous communication in our society that broadcasts incidents of violence that happen across the country gives us the impression that violence is rampant and growing. Not only do we hear about violent crime that occurs outside of our social circle, but even within our local communities, the news focuses on this, whether it is a sexual assault, a house break-in, a murder, or a robbery. So even if crime is down, we do not appreciate this, as crime is constantly in our faces. As a result, our interactions with others whom we do not know are filled with fear, curtailing our ability to develop connections with other people.

SOME SOCIAL INDICATORS

There are many other signs that demonstrate that we are living more isolated lives than in the past. Robert Putnam, in his fascinating book *Bowling Alone*, reviews data from many surveys that reveal the collapse of American community life.[14] Looking at involvement in many community activities, he makes the point that social capital and connections among individuals in a community have declined. For example, the percentage of parents involved in parent-teacher associations has declined dramatically since around 1960, when almost 50 of every 100 families were involved in such associations; 40 years later, at the turn of this century, this number had dropped to fewer than 20 for every 100.

Surveys have also revealed that active participation in a variety of clubs, civic groups, charities, and fraternal and veterans organizations has been dropping. The operative word here is *active*, and here this means having served on a committee or having taken a leadership role. From the early 1970s to the early 1990s, the percentage of people who took an active role in any local organization had decreased by 50 percent. Apart from active involvement, mere attendance at club meetings has also declined. In the mid-1970s, American men and women attended on average about 12 meetings each year, or about one per month. By 1999, attendance had decreased to only five meetings each year. It has also been found that in 1975, 64 percent of Americans reported having attended at least one meeting during the past year, but in 1999, this had decreased to only 38 percent. Or to talk about it a different way, back in the 1970s, two-thirds of Americans attended club meetings, whereas about 25 years later, two-thirds of Americans stated that they never attended a club meeting. This same trend can be seen in religious participation. When looking at actual church attendance and involvement as opposed to simply church membership, it has been shown over the past 30 to 40 years, attendance and involvement in religious activities among adults living in the United States has decreased by 25 to 50 percent.

Visiting with friends and neighbors is also down. From the mid- to late 1970s to the turn of the century, individuals who report entertaining friends at home decreased by 45 percent, from an average of 14 to 15 times per year to only eight times per year. It would be nice if this were replaced by going out with friends, but that activity has not shown any increase. It has also been ascertained that going on picnics with others has declined by about 60 percent during the past 30 or so years. Spending a social evening together with a neighbor has declined during this time period as well by about 33 percent. Card playing with each other as well as sending greeting cards to others in our social network show the same trend.

Even families doing social things together have shown a downward trend. Families that report that their whole family generally eats dinner together has decreased by one-third from the late 1970s to the turn of this century. From the mid-1970s to the late 1990s, polls have shown that among families with children between the ages of 8 and 17, the percentage of those that report vacationing together has dropped from 53 to 38 percent, reflecting an almost 30 percent drop. Watching television together has decreased from 54 to 41 percent, and just sitting around and talking to each other has decreased from 53 to 43 percent. All these data point to the fact that as a society, we appear to be less socially connected with each other.

In summary, while we need and enjoy social interaction, it appears that we now tend to be more isolated than in the past. This has occurred for a variety of reasons that include economic and modern technological factors, the urbanization of our immediate environment, perceived violence in our communities, and our changing family structure, to name just a few. The fact is that as much as we like and crave contact, we currently live in ways that don't foster this and that inhibit our social side and being able to have close connections to others. As will become apparent, our greater isolation is relevant to our obsession with celebrities.

8

WHAT MAKES US FEEL GOOD?

Advertising has us chasing cars and clothes, working jobs we hate so we can buy shit we don't need. —From the movie *Fight Club*, based on the novel by Chuck Palahniuk

It's not how you feel, but how you look . . . and darling, you look MAH-ve-lous. —Billy Crystal

The end of labor is to gain leisure. —Aristotle

A second change in our culture that is relevant to our obsession with entertainment and celebrities is our increased focus on personal life fulfillment and inner happiness. As reviewed in chapter 6, we all have a need to develop and maintain a healthy and positive self-regard, and people will do different things to achieve this. However, today, there is a greater preoccupation with self-fulfillment and one's personal satisfaction with life. Furthermore, in a general sense, the route and means to feel good have come to be based largely on consumption, although a search for meaning in other ways is still an important motif, as can be clearly seen in the range of psychotherapies and self-improvement guides that are available to assist people in achieving happiness. There is also an increased focus on our external physical appearance as a way to augment our feelings about ourselves. These changes have occurred largely as a result of our changing work environment.

Prior to 1750 and the industrial revolution, there was no separation of work and family life. While there was a division of labor within the family based on age, sex, and what work people could reasonably be expected to accomplish based on their abilities, there was a unity between the family and the world of the production of goods. Family units produced commodities that were contributed to society; some constructed tools, others made clothing, and others crafted silverware, to name just a few. In addition, many individuals were self-employed, and each had their particular trades and crafts, using their own tools to make products. The family and the entire household made up the basic economic unit as opposed to people leaving their homes to work and make money, a totally separate activity divorced from one's family life. Furthermore, one's working and personal life were one and the same. For most, life was work, and work was life.[1] In fact, the concept of an inner, personal, subjective life didn't even exist as we think of it today. For example, the word *self-esteem* was first coined by William James, the father of American psychology, at the turn of the twentieth century.[2] This, however, was about to change.

The industrial revolution, which began in England around 1733 with the invention of the cotton mill, took off in the United States shortly thereafter. From 1775, when the first reliable steam engine was invented, until the Model T Ford was manufactured in 1908, many modern conveniences that we take for granted were invented, whether this was the sewing machine, the telephone, the phonograph, incandescent lightbulbs, electric motors, or the first airplane. In addition, it was during this time that a variety of different kinds of commodities began to be produced on a large scale on assembly lines, which removed the manufacturing of many goods and wares from the family and one's own private efforts.

For example, in Lowell, Massachusetts, a major textile manufacturing plant was built in 1823, and by 1840 a total of 32 mills existed in the city, employing over 8,000 employees. Many of these employees were women who had previously lived in the countryside, and rows of boardinghouses and tenements were built to accommodate their need to have a place to live.[3] Over the years, huge cotton mills were built in other areas, also employing large numbers of workers. This pattern soon spread to other industries, and during the century more crafts and products that were once made in people's homes on a small scale instead began to be made in mass production factories. The change in how products were produced also led to a change in the skills that were required to be employed. In particular, the precise skills that people honed to make and produce a variety of goods, such as clothing, pottery, and glass objects, were no longer required, as these products began to be mass-produced by newer technological innovations. Large-scale manufacturing needed people to work on assembly lines, being responsible for one small part of the end product rather than for the entire entity.

The shift in our working life can be seen simply in the number of people who were self-employed in the not-too-distant past compared to now. In 1948, or shortly after World War II, almost one out of every five people, or 18.5 percent of those who worked, were classified as self-employed.[4] Move the clock forward to 2004, and this percentage had dropped to 11 percent, or about one out of nine people.[5]

What has occurred is that for many people (but certainly not all), what they do for work has simply become something that they do to survive economically rather than as a means to define themselves and who they are. As a result, the pride and recognition that one can receive through work no longer exists, and this can impact one's identity, sense of self, and self-esteem. In addition, whereas a person's personal life and what the individual did for work used to be fused together (again, life was work, and work was life), for many people a split began to take place. Work became an activity that one did to make money, and a completely separate sphere of personal life that was focused on achieving individual fulfillment began to emerge. When reviewing the changes in personal identity spawned by capitalism and the industrial revolution, it has been noted, "one's individual identity could no longer be realized through work or through ownership of property: individuals now began to develop the need to be valued 'for themselves.'"[6] As a result, over time, a search for a personal identity that had nothing to do with work was born, and an increased preoccupation and search for self-fulfillment and personal happiness was produced. While to some extent this "privilege" was always available or restricted to the wealthier members of society, the pursuit of fulfillment outside of work got extended to the working class and to more members of society due to how the industrial revolution affected many people's working lives. What, though, was a person to do to obtain personal fulfillment?

CONSUMPTION

While modern technology has enabled companies and corporations to mass-produce most anything and the list of manufactured products is almost endless, the products must be sold to make it all work. Unless people are buying and consuming, a capitalistic and consumer-oriented structure cannot be sustained if there is no demand for the merchandise. To ensure the success of capitalism, members of the working class needed some leisure time and the wages necessary to increase the market for all the goods that were being produced.

In this regard, in 1863, Ira Steward, an American labor spokesperson, called for a reduction in hours and increased wages that would enable the workers, "through their new leisure, to unite in buying luxuries now confined to the wealthy."[7] Edward Filene, the founder of the department store Filene's, also advocated for workers to have more wealth and more time for leisure and stated the following: "Mass production demands the education of the masses . . . the masses must learn to behave like human beings in a mass production world."[8] By this, he meant that the masses must be taught to consume what was being produced. In fact, he explicitly stated that companies needed to "sell to the masses all that it employs the masses to create."[9] In addition, through advertising, which will be more fully reviewed in the next chapter, people became convinced that the way to happiness and fulfillment was through consuming and buying fancy goods and products.

Concerning how capitalism has changed the family as well as personal life, it has been noted that "mass production forced the capitalist class to cultivate and extend that market, just as it forced it to look abroad for other new markets. As a result, American domestic and personal life in the twentieth century has been governed by an ethic of pleasure and self-gratification previously unknown to a labouring class. Working people now see consumption as an end in itself, rather than as an adjunct to production, and as a primary source of both personal and social (i.e. 'status') identity. This is often expressed within the 'middle class' as 'lifestyle,' a word that is used to defend one's prerogatives regardless of the demands of society."[10]

Essentially, there has been a general shift in the way people try to feel good about themselves and their status in life. Whereas fulfillment was often and largely tied to work and what a person did to make a living (if an inner dialogue about life fulfillment even took place), currently, for many people, feeling good about oneself is entwined with what can be bought and consumed. Buying a new car, fancy jewelry, the newest iPhone, or the latest fashion style has become the way to bolster a positive regard about oneself. In fact, many have suggested that consumerism has gotten so extreme that it has the potential to destroy Earth as we know it. Rampant manufacturing and consumerism leads to the destruction of the world's forests, the pollution of our air and water, and climate change. Over 15 years ago, the Union of Concerned Scientists, consisting of a group of scientists across the planet, warned that unless developed nations changed their course of overconsumption, earth as we know it would be indelibly changed if not irretrievably mutilated.[11]

In addition to consumption, the industrial revolution also led to the creation of greater free time and the pursuit of recreational activities. To begin, working hours were reduced, and thus people had more time to spend on leisure. The Bureau of Labor Statistics collects all kinds of data on businesses and the people who work in a variety of different occupations in the United States. It looks at average pay, average hours worked, benefits offered, and a variety of other factors. Relevant to this discussion is the average number of hours worked per week in the United States. Around the turn of the century, the average number of hours worked per week was around 59.[12] Over the next 50 years, it dropped by about one-third to an average of around 40 hours[13] and has remained relatively consistent to this day.[14] That is close to 20 hours per week, or about 1,000 hours less time devoted to working each year.

Furthermore, with the explosion of modern technology that has occurred, life is now much easier than it was in the past. As a result, we have much more time for the pursuit of pleasure and recreation. Let's take one example of how modern technology has provided us with significantly more free time: the heating of our homes. For most of us, heating our homes now simply takes a flick of the wrist to move the dial on the thermostat. Compare this to the effort it took to heat a home before we learned how to harness and deliver heat at our beck and call: it would take days or weeks (if not months) to cut down trees, which in turn needed to be cut into pieces, which then needed to be transported, split, stacked, and dried. Then, on a daily basis, wood needed to be carried into the home and burned, requiring still more time and effort.

Another example is the time it takes to ensure our supply of food. In the past, getting enough food together to be able to survive and to continue to eat over the winter entailed a huge amount of work. This could consist of plowing one's property, planting seeds, caring for and harvesting what was grown, caring for and killing one's livestock, and preparing the meat for consumption. A person might be involved in the canning of some vegetables or making some jellies out of some fruit that was grown. All of this was out of necessity: if a person didn't prepare, he or she could not survive and be sustained over the winter.

Today, a person gets into his or her car, travels to the grocery store, buys what is needed, and, presto, cooks and eats a meal. Or maybe the person shops only once per week so that all the food is already purchased and ready to be cooked; this requires simply opening the refrigerator (also a timesaving invention) or cabinet and choosing what was already bought. Or perhaps the person is lazy and bought a TV dinner, which requires only heating it up and not wasting time preparing and cooking the food. The person may also own a microwave oven so that the meal can simply be placed in the microwave; a button is pressed, and within a few minutes the person is delighted with a hot meal. The individual may also own a dishwasher, another timesaving invention that eases the cleanup effort and saves even more time. But maybe even that is too hard; instead, a quick phone call is made, and within half an hour, a piping-hot pizza is delivered to one's home. In many ways, life is a bit easier now than in the past, giving us much more leisure time.

Think about this: in the 1700s, Mozart, just to survive (and barely survive), had to write pieces of music geared to the aristocrats who paid him to do this. That was the only way for him to make money, as there wasn't a large group of people who had the time or money to see him perform. However, 25 years later, Beethoven could fill a concert hall with hordes of people who had the time and money to come to listen to him. Paganini, a name much less familiar than Mozart and whom many people may not have even heard of, could also fill concert halls and live a good life, as there were people who had the time and money to attend a concert. There were also others with questionable talent who made a good living, as the demand for entertainment exceeded the available talent.[15] Life had changed, and there was now a group of people who had the time to be entertained. Too bad Mozart wasn't born a few years later, as he would have had a much easier life.

So we see that as a separation between work and personal life occurred, pleasure and fulfillment began to be marketed through advertising and convincing people that the way to feel good about one's life could be obtained through consumption, consumption, and more consumption. Buy and drive the nice car, and in return you will feel good about yourself. Or buy the fancy diamond bracelet or the bigger and newer television, and, bingo, you will feel good. More energy was also placed on obtaining satisfaction by doing something gratifying during one's free time. So, in a general way, satisfaction with life, or feeling good about oneself, not only became a prominent motif in society but also became married to what one consumed and what could be experienced in free time outside of work.

The general interest in an inner and subjective sense of self can also be seen in the birth of the modern psychotherapy movement, which began with the theory of mental functioning of psychoanalysis put forth by Sigmund Freud around the turn of the twentieth century. Since that time, hundreds of other theories about why people think and behave in particular ways have been developed, and attached to each of these theories are therapies that are designed to help people learn about themselves and achieve greater life satisfaction and fulfillment. This focus on one's subjective sense of self and inner happiness continues to this day, and thousands of self-help books written to enable people to obtain greater joy in life are available. Some have even suggested that the focus on "me" represents a negative trend in society, as greater benefit could occur through an emphasis on caring for others.[16] Regardless, it is clear that there is an enhanced focus on feeling good about oneself and how to obtain personal fulfillment and inner happiness.

A FOCUS ON THE EXTERNAL

Another shift that has taken place as a way to augment and solidify our self-esteem is a focus on the external. Our looks and outward appearance and how we present ourselves to others have become increasingly important. As mentioned in chapter 2, our worship of beauty has always been omnipresent, but over time, wanting to look beautiful and our focus on external appearances has strengthened immensely and has become even more of an obsession. We have become preoccupied with how people (as well as ourselves) look and present themselves on the surface and how hip or charismatic they or we are. Let's take a look at why this has taken place.

As mass production began to occur, factories opened, and to secure work, people left their farms and moved to the city. In 1910, about 33 percent of the labor market worked on farms. However, by the end of the century, only 1.2 percent were employed as farmers or farm laborers, a drop of 96 percent.[17] With this changing work environment precipitated by the industrial revolution that brought an influx of people into the city, how were people to stand out in the crowd, develop a unique identity, and define who they were? Among this swarm, how were people to meet others and develop friends when there were so many potential possibilities? One way was to focus on their skills of self-presentation.

As the twentieth century approached and even to this day, people were encouraged to impress others based on an appealing appearance, the development of charm, and making a good first impression. Style, a sense of humor, and charisma began to be more important, and while it was still important to be honest and sincere, these traits had to be externalized to others so that they could be seen. A person who was sincere and honest but who could not effectively demonstrate these traits to others was not as valuable as the person who could, without effort, show this side to the public. A significant shift began to occur from the depth to the surface—how one presented to others became most important.[18]

Furthermore, as the manufacturing of products began to dwarf need, these products had to be marketed, advertised, and sold. To accomplish this, companies needed attractive, engaging, and personable people to interest others to buy the products. The better a person was at doing this, the more valuable that individual was to the company. For obvious reasons, celebrities were used to market a variety of products,[19] as were others who exuded charm. As a result, physical attractiveness became increasingly important, and the external attributes that people possessed dominated previously valued internal ones, such as honesty, integrity, and dependability. This remains true to this day, as evidenced by the gigantic advertising and marketing industry, which typically uses engaging, sexy, and attractive people to sell whatever merchandise is being sold.

Around this time, books and magazine articles began to get published, instructing people how to develop a personality to win over friends and to be a complete success in the business world. In this regard, personality was a general term that described how a person

presented him- or herself, and having charisma or a charismatic personality became the goal. Experts in personality development helped people cultivate a magnetic personality, which consisted of perfecting one's
inner being and effortlessly being able to show others his or her true
and wonderful self. It became all about *the image* and that is true to this
day. Having a good personality meant that the person engaged well with
others and was friendly, likable, funny, charismatic, and charming.
Depth did not matter; what mattered was a person's skill at external
presentation.

Relevant to this discussion is Dale Carnegie (1888–1955). Carnegie
was a pioneer in public speaking and teaching others how to develop
and improve their personalities. He obtained fame by showing other
people how to achieve success, and his book *How to Win Friends and
Influence People*,[20] published in 1936, has sold more than 10 million
copies. Dale Carnegie courses and seminars have been and continue to
be offered to help others develop the leadership attitude as well as the
executive image. Here is a passage from the Dale Carnegie website:
"You'll gain dexterity and grace in dealing with new or trying situations;
recognize how you come across to others; speak honestly and confident-
ly; become conscious of body language; master your emotions; give and
receive criticism constructively; present yourself as powerful—not in-
timidating; and say what you need to say without offending or creating
conflict."[21] I think this kind of training can be valuable, and especially in
society today, it can be essential. However, the point is that this is all
about how to interact with others and showing and cultivating the best
image possible, which has become a way to feel good about ourselves.

Compare the title of Carnegie's book to some books that were sold
in the nineteenth century that were written to help people develop
their character. Some examples include a self-help book by Cecil B.
Hartley titled *The Gentlemen's Book of Etiquette, and Manual of Politeness: Being a Complete Guide for a Gentleman's Conduct in All His
Relations towards Society . . . from the Best French, English, and
American Authorities*.[22] Here is another title by George Winfred Hervey: *The Principles of Courtesy: With Hints and Observations on Man-*

ners and Habits.[23] And here is one more by G. S. Weaver: *Hopes and Helps for the Young of Both Sexes: Relating to the Formation of Character, Choice of Avocation, Health, Amusement, Music, Conversation, Cultivation of Intellect, Moral Sentiment, Social Affection, Courtship, and Marriage.*[24] It is hard to imagine a book coming out with those titles today.

While we are increasingly focused on our external appearance, our image, and how we portray ourselves to others, what is also true is that when we look to others, in a parallel way we are grabbed by and enamored with people who look good and present themselves well. Whereas in the past we were more interested in a person's internal attributes, in this day and age it is the external image that has become most important. We no longer care as much whether a person is good, bad, self-centered, caring, or particularly intelligent. Rather, we are more concerned with whether the person is attractive, cool, or charismatic or can make us laugh.

This shift from internal traits to external presentation can be clearly seen in the following excerpt, which was from the personal agenda of an adolescent diarist from a book published in 1892 called *The Body Project: An Intimate History of American Girls*: "Resolved, not to talk about myself or feelings. To think before speaking. To work seriously. . . . To be dignified. Interest myself more in others." When girls in the nineteenth century thought about ways to improve themselves, they almost always focused on their internal character and how it was reflected in their outward behavior.

A century later, American girls think very differently. In a New Year's resolution written in 1982, a girl wrote, "I will try to make myself better in every way I possibly can with the help of my budget and baby-sitting money. I will lose weight, get new lenses, already got new haircut, good makeup, new clothes and accessories."[25] Now if that doesn't say something, I don't know what does.

In summary, over the years there has been a shift in how we try to feel good about ourselves. First, there is an increased focus on buying and possessing "things" to help us feel positive about our lives as well as an increased emphasis on enjoying our free time for the pursuit of leisure. Second, there is an enhanced obsession with our external appearance, body image, and how we present to others. Being good looking, charismatic, and engaging is a focus and desired goal, as is the possession of material goods. In a similar vein, individuals who possess these attributes will be sought after, adored, and desired. Sadly, a person could be caring, intelligent, thoughtful, and loyal, but in today's world this may not get the person too far without those other, more external characteristics. While those internal traits may help and be useful in certain realms, it will be hard to beat the attractive person who is charismatic and wealthy. A shift from internal to external, from depth to surface, has taken place, and this has particular relevance to our preoccupation with being amused and our obsession with celebrities.

9

MASS MEDIA

Whoever controls the media, controls the minds. —Jim Morrison

Whoever controls the media, the images, controls the culture. —
Allen Ginsberg

To understand our obsession with celebrities, we need to appreciate
the influx of mass media and its impact on our essence and consciousness. Mass media has the power to reach out broadly to audiences
across the nation or world—television, radio, the Internet, newspapers,
and magazines. Within minutes after an event happens across the
world, we become aware of it because of mass media. This includes
catastrophic and major events, such as natural or manmade disasters,
declarations of war, explosions of bombs, or the death of some powerful
political figure. Likewise, this also includes more trivial occurrences,
such as the color of a tie that some noted individual wore at an event
1,000 miles away, the food that some well-known individual ate at some
celebration, or a mother who lost custody of her children because of
mental illness. A murder happened, a suicide took place, a store was
broken into, or a pipe in a restaurant exploded. Over the years, the
amount of information that we are exposed to has increased exponentially. In fact, there is so much information that gets transmitted that it
is hard to keep up with it.

Is all of this information newsworthy? But this raises the question: what is news, or what is newsworthy? How about anything a good editor wants to print, as expressed by Arthur MacEwen, who was named the first editor of the *San Francisco Examiner* by William Randolph Hearst? Or another definition of news: "News is anything that makes a reader say, 'Gee whiz!'"[1]

Mass media began around the early to mid-nineteenth century. In the 1830s and 1840s, the telegraph first began to transmit reports of affairs from far away, and it was in 1846 that the first presidential message was transmitted by wire. Around this time as well, the newspaper industry began to greatly expand. High-speed presses were developed, as was the rotary press, which could churn out newspapers at rates of speed unheard of before this time. The Associated Press was founded in 1848, and news in general became a part of our society. Daniel Boorstin coined this period the beginning of the graphic revolution, where news and images of events grew at an amazing pace.[2] In 1783, there were 43 newspapers in the United States. Thirty-one years later, in 1814, there were 346 different newspapers. Another 36 years later, in 1850, newspapers numbered 2,526. And 30 years later, in 1880, 11,314 different newspapers were in existence. Over time, more inventions followed, further expanding our ability to rapidly disseminate news from all over the world. Some examples include radio transmission at the turn of the century with the first commercial radio station in 1920. Three years later, there were over 600 radio stations. Television came into existence in 1941 and color television 20 years later. In 1950, just about 9 percent of all homes had a television; in 1960, it was closer to 90 percent, and now almost every home has one if not two or more. Even in hotel rooms, there may be one in the bedroom and a small one in the bathroom. In 1992, the first 24-hour news station appeared, and around this time, the Internet also came into existence. Whereas in 1997 only about 18 percent of households had Internet access in the United States, its penetration reached approximately 75 percent of all households by 2012.[3] All of these inventions and new ways to transmit more lifelike information have created an almost unlimited ability for us to know what is going on around us, whether close at home or far away. At the same time, mass media has also completely infringed on our psyches, and we are continuously exposed to a boundless range of information and images that can barely be absorbed.

THE POWER OF MASS MEDIA

So why does this matter, and why is this important? It matters because what we see and what we are exposed to influences both what and how we think. It can also exert control over us in ways that are underappreciated and that are just beginning to be fully understood. The power of the media is truly gargantuan.

As an example, before mass media, within a typical day, most people would generally think about their immediate surroundings, the people they interacted with, and what occurred in their lives. Sure, other, more worldly events and happenings would sometimes enter the field, and there were certainly people involved in more creative activities and their own internal thought processes. But overall, what most people encountered face-to-face in their daily lives were the things that filled their consciousness.

Jump to the present, and it is totally different. While we still think about these same things, like our workdays, our romantic encounters, our immediate friends, and happenings of the day, today we are exposed to a new level of awareness. Just a few examples: we can witness a political demonstration in some faraway country that is happening as we watch, we hear about a woman who had eight babies through fertility treatment who lives thousands of miles away and the fact that she already had six young children, a war that is occurring far from our shores is now living room entertainment, a family whom we will never know encountered a bear when on a camping trip, or a man died while climbing Mount Everest.

Mass media has dramatically changed the nature of our social intercourse and interactions with each other. When we meet with friends, work colleagues, and other acquaintances, the focus of conversation now often has less to do with our daily lives, as the focus often turns to the events of the day that occur in society and the world at large. We discuss current events to the exclusion of what is happening in our personal lives, and often what is discussed may be rather trivial. Sadly, too many get-togethers come and go with no one learning anything newsworthy about each other. To some degree, this also diminishes the closeness we once shared. What is featured in mass media inadvertently often dictates what we talk and think about.

Do you remember Terri Schiavo? Had it not been for the media, her name and case would have remained obscure. For those who do not remember, the Terri Schiavo ordeal was a seven-year legal effort by her husband to have her disconnected from life support, as she was diagnosed as being in a persistent vegetative state. He was opposed by Terri's parents, but finally, her husband won, her feeding tube was disconnected, and she died in March 2005.

When this legal battle reached its crescendo, Terri was a household name. Here was a private matter of a woman and her family who lives in Florida, and regardless of where people lived, everyone knew of Terri and had an opinion about her fate. Due to this story being picked up by the media, advocacy groups, pro-life organizations, disability rights groups, and even President George W. Bush got involved. This demonstrates the far-reaching impact of the media, as without media coverage, almost no one would have known anything about Terri. Terri's plight was the subject of discussion among households due to the power of the media.

In regard to how the media controls our thinking, I live in the state of Massachusetts, and our major athletic teams are the Patriots, the Red Sox, the Celtics, and the Bruins. When any of those teams are in the playoffs, the Patriots, Red Sox, Celtics, and Bruins dominate the news. All the Boston newspapers and local television news stations focus on this. When in conversation with other people, it is also a main topic of discussion. Now, certainly, even without the media, it is possible that how the city's team may fare in the big game might be a conversation item. However, it is the media that blows it up big-time and largely fuels and generates all of the hype and subsequent dialogue.

When our local teams are not in contention, the playoffs get minimal coverage, and discussion about this among us New Englanders comes crashing to a halt. Given that our teams are out of it, talking about these sporting events will naturally decrease. However, if the news focused on it more, it is likely that we, in turn, would continue to think and talk more about these championship series as well despite our teams being out of contention.

The extreme power of the media is even recognized in the U.S. Constitution. Embedded in the First Amendment to the Constitution, documented in 1791, is the freedom of the press. That is, people should be free to express any and all opinions in written materials as well as in the media, which is the only way to ensure democracy. Any limitation on expression curtails what people reflect on and can be used to restrict and control our thinking. Communist countries understand this very well, which is why they tightly control and regulate the media. It was Napoleon Bonaparte who uttered the following: "I fear three newspapers more than one hundred thousand bayonets." Napoleon knew what he was talking about—the power of the press is monumental. And this was stated about 200 years ago. If Napoleon lived in today's environment, I can only imagine what he would say.

I would even suggest that for many people, especially those who are less connected to others and tend to live more isolated lives, the new social connector to the world is the various forms of mass media that exist. For some, their primary means of social connectedness to the world has become their involvement in what mass media deems important to print and broadcast. Topics of conversation concern what took place on *The David Letterman Show*, *Saturday Night Live*, or some other television program. Other conversation topics could be what Brad Pitt and Angelina Jolie are doing, how much money Paul McCartney had to pay in his divorce, or how much some sports team is paying an athlete to play for them, who is injured, who has been traded, what team is doing well, what team is doing poorly, and who is in a slump.

Other, more substantive topics could include what is happening on Wall Street, the spread of nuclear technology, or the political unrest in another country. The point is that what is featured in mass media, whether insignificant or significant, are the topics and foci of interest. We are sponges, and we soak up what we are exposed to, determining what we think.

The overwhelming influx of the news we hear in the media has also changed our thought processes and how we learn. While exceptions exist, more commonly, instead of attending to just a few events in a more in-depth way, we instead learn about a far greater number of events in a more superficial way. As we are exposed to so much information, it is impossible to read a lengthy article or to listen to in-depth discussions of all of these events, as that would simply take too much time. Consequently, we hear and take in sound bites or read brief blurbs to absorb a greater number in one sitting. Over time, this has changed how we learn about the events that occur in the world. Furthermore, as there are so many events that we can hear or read about, we have a tendency to forget past events, as there is another, more recent incident that we are exposed to and that is highlighted in the media. Rapidly, news becomes old news, as there is a more recent occurrence that takes center stage. The earthquake in Haiti is soon forgotten, as the tsunami in Japan, the political unrest in the Middle East, or the tension between North Korea and the United States becomes the newer news of the day. So not only has the media transformed what we think about, but it has also changed our actual learning style.

SOME UNINTENDED CONSEQUENCES OF THE MEDIA

Another way to appreciate the power of the media is to look at the relationship between exposure to media and children's health. Youth ages 8 to 18 spend a little over seven and a half hours each day using various forms of media, including television, the Internet, movies, video games, music, and websites. That equals more than 53 hours each week. And if you include multitasking, or using more than one medium at a time, it is estimated that kids can jam in about 10.75 hours into that seven and a half hours. This is more time than they spend on a weekly basis with parents (17 hours) or even at school (30 hours).[4] A lot of people are concerned about the impact that exposure to the media has on today's youth.

In a recent meta-analysis that looked at numerous studies that have attempted to explore this topic, it was found that viewing tobacco use in the media had a significant association with youth's tobacco use. A relationship was also found between viewing scenes of alcohol use in film or the number of hours spent watching television and an increased use of alcohol. Watching sexual content on television was also associated with initiating sexual intercourse and other sexual activities. With adolescents, researchers have found a relationship between watching greater amounts of "sexy" television and earlier initiation of sexual intercourse.[5] In addition, in a one-year study, it was found that frequent watching of rap videos by 14- to 18-year-old adolescents was associated with engaging in higher-risk sexual behaviors as well as contracting a sexually transmitted infection.[6] So without even trying to get youth to smoke, drink, and have sex, simply watching these kinds of visual images had an impact.

Even among college students, we see the effect of viewing certain kinds of content in the media. In one study, two control groups of college students watched movies with commercials. Some of the movies showed a lot of alcohol use, whereas others did not, and some commercials advertised alcohol, whereas did not. In addition, in this experiment, alcohol and other soft drinks were available while watching the movie. What the researchers found was that viewing a movie in which the use of alcohol was portrayed led to greater amounts of drinking than when the movie did not portray alcohol use. In fact, it was found that the group in which the use of alcohol was portrayed in movies and commercials drank one and a half more glasses of alcohol than the group that did not watch movies and commercials portraying this.[7]

What we see in the media also can greatly affect how we view our body image and overall attractiveness. Jean Kilbourne is a psychologist who has studied the impact of the media and, in particular, how this may affect how girls view both their body image and themselves. She believes that the incessant images shown to teenage girls that show flawlessly beautiful woman who happen to be ultrathin greatly influence how girls view themselves.[8] In support of this is a study that found that as time spent reading magazines, which typically show thin and attractive women, increased, dieting among girls increased.[9] Other studies have shown that after reading women's magazines, college girls tended to feel less satisfied with their own bodies.[10] In fact, Kilbourne believes that adolescent girls' obsession with thinness is tied to being inundated with images of women who are beautiful and thin.

Why thinness is a necessary part of being beautiful is a complicated subject, and a thorough discussion of that could fill another book. Regardless, the reality is that in this country, beauty and thinness are connected, and the viewing of such models of beauty in the media affects our psyches. Some startling statistics include the fact that 40 to 80 percent of fourth-grade girls are dieting, and one-third of 12- to 13-year-old girls are trying to lose weight by dieting, vomiting, using laxatives, or taking diet pills.[11]

Furthermore, it isn't only girls who are affected. There have also been some studies that have looked at boys and how what they read may affect their body image. Boys who read *Electronic Gaming Monthly* and *Game Informer*, magazines that show hypermuscular video game characters, reported greater body dissatisfaction than boys who read sports, fitness, and fashion magazines.[12] Second-, third-, and fourth-grade boys have also been studied to explore the relationship between what kind of magazines they read and their body image perceptions. What was found was that the boys who read primarily gaming magazines reported greater concern about their body size compared to boys who read fashion and fitness magazines.[13]

Much has also been written about the possible relationship between watching violence and aggressive acts in the media and people's own levels of aggression and violence. That is, does watching violence cause people to act more aggressively? This is a complicated relationship to ascertain because more aggressive people may tend to watch violent media. It follows that if people who watch violence are more aggressive, it may be not the watching of violence that caused the aggression but rather that these people were already more prone to violence to begin with. In addition, violence in the media can consist of many things: it can be violence between people, violence among cartoon characters, playing violent games, watching realistic violence, watching less realistic violence, observing funny violence as in *The Three Stooges* as opposed to violence designed to truly maim and kill others, watching violence associated with bombings in war, or even seeing sexual versus nonsexual violence, to name just some variants.

Nonetheless, despite the difficulties in trying to understand the causal relationship between watching violence in the media and acting more aggressively, it is clear that viewing violence increases aggression. While not every person who watches media violence will become violent and aggressive, just as not every person who smokes cigarettes will develop lung cancer, there clearly is a causal link between watching violence and becoming aggressive and violent.[14] Again, the power of the media cannot be overstated.

WHAT IF MEDIA TRIES TO INFLUENCE PEOPLE?

So far, I have been discussing how what we read and watch can impact and influence both our thinking and our behavior. Without *purposely trying to make us think and act in certain ways*, what is portrayed in the mass media has its effect on our psyches and influences what we think and what we do. But what if mass media *actually tries to influence us*? Could its effects be further enhanced? I believe that the answer is undoubtedly and without question yes.

The most obvious way that the media can be used to influence and control us is through direct advertising, which is a giant business. It was estimated in 2009 that companies spent about $260 billion a year on advertising.[15] It has also been stated that 70 percent of our newspapers[16] and 40 percent of our mail[17] consists of some kind of advertisement. In fact, it has been stated that "to not be influenced by advertising would be to live outside of culture. No human being lives outside of culture."[18] Margaret Mead, the American cultural anthropologist, stated that children are no longer brought up by parents. Instead, they are brought up by the mass media.[19]

One example that demonstrates the enormity of advertising as an enterprise is the advertising that takes place during the Super Bowl. In 2013, during the Super Bowl, companies shelled out over $4 million for a 30-second ad.[20] That is almost $130,000 per second. And that doesn't include the $1 million to $2 million it takes to produce that 30-second ad. Companies would never spend this kind of money if depicting and displaying their goods on television didn't have the ability to influence us. Advertising obviously has a tremendous influence on consumerism and on our buying behaviors. Very simply, without advertising, we would never know what products to buy. There are many examples of how advertising has been used successfully to influence us, but here are a few that show not only how advertising affects what we buy but also how it can have huge implications on our health and lives.

SMOKING CIGARETTES—JOE CAMEL

Joe Camel was an advertising campaign implemented by R. J. Reynolds for Camel cigarettes from the late 1980s to the mid-1990s. Joe Camel was a really cool camel and was the mascot for Camel cigarettes who appeared in magazine advertisements, on billboards, and in other print media. In late 1991, the *Journal of the American Medical Association* published three articles that concluded that Joe Camel was as well known to six-year-olds as was Mickey Mouse.[21] Another article reported that Camel's market share among underage smokers grew from .5 to 32.8 percent.[22] Shortly after, a lawsuit was filed against R. J. Reynolds that stated that the Joe Camel campaign was targeting youth, and it demanded that this advertising campaign cease, that R. J. Reynolds surrender profits made through sales to underage buyers, and that they develop a different advertising campaign. This lawsuit also alleged that in 1988, Camel cigarette sales to youth were only $6 million, whereas in 1992, sales of Camel cigarettes to youth totaled about $476 million. Over time, a number of other cities and countries filed similar lawsuits, as did the Federal Trade Commission, which alleged that this campaign made children smoke. What eventually occurred is that in 1997, R. J. Reynolds settled and decided to discontinue the Joe Camel advertising campaign and also agreed to spend about $9 million to prevent youth from smoking.[23]

In fact, the clout of advertising through the media is so great that how cigarettes can be marketed in general has been curtailed over the years. For those who remember, cigarette advertising was ever present on television and radio. Who remembers the following advertising lines: "Us Tareyton smokers would rather fight than switch" or "Winston tastes good like a cigarette should"? These ads were popular on television in the 1950s and 1960s, and what changed everything was when Congress banned the advertising of cigarettes on television and radio on January 2, 1971.[24] In fact, prior to the banning of such advertising, in the late 1960s, the Federal Communications Commission ruled that television stations had to air antismoking ads at no cost to offset the effect of paid advertisements.

Advertising has continued in magazines, in newspapers, and on billboards, but as most everyone knows, a message of how cigarettes are detrimental to a person's health must appear on all products sold. Also, in 2003, tobacco companies and magazine publishers agreed to stop placing smoking ads in school library editions of several magazines that are often read by young readers, such as *Time*, *Newsweek*, *Sports Illustrated*, and *People*.[25]

Placing even more controls on cigarette advertising occurred with the passage in June 2009 of the Food and Drug Administration's Tobacco Regulation Bill, which provides the government with tremendous power to regulate tobacco advertising. Under this bill, the Food and Drug Administration can compel tobacco companies to eliminate misleading labels such as "light" and "mild," and it also can force tobacco companies to increase the size of warning labels.[26] All of this demonstrates the effect of advertising in the media and how this can be used and has been used to influence our behavior.

OVEREATING AND OBESITY

Another huge public health concern is overeating and obesity. It is estimated that childhood obesity has more than tripled in the past 30 years. In particular, from 1976–1980 to 2009–2010, the prevalence of obesity among two- to five-year-old children increased from 5 to 12.1 percent. Among youth aged 6 to 11 years, obesity increased from 6.5 to 18 percent. Among 12- to 19-year-old adolescents, during this same time period, it is estimated that the prevalence of obesity has increased from 5.0 to 18.14 percent.[27] While this can be caused by many factors, including greater levels of inactivity and staying inside due to living in unsafe neighborhoods[28] and watching more television and surfing the Internet, one big factor that researchers believe plays a key role is advertising junk food in the media. As noted by the Institute of Medicine, exposure to advertisements in the media can greatly affect people's decision making. In particular, the Institute of Medicine found that the advertising of food and beverages on television influences children ages 2 to 11 years to buy and prefer high-calorie and low-nutrient foods and beverages. It was found that the most prevalent items teens purchase with their own money were candy, carbonated soft drinks, and salty snacks and chips. In addition, without parental oversight, of all the money children and youth spend annually, the four top items that youths ages 8 to 12 years purchase are high-calorie and low-nutrient food.[29] While the Institute of Medicine is not calling for a complete ban on such advertisements, there is sufficient concern to suggest that this kind of marketing needs to be looked at and that perhaps some controls should be put in place, similar to how controls have been enacted regarding the advertising of cigarettes.

GETTING ELECTED

The power of advertising is also evident in politics. Without advertising, candidates cannot get their messages out, and no one would ever know who the candidates were. Without huge dollars, no candidate has a chance, as television advertising is expensive. It is no wonder that many of our elected officials are very wealthy and place enormous sums of their own money into their campaigns. Additionally, it is not surprising that money is the tool used by lobbying groups to influence candidates who will support their agendas. Not only are ads designed to simply get a candidate's message out, but they are also carefully crafted to influence our decision making. How to either portray one's own message in a desirable way or devise a message to turn voters off to another candidate, or what is known as negative advertising, is a huge enterprise. While this doesn't always work, valiant efforts are undertaken, so much so that in some campaigns negative advertising is the norm.

If we just look at Barack Obama and John McCain, the Democratic and Republican finalists, respectively, in the 2008 election, Obama raised $138,231,595 and McCain raised $53,717,085.[30] Now that is just about $200,000,000 for just those two candidates, which is an enormous sum of money. Another way to look at it is that Obama spent $2.00 per vote, whereas McCain spent a little over $1.00 per vote. It is interesting to wonder whether the election would have been different had McCain been able to raise more money, but perhaps Obama was able to raise more money because more people wanted him to be elected president. One never will know, but regardless, in political campaigns, advertising in the media is crucial.

PROMOTING POSITIVE BEHAVIORS

The media can also be utilized to encourage and foster positive undertakings and to influence people to do constructive things that they otherwise might not do. Public service announcements designed to influence people to engage in healthy behaviors and to get involved in helpful activities also exist and are equally powerful. Antismoking advertisements, substance abuse prevention marketing strategies, increasing the use of sunscreen to decrease the risk of getting skin cancer, HIV and hepatitis prevention efforts, and advertisements encouraging women to get yearly mammograms, to name just a few campaigns, have all had some success in influencing people in positive ways. Antilittering campaigns are other examples of how the media has been used to benefit all of us.

In fact, researchers have looked at how to craft a message to increase the chances that a person will engage in the healthy behavior. For example, in researching the use of sunscreen, researchers have discovered that creating a message extolling the benefits of using sunscreen as opposed to the dangers of not using it have a greater chance of success.[31] This goes to show how, with careful planning and thought, the media can be used in ways that can help society and its citizens. Some other examples are discussed next.

"Only You Can Prevent Forest Fires"

One of the longest-running ads in history is Smokey Bear and his now famous line, "Only you can prevent forest fires." This advertising campaign was first introduced in 1944 by the Ad Council, an American nonprofit organization that distributes public service announcements for other sponsors and organizations in the United States, in an effort to educate the public on how to prevent forest fires. At that time, accidental fires accounted for 9 out of 10 forest fires and were responsible for destroying millions of acres of land each year.

Smokey Bear became so popular that he began to appear in cartoons and comic strips, and in 1952, after beginning to attract commercial interest, an act of Congress was passed to take Smokey Bear out of the public domain and place him under the control of the secretary of agriculture. This way, the money that Smokey Bear generated could be used for continued education on forest fire prevention. Over 50 years later, due to the concern about wildfires across the country, the slogan was changed to "Only you can prevent wildfires." So the question is whether something like this was successful. Since the beginning of the Smokey Bear fire prevention campaign until the year 2000, the numbers of acres lost to fire has decreased from 22 million to 8.4 million.[32]

"Keep America Beautiful"

Another successful advertising campaign began in 1961. "Keep America Beautiful" joined forces with the Ad Council to develop a campaign to fight pollution. Advertisements were created to show how litter, as well as other forms of pollution, was destroying our environment. The campaign's goals were to get the message across that every person needed to protect the environment and that protection of the environment was everyone's responsibility. It also sought to change behaviors that caused pollution.

Initially, "Suzy Spotless" scolded her father, who was a litterbug. A later ad showed pigs rummaging through trash that had been left behind by humans. About nine years later, a toll-free hotline offered free brochures, and within the first four months, over 100,000 copies were requested. Reportedly, the National Litter Index dropped for the second straight year. This advertising campaign continued to progress, and on Earth Day 1971, Iron Eyes Cody took over the scene along with his line, "People start pollution. People can stop it," and Cody became known as the "Crying Indian."

When this campaign was at its peak, over 2,000 letters each month were sent to "Keep America Beautiful" from people who wanted to get involved in their local areas to work on antipollution efforts. When the campaign ended, it was estimated that "Keep America Beautiful" local teams had helped reduce litter by about 88 percent in 300 communities and 38 states as well as in several other countries. In fact, *Advertising Age* magazine named this campaign one of the top 100 advertising campaigns of the twentieth century, and the ad won two Clio awards.[33]

"A Mind Is a Terrible Thing to Waste"

Many of you reading this might remember this now famous line. You may not be sure from where it stems, but the line is ingrained in our minds. For those who don't know, in 1972 the United Negro College Fund (UNCF), in conjunction with the Ad Council, implemented an advertising campaign to raise funds to send black students to UNCF-affiliated colleges. These are individuals who could not afford to go to college without financial support. Through the funds raised, tuition at these schools is generally less than half the average of other private schools.

"A Mind Is a Terrible Thing to Waste" became ingrained in our minds and helped generate huge sums of donations and money, and to this day this tagline continues to be used. Over the years, this campaign has helped raise over $2.2 billion and has helped more than 350,000 minority students graduate from 43 UNCF member colleges and universities. Today, UNCF enables over 65,000 students each year to attend college and get the education they want and deserve. Sixty percent of students supported by UNCF are the first in their families to ever attend college, and 62 percent are from families with annual incomes of less than $25,000. [34]

"It Shouldn't Hurt to Be a Child"

Another successful ad campaign was the effort to increase awareness of the problem of child abuse and to get people to obtain more information about this issue using the tagline "It Shouldn't Hurt to Be a Child." Prevent Child Abuse America, along with the Ad Council, created this ad campaign to inform people of the problem of child abuse. While this may be hard to fathom today, in the mid-1970s only 10 percent of adults thought that child abuse was a significant problem, although at the time over 1 million children in the United States were subject to abuse each year.

During the first month of the campaign, over 40,000 people sent letters to Prevent Child Abuse America. A survey conducted in 1981, after only five years into the campaign, found that 91 percent of the American public considered child abuse a major problem, whereas prior to this time, as mentioned, only 10 percent thought that child abuse was a significant concern. This campaign is credited to our current views on child abuse. For example, in 1996, a survey revealed that over 95 percent of adults believed that child abuse is a serious issue, 18,000 calls were made to the hotline, and more than 95 percent of adults surveyed said they believed child abuse was a serious problem. In 1978, the International Advertising Association's Public Service Advertising Award stated that this was "the best public service advertising campaign produced by an agency anywhere in the world."[35]

"Drinking and Driving Can Kill a Friendship"

A final example was the advertising campaign to decrease drinking while driving. In the early 1980s, the Ad Council and the National Highway Safety Administration launched the Drunk Driving Prevention Campaign. The tagline "Drinking and Driving Can Kill a Friendship" was targeted to 16- to 24-year-olds who were involved in 42 percent of all fatal alcohol-related car accidents. The intent of this ad was to bring the issue of drunk driving to the front of people's minds and to decrease driving while under the influence of alcohol. The Department of Transportation reported a 25 percent decrease in the number of drunk drivers killed in car accidents between 1980 and 1990, and this ad was believed to have been largely responsible for this. In fact, this public service announcement won the Clio award for best ad campaign.

The "Drinking and Driving Can Kill a Friendship" tagline was modified with a new, perhaps more familiar tagline: "Friends Don't Let Friends Drive Drunk." The intent of this line was to encourage friends to not allow their friends to get behind the wheel if they had been drinking. This public service announcement hit the airwaves in 1990, and it is believed that this campaign helped create a 10 percent decrease in fatal car crashes between 1990 and 1991.[36]

SUMMARY

Our inundation with images, sounds, pictures, and printed materials within the overall rubric of mass media is astounding. We are immersed in a sea of media, influencing us on many levels. The power of the media is further amplified when experts are intent on influencing public opinion by redirecting our views and decision making and thereby encouraging us to engage or not engage in certain behaviors. The scary thing is that we often are not aware of how what we see, read, and hear affects us, as we are completely surrounded by mass media, which has simply become a part of our lives. In the next part, when we attempt to understand our fascination with celebrities, we will see how the role of mass media cannot be underappreciated or understated. It adds jet fuel to the fire.

Part III

The Perfect Storm

10

ENTERTAINMENT ADDICTION

The effect of the mass media is not to elicit belief but to maintain the apparatus of addiction. —Christopher Lasch

Film is a powerful medium, film is a drug, film is a potential hallucinogen—it goes into your eye, it goes into your brain, it stimulates and it's a dangerous thing—it can be a very subversive thing. —Oliver Stone

I could have been a doctor, but there were too many good shows on TV. —Jason Love

In this and the next several chapters, I will bring together the ideas that I have written to help us understand our obsession with being entertained and our fascination with people who entertain us, whether they appear in movies, on television shows, on the athletic field, or in concert halls. We are also enthralled with some who have no particular talent at all other than being in the news and featured in the media. To understand this phenomenon, the metaphor of the "perfect storm" elegantly captures what has taken place. That is, a number of elements have come together to create this national obsession and preoccupation.

In fact, when trying to understand why a person acts in a particular fashion, many factors often play a role. A professor of mine once told me that the biggest danger in the field of psychology is reductionism, or trying to understand something by a single core source. For example, it might be suggested that a man develops distant relationships with others because when he was growing up, his father left the home and abandoned him, and to cope with this loss, he learned never to allow himself to get close to others. While this experience may be relevant to his isolation from others, to suggest that this individual acts in a particular fashion due to one specific event that occurred in the past is simply too naive. Rather, it is a range of things that have all come together to cause this trait, which can include his relationship with his mother, less-than-satisfying early peer relationships, a concern about body image, and experiences that occurred in school, to name just several factors. The outcome of being abandoned by one's father could have a dramatically different impact on another person who had other life experiences.

Regarding celebrity obsession and our fascination with celluloid images, this same kind of thinking is essential. There are numerous elements that have coalesced and that must be fully appreciated if we are to understand and make sense of this spectacle. It is equally hard to say which are the most important factors, and it was difficult to decide in what order to present them. However, while it can be challenging to separate all the components—the various traits that we all possess, the forces that impinge on us in our society, and the power of the media—for the sake of clarity, these must be reviewed sequentially. As you read this and the next four chapters, keep in mind that at all times, all these elements are operating simultaneously.

That being stated, if there are two overriding forces that are most important to understanding our obsession with celebrities—that is, if they did not exist, we would never be where we are—it is our craving to be entertained, coupled with and capitalized on by the power of the entertainment industry.

THE ENTERTAINMENT MACHINE

As reviewed in chapter 1, we have a huge need to be entertained, and we hate to be bored. That cannot be denied, and it if weren't for that, we would never be in the situation we are in. While it is possible to enjoy and seek entertainment without being particularly obsessed with those who do the entertaining, one would never be infatuated with celebrities if entertainment were not important. That is, if a person did not watch television, go to the movies, view sporting events, or listen to music or if the desire to view these kinds of events was not particularly strong or important, the individuals who work in these venues would not be known, and thus there would be no interest in them. While our lust to be entertained has always existed, our wish to be entertained has grown even stronger, and this is relevant to our obsession with the comings and goings of people who work in the entertainment field. Consequently, we must first comprehend how we have come to be so preoccupied with being amused to understand our obsession with these individuals.

What has taken place over the past 100 years is that the entire media and entertainment machine has become increasingly powerful, intoxicating, and potent. Success in this industry is grasping our attention, and enormous amounts of money, talent, and time are utilized to do everything possible to engage our focus and interest. In fact, the ability of this entire industry to capture our brains is remarkable. Neil Postman, in his book *Amusing Ourselves to Death*,[1] suggests that the origins of the entertainment industry had its beginnings with the invention of the photograph. As opposed to the written word, a photograph immediately taps in to our sensory experience, and viewing a photograph requires much less analytic thought and reasoning than does reading about the same event, as it impacts us much more intensely and immediately. For example, we can see a picture that shows the destruction caused by a tornado, and immediately we can be affected by it. In contrast, reading about a tornado's destruction requires considerably more thinking, and it feels like we are more removed from the event than when seeing a photograph or, better yet, watching a movie of it. In a similar vein, seeing a picture of a beautiful landscape is much more captivating than reading about it. In fact, something is lost when an attempt is made to describe with words a stunning scene of nature.

Neal Gabler, in his book *Life: The Movie*,[2] has noted that in America, with the invention of photography, there appeared to be a new emphasis on seeing and visual images.

With photography came moviemaking, which began in the late nineteenth century and quickly became a national preoccupation, as movies captivated our need to be entertained, which can be seen in the rapid expansion of movie theaters across the country. In 1907, there were approximately 5,000 movie theaters, and four years later, that number more than doubled to about 11,500. Three years later, there were about 18,000 theaters, and it was reported that there were 7 million admissions per day.[3] While initially movies were frequented by the working class in storefront nickelodeon theaters, it didn't take long for movies to spread to the middle class in more upscale establishments. When talking about movies, Gabler noted that "no other entertainment could provide the same immediacy, the same vast scale, the same phenomenological impact as the movies."[4] What has occurred over time is that the moviemaking industry has made watching films even more compelling than it was when they first came into existence, although it is clear how much this form of entertainment was able to capture our need for amusement even when movies first came into existence. I equate this change to the shift that has occurred in the use of the active ingredient in the coca leaf.

About 5,000 years ago, in South American Indian culture, people used to chew coca leaves, and they would experience a minor effect from the tropane alkaloid in the leaves of the coca plant. People chewed the leaves, which can produce a stimulant effect similar to strong coffee. It was used for medicinal purposes, for energy, as an anesthetic, and to aid blood clotting. It also was viewed as having mystical and religious value. Chewing the leaves enabled people to work, as it combated fatigue and promoted a sense of happiness and well-being. Coca leaves also had nutritional value, as the leaves contain many essential proteins and minerals. Essentially, the use of the coca leaf was integrated into their society. It gave people a lift, helped them do their chores, and didn't cause too many problems; coca leaf chewing was simply a part of the culture.⁵ However, as we now know, cocaine, or the extracted alkaloid from the coca leaf, is a powerful substance that can destroy a person's life. Whether snorted, smoked, or injected into a vein, it has a very different and much more powerful effect than chewing a coca leaf. Taken in this purified form, it can cause cardiac arrhythmias, paranoia, and death, along with severe addiction.

In a similar fashion, at the present time, watching a movie, as well as viewing any other form of entertainment that has been enhanced and amplified by the technological advances used in filmmaking, is a totally different experience than it used to be. Movie and television directors, along with their entire support staff, are talented and know how to use the camera to create a picture to evoke our emotions. The use of special effects, more complex film editing techniques, musical scores, better ways to pace the storytelling, the use of montage, fadeaway shots, and continuity editing, to name just a few techniques, are all used to enhance the visual and sensory experience of watching a film. A film can impact us on many levels and place us in different mental states, and what is produced can make us laugh or cry, enrage us, or make us feel more sexual. Today, watching a movie is a totally engrossing experience that can completely seize a person's psyche. Viewing a movie now is more akin to a person's smoking crack cocaine or mainlining it intravenously and getting totally wired as compared to chewing on a coca leaf. This is no small-time buzz but rather a major adrenaline rush.

Regarding the hypnotic effect of movies, Hugo Munsterberg, a Harvard psychology professor, wrote, "Sensory hallucinations and illusions have crept in; neurasthenic persons are especially inclined to experience touch or temperature or smell or sound impressions from what they see on the screen. The associations become so vivid as realities, because the mind is so completely given up to the moving pictures."⁶ When movies first appeared, they did not have all of the technological advances that current directors utilize, but viewers still needed to be cautioned that what they saw was not real. In 1907, *Movie Picture World* had to remind readers, "You will learn that the comic, the tragic, the fantastic, the mystic scenes so swiftly enacted in photographic pantomime are not real but feigned."[7]

The ingenuity of the filmmaking industry can even be seen in the making of commercials, as these same techniques are used to take the creation of commercials to a higher level, all in an effort to captivate our attention, temporarily entertain us, and make us want to buy whatever product is advertised. Just think of the dollars spent on commercials during the Super Bowl, which are miniature works of art in their own right. It is not uncommon for people to talk about what commercials they have seen, and commercials that have appeared during the various Super Bowls can be viewed online both before and after the Super Bowl.

Beyond a shadow of a doubt, the telling of a story or even the selling of a product through visual images has been enhanced over the years. The evolution of this art through advanced techniques has captured our minds in ways not previously possible, and due to our need to be entertained, we have been captivated by this technology. Regarding the interplay of our instinctual need for entertainment and the media, Walter Lippmann, journalist and media critic, wrote, "The philosophy which inspires the whole process is based on the theory, which is no doubt correct, that a great population under modern conditions is not held by sustained convictions and traditions, but that it wants and must have one thrill after another. Perhaps the appetite was always there. But the new publicity engine is peculiarly adapted to feeding it."[8] While this was written in regard to the sensational storytelling in tabloids that focused on real-life tragedies, murders, and other lurid events, it clearly is relevant to our being entertained in all media venues: our need for entertainment has been captivated by the power of the media machine.

The entertainment machine is even able to transform some individuals into "musicians." These are people who are able to sing moderately well, although their talent may be modest at best, but they have learned to use the entertainment machine for maximum benefit. When they perform or make a music video, with the use of fantastic lighting, choreographed dancing, a team of other performers, and other special effects, they are transformed into musicians. Such individuals are more like actors than musicians, and their concerts are more akin to a show than to a musical performance.

Our greater free time is also of paramount importance to our obsession with being entertained. As reviewed in chapter 10, beginning with the industrial revolution and the advent of technology, we have more leisure time than we had in the past. Life was much harder, and much of the day was spent working and taking care of one's household duties. Simply put, if we were busy with other activities and did not have the time to be entertained, the entertainment machine as it is today could not exist. People would not be available to be entertained or as interested in being entertained, as they would be involved in other pursuits. Entertainment can take place only in a social context in which people are accessible for this endeavor.

ADVERTISING

As was reviewed in the previous chapter, advertising is a powerful force, and many companies, including the television and motion picture industries, use this for maximum effect. Not only is the watching of entertainment much more engaging, but advertising has further increased its hold on us and has made watching entertainment something not to be missed. On television, programs, sporting events, and movies are heavily advertised, and in newspapers, movies are promoted with ads that abound with hyperbole. Here is just a sampling:

- The best romantic comedy in decades!
- The funniest film of the year!
- Fabulous, fun, and fresh!
- Bloodthirsty fun!
- As exhilarating, captivating, and enjoyable as a summer romance in an exotic city!
- A sexy, funny romp!
- Raunchy merriment!

- See it. In fact, see it twice. Epic. One of the best movies of the year!
- A crazy-quilt comic thriller!

Here is an interesting statistic: in 2003, it was reported that the six major studios—Disney, Warner Bros., Sony, 20th Century Fox, Universal, and Paramount—spent about $34.8 million to advertise a movie and at the box office earned, on average, just $20.6 million per title, a loss of about $14.2 million per picture. As crazy as this sounds, the studios spent more money to lure a person into the theater than they received at the box office. The costs of advertising can be justified, as a big opening weekend can help generate additional dollars through future sales in terms of video rentals, video movie sales, pay television, and the foreign markets.[9] The point is that entertainment advertising further grabs our attention and increases our need and desire to be entertained.

The sporting industry has also capitalized on our need to be entertained and uses advertising to elevate our interest. Whenever a big game is advertised on television, whether it is the Super Bowl, the NCAA basketball final, the World Series, the National Basketball Association finals, a big boxing match, or even a well-known golf tournament, these events are made into extraordinary and colossal happenings and something that simply cannot be missed. The promotion of the Super Bowl takes the prize, and it has truly become a bigger-than-life event.

The Olympics is another great example. When the Olympics aren't taking place, who thinks of these events or the athletes who compete in them? Certainly some people do, but unless you are closely affiliated with those sporting events, they are not topics of interest. However, when the Olympics begin, they dominate our thinking, and suddenly the Olympics are on everyone's mind. They are not to be missed, and this is strictly due to the fact that the Olympics are publicized and can be seen on television. There are numerous other Olympic-type sporting competitions that happen throughout the year that most people never think about because they are not broadcasted. These are the same competitive sporting events that take place in the Olympics, but without all the advertising, they remain largely anonymous. The ability of the advertising industry to magnify and promote an event is truly astonishing.

BEING ENTERTAINED AS AN ADDICTION

As reviewed in chapter 4, we have a vulnerability to addiction. Whether it is using heroin, alcohol, or cocaine; gambling; eating too much or too little food; eating junk food; engaging in sex; viewing pornography; smoking marijuana; smoking tobacco; exercising; watching football; surfing the Internet; or taking steroids, we are vulnerable to getting addicted to things. Our brain is an organ that gets modified by our life experience. It remembers what gives us pleasure, and we want to repeat over and over the things that make us feel good.

In general, when we think of addiction, we typically think of things people do that cause them harm and are done to excess, including many of the behaviors and activities just listed. However, even a positive activity can be addictive-like if it is done in excess and causes an individual or someone else harm. For example, even a healthy, constructive activity can become addictive-like and turn sour if the balance isn't there (e.g., a compulsive golfer who must play golf incessantly to the point that it is hurting his or her marriage or a person who is physically active and who is starting to injure him- or herself due to too much exercise and refuses to stop despite being told to rest).

While addiction to the media may be too strong of a word, here are some statistics about watching television that are cause for concern:

- According to the A. C. Nielsen Company, the average American watches approximately 153 hours of television at home every month.[10] That's about five hours of television each day, or two and a half months of nonstop watching per year. In a 70-year life, that equals about 14.5 years glued to the tube.
- Percentage of Americans who say they watch too much television: 49.

- Number of minutes per week that parents spend in meaningful conversation with their children: 3.5.
- Number of minutes per week that the average child watches television: 1,680.
- Percentage of parents who would like to limit their children's watching of television: 73.
- Percentage of four- to six-year-olds who, when asked to choose between watching television and spending time with their fathers, preferred television: 54.
- Hours per year the average American youth spends in school: 900.
- Hours per year the average American youth watches television: 1,500.[11]

If watching television isn't an addiction, it sure sounds like one.

Certainly, one sign of an addiction is experiencing harmful effects related to the compulsive behavior. In this regard, many researchers have, at least in part, explained the obesity problem in the United States as being caused by our inactivity and watching too much television. One study looked at over 7,000 children from kindergarten to grade 5 and assessed the association between hours watching television and the increase in the Body Mass Index (BMI). They found that the number of hours of watching television was significantly associated with the acceleration of BMI growth from kindergarten to grade 5.[12] The author concluded that hours watching television may be contributing to the overweight and obesity problem among today's children. Another study showed this same relationship among three- to seven-year-old children: as the amount of hours spent watching television increased, so did the risk of becoming overweight and of increasing BMI.[13] On the flip side, in a study that worked with four- to seven-year-old children that helped them reduce their television viewing and computer time, it was shown that reducing television and other screen media use was associated with a decrease in BMI.[14] The same findings were demonstrated in a similar study among almost 200 nine-year-old students that helped them reduce the amount of time they spent watching television and videos and playing video games.[15] And it's not just children: a relationship between the number of hours of watching television and obesity has also been found among older adults. [16]

So whether or not seen as an addiction, television can powerfully grab our attention and can have a deleterious impact on our health. And without a doubt, there are other activities that might be better for a person's brain, soul, and overall development. It has been found that happy people watch about 30 percent less television than do unhappy people, [17] although the reasons for this are not clear, as there are many possible relationships between watching television and overall happiness. For example, it is conceivable that being happy leads to less viewing, as people have other, more rewarding activities to do. It is also possible that being unhappy leads to more viewing, as it works as a refuge from one's life. It could also be the case that watching television causes one to be unhappy, and there could many reasons why this is the case. Regardless, while the causal relationship is not clear, this finding is still a cause for concern. Regarding watching television, here is a quote from David Satcher, the former U.S. surgeon general: "Given our national television habit, it is no surprise that we are raising the most sedentary and most overweight generation of youngsters in American history. As they grow, these children will run increased risks of heart disease, diabetes, and other health problems—unless they turn off the tube and become physically active." [18] Those are pretty strong words. Our national television habit (or addiction) increases the risk of heart disease, diabetes, and other health problems.

Another sign of addiction is experiencing a withdrawal syndrome when a person is denied or can no longer use the addictive substance. With some addictions, the withdrawal is physical and can be very dangerous. For example, withdrawal from alcohol and benzodiazepines, or antianxiety medications, can cause a physical withdrawal syndrome that can be life threatening without proper medical management. Withdrawal from heroin and other opiates is physical and uncomfortable but typically not life threatening, and the same is true with withdrawal from nicotine.

With some other addictions, withdrawal is uncomfortable and painful but not truly physical. An example is the compulsive gambler who stops gambling. While there is no physical withdrawal, clearly there are psychological withdrawal symptoms, such as depression, anxiety, tension, and cravings to continue to gamble. Individuals dependent on cocaine also do not experience a physical withdrawal yet can feel uncomfortable with sleep problems, depression, and cravings to continue to use cocaine.

If people can no longer get their need for entertainment met, what happens? Do they experience a withdrawal? This is a difficult question to answer, as I don't think there has ever been a research study that has looked at what happens to people if their ability to be entertained is taken away. However, there is some research that has looked at what happens when a person can no longer watch television. Two studies have paid people to no longer watch television to see what would happen if this form of entertainment were taken away. In one study, families were paid $150 per month to discontinue watching television, and in another, families received $200 per month. After two months, both studies ended because the families couldn't continue not to watch television despite being paid.[19]

Other studies have looked at what happens to people when their television sets were broken or stolen. In general, people reported the first few days to be the toughest. They reported that their routines were disrupted, they didn't know what to do with their time, they experienced anxiety and more hostile behavior, and many felt bored or irritated. By the end of the first week, things got somewhat easier, and by the second week, some readjustment occurred. Reportedly, about a quarter of the family members in the home experienced extreme disruption and discomfort; about 40 percent experienced substantial disruption, including some anxiety and unhappiness; almost 30 percent felt moderate disruption; and less than 10 percent reported few problems.[20] This certainly sounds like a moderate withdrawal syndrome.

The amount of money people will spend to be entertained also demonstrates our addiction to being amused and how important entertainment is to us. Fenway Park, the home of the Boston Red Sox, renovated the suites in the stadium, and in 2007 the asking price to have the season-long luxury of watching the games from this suite was $283,000. In addition, to purchase a suite, the commitment had to be for 10 years. Now that is close to $3 million, which is an amazing amount of money, and, reportedly, there was a waiting list of 15 companies in line to purchase these suites.[21] Being able to be entertained in such style is a mark of status and prestige, and that people will spend such sums of money to do this is a reflection of how obsessed we are with watching sports and being entertained.

Our addiction to being entertained can also be seen in the money that those in the entertainment field make. In addition to the revenue that is generated simply as a result of our need for entertainment, in some venues it also has a lot to do with the money that is made from advertising. Particularly in the sporting business, advertising is a tremendous source of revenue, and companies are willing to advertise their products in these venues and spend exorbitant sums of money because watching sports is such a national preoccupation. If we as a society were not so preoccupied with being entertained by watching sports, companies would never spend this money, and athletes would never make the huge salaries that they do. How sports-as-entertainment has expanded over time can be seen in the following: in 1930, when Babe Ruth made his highest salary, he earned $80,000,[22] or the equivalent of about $1.16 million in 2014, which is a little more than one-third what the average baseball player earned in 2013.[23] Companies and businesses involved in the advertising and marketing of the sporting industry have increasingly learned to exploit our addiction to being entertained.

Finally, as with any addiction, as tolerance develops, we need more and more (if not stronger and more potent forms) of the addictive substance. A person who is addicted to alcohol will drink more and will often use more potent forms of alcohol to get the same feeling of intoxication. A person who has become addicted to heroin may start off snorting the drug but often progresses to injecting the drug to achieve a more powerful high. In addition, greater quantities of the drug will also get used.

Similar to an addiction to a drug, with entertainment, for our interest to be sustained, we constantly need more powerful and novel amusement to satisfy our senses as we grow tolerant to earlier forms of entertainment. This has been accommodated through wide-screen, high-definition, and 3D television as well as more intense action-packed films and the use of special effects. We also are exposed to more sex and violence in television and film in order to sustain our interest. Whether art imitates life or life imitates art is not clear, and there is likely some truth to both. Regardless, sex and violence are often used as a way to ensure that our attention is captured. Whereas we used to have *Leave It to Beaver*, *Dennis the Menace*, *I Love Lucy*, and *The Dick Van Dyke Show*, now we have *Sex in the City*, the *Real Housewives* series, and crime shows too numerous to count that often show violent murder and other shocking crimes. Even the making of commercials has changed over the years. In order to captivate our attention and interest, today's commercials must use all of the same techniques that television and movies utilize, and more novel and outlandish ways to get a message out have become the norm. Our need for entertainment and the entertainment machine feed off of each other: as we need more novelty to sustain our attention, we are given more stimulation, and the more we are given, the more we need.

In summary, our need to be entertained, coupled with the time we have to be entertained, has been captured by the ingenuity, refinement, and power of the entertainment machine. In addition, this process has been further strengthened by creative advertising, which further engages us. Finally, our addictive vulnerability has solidified and fortified the hold that entertainment has over us. That is, we have become addicted to entertainment, and there is a national preoccupation and obsession with being entertained and amused. Just like a person can get addicted to a drug to obtain pleasure in the world, we as a society have literally become addicted to being entertained. Gabler was right when he stated that Karl Marx was wrong: religion is not the opiate of the masses; instead, it is entertainment.[24]

11

ENTERTAINMENT AS LIFE FULFILLMENT

It seems that entertainment is what most excites us and what we value above everything else. —Carroll O'Conner

Entertainment is the primary standard of value for virtually everything in modern society. Those things that entertain are, with rare exceptions, the most highly prized. —Neal Gabler

As reviewed in chapter 6, a primary mission for all of us is to maintain a positive self-concept and healthy self-esteem. Without this, we likely will struggle with depression and despair. Additionally, as outlined in chapter 8, a shift has occurred in *how* we try to accomplish this. Due to the changing nature of goods production that occurred during the industrial revolution, which led to the creation of a personal life separate from work and, for many, afforded less opportunity for pride and personal identity to be realized through work, a search for a personal identity and an increased preoccupation with fulfillment and personal happiness was generated. Furthermore, through advertising, people became convinced that the way to happiness and fulfillment was to look outside oneself and to consume, and this continues to this day. We deserve the good life, and the good life is buying and possessing all there is to offer, whether this is the newest and biggest gas grill, the newest car, or the latest phone. These possessions are supposed to give us fulfillment and happiness, but unfortunately they do not. The reality is that while the average income for Americans has basically doubled during the past 40 years, there has been no noticeable increase in overall happiness. Certainly, if a person has little or no money and, as result, almost no material possessions, this will factor into the person's happiness. However, once a person has an ample amount of money to live fairly comfortably, more money and, in turn, more possessions don't do much to increase happiness. A researcher who has explored this issue noted that "we are twice as rich and no happier."[1] As a society, however, despite this relationship, we continue to look outside of ourselves and to consume as a way to attempt to achieve happiness.

Building on the ideas reviewed in the previous chapter, not only has our need for entertainment been exquisitely captivated by technology and advertising, resulting in an addiction to being entertained, but, presently, *experiencing entertainment has evolved into a particular form of consumerism and has become a key if not primary way that we attempt to feel good about ourselves.* In addition to buying the newest product on the market in an effort to achieve fulfillment, we also attempt to meet our needs by viewing the latest piece of entertainment that is promoted, whether this is a movie, a television show, a sporting event, or a concert. Viewing the importance of entertainment from a cultural and historical perspective beginning in the mid-1800s, Gabler wrote of the working class, "Though he may have been deprived of wealth, social mobility, or political power, the common man learned to quickly compensate for his impotence in those areas by channeling his energies instead into the one arena in which he did seem paramount, culture, and into the one form of culture that was truly his own, entertainment."[2] Being able to view and experience entertainment and entertainment that was his or her own gave the individual a sense of power and control.

Our obsession with entertainment can be seen in the sheer number of television stations and shows that exist as well as the staggering number of movies that are released. Approximately 450 movies are released in the United States every year, or over one movie every day.[3] There are also all of the spectator sporting events we can watch, either live or on television: baseball, football (college and pro), tennis, basketball (college and pro), soccer, hockey (college and pro), golf, bowling, wrestling, boxing, and women's wrestling and boxing. Other entertainment venues are all of the various music and live theater performances, dance events, and magic shows that exist. We also cannot forget movie and television series purchases and rentals, giving us other options in case there still aren't enough things to watch. It seems that there is a complete immersion in being entertained.

Not only has being entertained become the way we feel good about ourselves, but being able to experience certain kinds of entertainment can also provide us with status, helping to augment our identity and self-esteem. Being able to get tickets to see a big baseball game or the World Series, getting tickets to the Super Bowl, being able to watch a television show live in the studio, or obtaining great seats to a concert gives us bragging rights and helps us achieve status over others. Either the person has a lot of money or he or she knows a person who has connections, and, consequently, this bestows on the person prestige and rank. In addition, giving tickets to others can also be used as a way to achieve high stature.

Now, there is nothing wrong with allowing oneself to be entertained. Having an interest in being amused and stimulated has always been a part of society and culture, as this need is in our genetic makeup. There is also nothing inherently harmful in doing this, as getting outside of ourselves and zoning out is important too. While being entertained by formal entertainment that is external to us is one mechanism, there are also many ways to entertain ourselves by utilizing our own internal resources. A person may take pride in tending to and growing a vegetable or flower garden, another person will have an avocation of taking photographs, and others will get their joy and fulfillment in being a parent. Some people volunteer and help those less fortunate, giving them internal satisfaction and energizing them about life. For good reason, children should be encouraged to get involved in extracurricular activities that give them pleasure, as this can be an important source of happiness. Furthermore, excelling at and mastering these pursuits can also help augment self-confidence and self-esteem, especially when these achievements are acknowledged. However, what has happened is that viewing some type of entertainment has become a quick fix, like a drug, to take us outside of ourselves and to give us a temporary *feel-good feeling* to the exclusion of other activities that could potentially be more fulfilling and satisfying.

In support of this, when looking at what we do for leisure, it has been shown that far and away, the greatest amount of time is spent watching television, a rather passive activity, at 2.8 hours per day, amounting to a little over half the amount of time we spend on all leisure activities combined. In addition, between 2003 and 2013, watching television increased by 7 percent.[4] It has also been shown that from 2012 to 2013, individuals who reported that they engaged in volunteer work dropped 1.1 percent from 2012, to 25.4 percent, and this was the lowest rate since such data were first collected in 2002.[5] Further evidence that we look outside of ourselves to meet our needs is the observation that from the early 1960s to the late 1990s, attendance at major sporting events has almost doubled. Surveys have also shown that from 1986 to 1998, there has been an increase in per capita attendance at museums, concerts, and movies while at the same time, church attendance, home entertaining, and attending a club meeting have dropped.[6]

Additional support for the idea that being entertained and having time for leisure has become increasingly important comes from a study that compared three groups of individuals: those born in 1958–1959, those born in 1973–1974, and those born in 1988–1989.[7] A variety of questions were asked regarding the importance of leisure time and work, as were questions about what people looked for in work. These questions were part of a large study called Monitoring the Future, which is conducted by the National Institute on Drug Abuse every year and that first began in 1975. The Monitoring the Future study assesses eighth, tenth, and twelfth graders who live across the United States on a variety of things, most notably their drug use attitudes and behavior. The study discussed here used data from this study and compared twelfth graders' responses to these questions to assess any changes over time.

What was found was that in a progressive fashion, individuals born later were more likely to value leisure at work than did individuals who were born earlier. In addition, the individuals born later were less likely to want to work overtime and were more likely to say that they would stop working if they had enough money. It was also found that a greater percentage of individuals born in 1958–1959 stated that they expected work to be a central part of their lives compared to individuals born more recently. Finally, in response to the statement "Work is nothing more than making a living," it was found that among the three cohorts, as individuals were born later, there was a progressively greater agreement to this question. All of this suggests that, compared to the past, work has less importance among young adults today and that what one does for leisure and having time for leisure is the greater priority.

BEING ENTERTAINED IS LIFE

Gabler has suggested that life itself has morphed into one big entertaining movie and that our necessity to be entertained has collapsed onto life itself. What he means is that our requirement to be entertained is so gargantuan that we attend only to events that are entertaining and that being entertained has become our primary preoccupation, an end in and of itself, as opposed to a diversion from life. As a result, everything must be made into entertainment because if it isn't entertaining, no one will take notice. Gabler has aptly stated that entertainment "is arguably the most pervasive, powerful and ineluctable force of our time—a force so overwhelming that it has finally metastasized into life."[8] Vargas Llosa, who won the Nobel Prize in literature in 2010, resonates with this idea and stated that "the audiovisual revolution, which is fantastic from a technological point of view, has introduced the idea that the main goal of culture is entertainment."[9]

While our indelible need to be entertained can be seen in our obsession with formal entertainment, such as television shows, movies, sporting events, and concerts, Gabler goes much further and states that even real-life events have been made into entertainment. In this regard, real-life news must be entertaining for people to take notice, and as a result, for obvious reasons, television news anchors are not chosen for their intelligence or deep thinking but rather for their looks and ability to engage and entertain us. Newscasters who get too old are often replaced by someone younger. Even weatherpeople must entertain us and not simply present the weather. Furthermore, we focus on sound bites, headlines, and images instead of more in-depth storytelling and elucidation.

Television news stations must make even war and other disasters into entertainment, as each station has to compete with the other stations for viewers and people will watch only if the news is presented in an entertaining fashion. News stations bring us live, up-to-date coverage of the latest disaster so that we can feel like we are really there. Great efforts are undertaken to get as close to the event as possible and to have the best photos to satisfy our need for entertainment and novelty. Phrases such as "Breaking News" are used, as is hyperbole, to grab our interest and attention. In addition, different channels often create their own logos and phrases all in an effort to make the news entertaining. In the Gulf War in 1991, "Crisis in the Gulf" was the phrase used by ABC and CNN. CBS used "Showdown in the Gulf" as the war was building and "War in the Gulf" once it began. "America at War" was the phrase used by NBC. Hurricane Katrina has also had its share of logos: one year after the hurricane, CBS used "Disaster in the Gulf—One Year After," and two years after that, ABC used "Katrina—Where Things Stand." In addition, the logos can fade in, fade out, and change color, making watching the coverage appear almost movie-like. During the Gulf of Mexico oil spill in 2010, New England Cable News, on a daily basis, showed on their station the caption "The Gulf Oil Crisis— Day ———," and behind these words was an animated picture of a moving blob of oil. On ABC's *The Today Show*, the introduction "Direct Hit: An American Tragedy in Joplin" was used to introduce the story of the 2011 destruction of Joplin, Missouri, by a tornado. These techniques were used to grab our attention and make the report and real-life events as *entertaining as possible*. Even everyday weather events are made into entertainment, and weatherpeople pique our interest with phrases like "And how much snow can we expect? How will be your evening commute? Coming up next!"

Politics, too, at least when candidates are running for office, has become a stage to see what candidate can be the most engaging and entertaining, as that is what will capture the most votes. Television changed the electoral process, as how a candidate presents and looks on television is of paramount importance. Commenting on John F. Kennedy's impact on the political scene and how this relates to entertainment, Richard Schickel, the documentary filmmaker, movie historian, and film critic, wrote, "What we are dealing with here is a recognition on the part of the candidate and his managers that traditional debts and alliances within the party and among various outside interest groups were, in the age of television, of less significance in winning elections, and in governance itself, than the creation of an image that gave the illusion of masculine dynamism without sacrifice of ongoing affection. Which is, one hardly need add, exactly what a successful male movie star recognizes his job to be."[10] Here we see how, to get elected, a candidate must be entertaining and generate enthusiasm, like a movie star, the ultimate entertainer.

Televised candidate debates are now media events and are more about how the candidate presents him- or herself than about actual substance. An adviser to Walter Mondale, when he ran for president in 1984, admitted that more time was spent talking about ties than East-West relations.[11] Writing about the 1988 presidential contest between Michael Dukakis and George H. W. Bush, Joan Didion, the American author and journalist, noted that much of what was seen in the media was staged "invented narrative" and that the idea was to create the right image that would appear on television.[12] In addition, time is spent on how to craft a message to get someone's attention or to say something that will create the right image. Two great examples are when Lloyd Bentsen turned to Dan Quayle in the 1988 Democratic vice-presidential debate and said, "I knew John Kennedy, and you are no John Kennedy" and when Ronald Reagan, in the 1984 debate with Walter Mondale stated, "I am not going to exploit for political purposes my opponent's youth and inexperience." Another example was a line delivered by Al Gore when he was running against George H. W. Bush in the 1992 election: "George Bush taking credit for the Berlin Wall coming down is like the rooster taking credit for the sunrise." These were great lines and could have been used in any movie. Politics as entertainment can also be seen in the "postgame" analysis of a debate that takes the same format as the postgame analysis of a football or basketball contest. Whether there were any knockout punches, who had the best lines, and who may have scored the most points often take precedence over what was actually discussed. It is no wonder that Bill Clinton was coined the "entertainer-in-chief" by Kurt Anderson of *The New Yorker*.[13] And it was Ronald Reagan who once told television journalist David Brinkley, "There have been times in this office when I've wondered how you could do the job if you hadn't been an actor."[14]

How the nature of political contests has changed and how it is now a focus on sound bites and images as opposed to serious debate can be starkly seen by contrasting most current debates and the ones between Abraham Lincoln and Stephen Douglas in 1858, when they debated each other seven times. In each debate, either Lincoln or Douglas spoke for one hour, followed by the other talking for an hour and a half and a rebuttal for another half hour.[15] In an earlier debate, on October 16, 1854, Douglas spoke for three hours, after which it was Lincoln's turn. However, when Lincoln was about to begin, he noted that it was approaching dinnertime and suggested that perhaps people wanted to go home for dinner, as the plan was for him to speak for about three hours, after which Douglas would be allowed an hour-long rebuttal. So people went home and then returned to hear several hours of additional talking, for a total of close to seven hours.[16] And at the time, they were not even running for president. Can anyone now imagine an audience listening to two candidates for three hours let alone seven? This was true politics as opposed to politics masquerading as entertainment, or "politainment," the blending of politics and entertainment.

In fact, the relationship between our need for entertainment and the entertainment industry or media machine is reciprocal. Certainly, the entertainment industry realized that it could make large sums of money by exploiting our need for entertainment by making real-life events entertaining. Very simply, the more entertaining something could be made, including life itself, the more viewers would watch, and this would generate larger amounts of revenue. At the same time, if we didn't have such a need to be entertained, the entertainment machine would never exist, as there would be no money to be made because there would be no interest or audience.

What has happened over time is that the entertainment machine has further intensified our need to be entertained because as we habituate to what we are exposed to, we require greater and more potent forms of amusement to sustain our interest. Essentially, the more it entertains us, the more we require, as we become less impressed with earlier and familiar forms of entertainment. This, in turn, fuels more intense and engaging forms of entertainment that are designed to continue to re-capture and sustain our interest. Thus, the entertainment machine not only entertains us but also enhances our desire. Our fixation on being entertained has not been caused by the entertainment machine, nor has the entertainment machine been caused by our need for entertainment. Rather, these two forces are intimately linked: each affects as well as strengthens the other.

In summary, as a result of the creation of a personal life dedicated to achieving personal fulfillment and the ability of the entertainment ma-chine to provide us with pleasure, being entertained has become our central preoccupation and the way that we attempt to feel good about ourselves and our lives. Even real-life events have been made into en-tertainment, as if they aren't entertaining, we have little if any interest. The entertainment machine is not responsible for this state of affairs, nor is our need to be entertained the culprit. Rather, these two ele-ments have a codependent, symbiotic relationship, and one could not

exist without the other. Regardless, life is now all about being entertained.

12

TRANSFORMATION AND OBSESSION

It's very easy to confuse Sean Connery with James Bond. Sometimes in the entertainment industry, people believe the cake is more real than the baker. —Judd Nelson

In the previous two chapters, I have discussed how we are addicted to being entertained, that getting our dose of diversion is a key way by which we attempt to feel good about our lives, and that entertainment has taken over and collapsed onto life itself. However, the entertainment industry not only has made the watching or viewing of celluloid more engulfing and satisfying but also has been able to make the people who appear in these venues into bigger-than-life figures and to transform everyday, ordinary people into images that we adore, admire, and worship. How and why this has occurred is due to a number of interrelated factors.

To begin, it is not difficult to appreciate that our obsession with being entertained can lead to an infatuation with and adoration of those who are doing the entertaining. As we are an idol-making and idol-worshipping species, we have come to admire and love those who appear in these venues, as they entertain us and give us that temporary pleasure and quick fix. In the 1850s, Jenny Lind, a Swedish opera singer known as the "Swedish Nightingale," became a celebrity fueled at least in part by the creative marketing of P. T. Barnum. When she arrived in

New York to begin her concert tour, she was greeted by thousands of admirers.[1] As noted in a *New York Herald* article, "Wherever her carriage goes, there is a crowd collected around it, and the people feast their eyes upon her as if she was an angel, and not a mere woman."[2] Fanny Elssler, an Austrian dancer, captivated audiences in the 1940s, and some coined the excitement surrounding her as "Elsslermaniaphobia."[3]

When motion pictures were first made, however, it was not this way, as those who appeared in them generated little interest. Why watching a movie or television show can now be such an engrossing experience and why we have become so enamored with the individuals portrayed in these venues is due to the change in how motion pictures are made. As we will see, with the advent of modern technology, the use of newer techniques, and the advancement in storytelling, ordinary and larger numbers of people began to be made into celebrities and capture the minds of viewers.

At the time when movies were first beginning to be produced, individuals who appeared in them used an exaggerated form of pantomime, an acting style that was typically used on the stage and that was artificial and unrealistic.[4] In addition, movies were more focused on simply bringing life to a reel.[5] The focus was on the event as opposed to the people enacting the happening. However, acting soon shifted to become more subtle, natural, and lifelike, and this more realistic, true-to-life portrayal of people rather quickly led viewers to become obsessed with the characters they saw in a film. Viewers began to feel as if they had a close and special relationship with these actors. Some fans who watched movies nearly every night in inexpensive nickelodeon theaters began to feel as if they knew, quite personally, the characters in films and the actors who played them. It has been noted that these newer techniques caused viewers "to become intensely involved in a narrative, to imitate actions on the screen, or to fall deeply in love with a celluloid image called a motion picture actor or actress."[6] Many moviegoers began to experience strong feelings of intimacy with the actors, as the characters' thoughts, feelings, and emotions could be deeply felt and experienced. Studios were inundated with requests from fans to reveal the names of these actors and actresses and to learn their birthdays, whether they were married, what they liked to do, and how old they really were.[7] Studios had to establish fan mail departments to respond to the thousands of letters that they received.[8]

In addition to the shift in acting, D. W. Griffith, an early pioneer in the motion picture industry, was responsible for developing newer techniques that encouraged viewers to enter a character's mind.[9] Point-of-view and close-up shots, along with the use of a variety of different camera angles, shifted the audience's attention away from the story and to the person playing the role. It has been noted that the close-up shot made a face big and gave it an appearance that was larger than life itself. With the close-up, the viewer's imagination was limitless, and a deep intimacy with the character could be achieved.[10] These techniques allowed viewers access to characters' thoughts and perspectives, and audiences were able to identify and sympathize with the men and women they saw on-screen. In turn, this helped foster attachments to them, and viewers began to wonder who these actors and actresses really were and what they were truly like in the real world.[11]

As well as the more refined processes of making a film and the more realistic portrayal of people, fierce competition among television stations and production companies to grab a larger share of the audience has led to better story writing and plots. The lines that actors and actresses deliver, the dilemmas they experience and overcome, the personal struggles they contend with, the decisions they must make, and the heroics they achieve have all become more engaging and engrossing. With the right makeup, the right close-up shot, the perfect line (along with a well-rehearsed delivery), or the flawless decision made, it is no wonder that we have come to worship and love these people. They do and say things that we have often thought or fantasized about doing and saying but, due to living in a society with more civilized rules of intercourse and contact established, simply cannot. They also find themselves in situations in which we can only hope to be in. Consequently, we vicariously identify with these characters, enhancing our obsession with them. I am sure that many of us wish we had thought of and delivered some of these lines in our lives or even been in these kinds of situations when these lines could have been used:

- "I'm going to make him an offer he can't refuse." (Marlon Brando in *The Godfather*)
- "So tell me Eddie, is that a rabbit in your pants or are you just happy to see me." (Johanna Cassidy in *Who Framed Roger Rabbit?*)
- "Go ahead . . . make my day." (Clint Eastwood in *Dirty Harry*)
- "You've got to ask yourself one question: 'Do I feel lucky?' Well, do ya, punk?" (again, Clint Eastwood in *Dirty Harry*)
- "You know how to whistle, don't you, Steve? You just put your lips together and blow." (Lauren Bacall in *To Have and Have Not*)
- "I came here tonight because when you realize you want to spend the rest of your life with somebody, you want the rest of your life to start as soon as possible." (Billy Crystal in *When Harry Met Sally*)
- "You don't understand! I could've had class. I could've been a contender. I could've been somebody, instead of a bum, which is what I am. Let's face it. . . . It was you, Charley." (Marlon Brando in *On the Waterfront*)

This is just a very small sampling. However, it is apparent that directors and producers of movies and television shows have made watching a celluloid story and entering another world for a small period of time so appealing, engaging, and interesting that it is no wonder that we are fascinated with the people who are in these works of art. Not only do these individuals get the best lines, but through the talent of a director and the cadre of people who work with them, we also feel for these characters and develop strong emotional bonds with them. Through this medium, they are allowed to do the most laudable things, to say the things we have always wanted to say, and to get themselves out of the most amazing dilemmas doing the most extraordinary things. We empathize and identify with these people and have come to love and respect what they do.

What is also relevant and adds to our fascination with such people is the shift that has occurred from internal to external, from depth to surface, that was noted in chapter 8. Whereas in the Puritan culture a person's honesty, integrity, and morality were most valued, now the people who grab our attention are those who present well and who are charismatic and engaging, and it is actors, actresses, and other entertainers who have mastered this. As has been noted by Warren Susman, the cultural historian who was a professor at Rutgers University, how people present, or their personality, which includes being charming and likable, is what became most valued.[12] The ability of actors and actresses to present themselves favorably is their specialty, sometimes even without a character to become or a great screenplay to guide their actions. However, with an appealing and charming character and great lines to deliver, it is no wonder that we idolize these people very much: they are chameleons and can become as engaging as the screenplay will allow them to become.

As a way to fulfill our unending need for entertainment, reality television shows have also entered the field, and producers of these shows use the same techniques to capture our minds and turn ordinary people into stars. Reality television first began around 1992 with the show *The Real World*, which simply consisted of group of seven young adults living together in a Soho loft in Manhattan. Then around 2000, the reality television show market expanded with shows such as *Survivor*, *Big Brother*, *America's Next Top Model*, and *Who Wants to Marry a Millionaire?*, to name just a few. We no longer need a trained actor or actress but, rather, everyday people who, when put in front of a camera with a good director and crew, can capture our interest. In addition, we no longer need the writing of a good story or plot; instead, get some women together who want to meet a future husband, and you have a show by simply filming their dates (*The Bachelorette*). Or get some men together who want to meet a prospective wife, and you have a show by simply filming their dates (*The Bachelor*). Or how about a contest about the person who can lose the most weight (*The Biggest Loser*)? Or as-semble people to cook meals and have a contest for the tastiest treat (*Hell's Kitchen* or *Top Chef*). There have also been other shows that simply follow the lives of ordinary people, such as Jon and Kate Gosse-lin or the Kardashian family.

Many individuals who have appeared on reality television shows have even become celebrities and stars due to the power of the enter-tainment machine and our need to be amused. You can take almost anyone, place them in some kind of drama or conflict, and add some sophisticated direction, camera shots, and angles, and they could be-come a star and an object of people's attention. The power of the entertainment machine cannot be overstated.

What also helps fuel our obsession is that we have an amazing vul-nerability to lose the distinction between what we see in the movies or on television and what is reality. We believe that a chic character in the movie is also that way in real life, and this may or may not be true. Or a sexy person in the movies is as bodacious in life, or the toughest guy in the movie is every bit as formidable when not on the screen. As re-ported by the Museum of Broadcast Communication, Marcus Welby (played by Robert Young) received thousands of letters in the mail asking for medical advice, demonstrating this phenomenon.[13] Was Mar-lon Brando as awe-inspiring as he was in *On the Waterfront*? I don't know, but who really cares? In the movie, he was, and that is all that matters.

One idea as to why we develop such strong connections to these people who we really do not know is because our brains are not wired to know the difference between real relationships and the images of peo-ple we see on television and film. As written by some researchers, "Our modern minds are not adapted to recently emerged environments, such as the media environment. The modern, mass-mediated environment mismatches with the environment of evolutionary adaptedness, in which our minds were shaped by natural selection. When we see an image of a media character (a celebrity), our brain processes this infor-mation as an encounter with a real person. As we get to know people through pictures and images of them, we actually come to believe that we personally know them as we are unable to separate the person from an image of the person."14

One example that aptly demonstrates our inability to distinguish between real people and images of people is a man's reaction to pornography. From an evolutionary point of view, when a man sees a woman who is of sexual interest, he gets an erection, as having a sexual encounter ensures his survival. A woman is a potential recipient of his sperm, and thus seeing a woman should and often does elicit arousal and an erection. From this perspective, there is no reason why a man should obtain an erection by viewing a picture of a naked woman: there is no chance of having sex, so, in theory, there is no reason to get aroused and get an erection. Yet when many men look at pornography, they do get aroused, demonstrating how the brain has trouble distinguishing between a picture and the real thing.

As with other kinds of people who entertain us, individuals who appear in sporting events can also become celebrities and figures of idolization. Not only do they entertain us (a reason to exalt and admire them in and of itself), but the entertainment machine can also help make athletes into larger-than-life figures. Often shown prior to the big game are the life stories and histories of certain athletes, including how they grew up, adversities they overcame, who their family is, and how they have come to be who they are on the field. Their on-field accomplishments are also highlighted and featured. These are people who have an athletic ability, but when their stories are told using the same elaborate techniques that are used to make movies, they too can be made into celebrities. Even during the sporting event, filming techniques used in movies, such as close-up shots, can help transform athletes into figures of idolization, as they allow us to enter the athlete's mind and experience his or her thoughts and emotions.

AND THEN THERE IS BEAUTY

As written in chapter 2, the human species loves a beautiful person, and we too are absolutely obsessed with looking our best. We are drawn to good looks, and we as a society have become increasingly preoccupied with physical appearance. We are inundated with advertisements to have the nicest hair, the smoothest skin, the whitest teeth, the best abs, and the sexiest lips and to be in the best shape. Our increased focus on physical appearance has occurred for a number of reasons, but one important factor is the sheer volume of people we interact with on a daily basis. We look to quickly size people up, and how people look is the quickest way to do this. If we can't get to know them, we can at least give them a quick eyeball, a surefire measuring stick.

In chapter 8, it was noted that our focus on external appearance also occurred due to our capitalistic society and our need to sell the products that are produced through advertising. Companies realized that charismatic and engaging people were needed to market their products, leading to a focus on looks, external appearance, and great presenting skills. A beautiful woman or attractive man always captures our interest and attention, essential to selling any product.

While not all celebrities are attractive, many if not most are, another reason why we are so enamored with such people. When it comes to celebrity status, the most attractive have the highest appeal, and, in general, one's celebrity status is augmented by beauty. It has been noted that when close-ups first began to be utilized in movies, many ordinary people who happened to look good came to Hollywood, and some of these stood out of the crowd and became stars,[15] and this is happening to this day. While there may be differences of opinion regarding the physical attractiveness of, for example, Cameron Diaz, Bradley Cooper, Reese Witherspoon, Brad Pitt, George Clooney, Angelina Jolie, Ryan Gosling, and Jennifer Lopez, they get considerable attention, at least in large part, because of their looks. Think about the Academy Awards ceremony. Although who will take home the Oscar for the best actor or actress or best supporting actor or actress (along with the many other awards) is relevant, underneath the actual ceremony is the fashion show. Women come to this event in their finest garb, and the news that is almost as big as who actually wins the awards is who had best outfit, who had the worst dress, and who looked the best and who did not. Even the designers of the best outfits get their due recognition. Outrageous dress is also the norm, and for some, showing the most skin appears to be the goal. The Academy Awards is as much about beauty as it is about filmmaking, and this is also one of the reasons people watch it.

It isn't just actors and actresses who need to be attractive, but we now have some newer celebrities: newscasters. As the purpose of news is to entertain us and to attract the most viewers, newscasters' appearances have become increasingly important. While not all newscasters are beautiful, most are quite attractive, and this is often a piece of why they were given the job in the first place. As has been written, if one were to trying to produce a television news show to attract the largest audience possible, a cast of "talking hair-dos" would be assembled who would have faces that "would not be unwelcome on any magazine cover."[16]

It is also clear that people are most attractive and handsome when they are younger, and this is when celebrity status is at its highest. Furthermore, as people age, the chances of becoming a major celebrity diminish for a variety of reasons, but beyond doubt, one reason is their attractiveness. As Faye Dunaway, Raquel Welch, Bo Derek, and Brigitte Bardot age, their stardom decreases, as society is looking for the next beauty to hit the scene, and youth is equated with beauty. The same is true with top models: as they age, they drift off the scene, and newer and younger ones take the stage, front and center. That supermodels exist and can even achieve celebrity-hood demonstrates how important simple attractiveness is in our society. The only thing such people offer is their beauty and photogenic appearance, and this goes a long way.

The importance of facial appearance and attractiveness is true even in politics. While we think that whom we vote for is a well-reasoned and carefully thought-out decision, much research has demonstrated that decisions are heavily influenced by the physical appearance of a candidate and the kinds of personality traits that the candidate's face projects.[17] Furthermore, it has been shown that the judgments we make based on facial appearance are done rapidly and can predict better than chance who will actually win the election.[18, 19] It has also been demonstrated that when deciding whom to vote for, certain facial features seem more important based on whether the country is at war or at peace.[20] There also appears to be a gender bias when determining whom we will vote for. While all voters are likely to vote for candidates who look more competent, male candidates who appear more approachable and female candidates who appear more attractive are more likely to gain votes. In addition, it has been shown that men are more likely to vote for attractive female candidates, whereas women are more likely to cast their vote for men who look approachable.[21]

In summary, not only are we addicted to being entertained (and being entertained sustains us and is our primary focus), but we also have become captivated by entertainers and those doing the entertaining. The techniques used to make any visual medium can transform an ordinary, everyday person into someone to admire and worship, at least in part, because we cannot distinguish between real people and those we see in photographic images. Their allure is further heightened due to our fascination with facial appearance and attractiveness, which most of these people possess.

This, however, is just one piece of the puzzle. The fact that through the media entertainers achieve wide recognition and notoriety is also relevant to our obsession with these individuals. In fact, the appeal of recognition and fame and the impact this has on people is so profound and significant, in terms of both how this affects our own behavior and our obsession with celebrities, that this will be the focus of the next chapter.

13

THEY GOT WHAT I WANT

I now perceive one immense omission in my psychology—the deepest principle of human nature is the craving to be appreciated. —William James

There are two things people want more than sex or money . . . recognition and praise. —Mary Kay Ash

As was reviewed in chapter 6, we all need a healthy self-regard and to feel good about ourselves, whether striving to succeed in business, developing valued relationships, or achieving recognition in recreational pursuits. In attaining our goals, we not only take pride in our accomplishments but also appreciate the recognition and approval we receive from others. Recognition makes us feel valued. In this context, recognition is not the simple notion of being recognized or seen. Rather, it is the deep sense that people value us and appreciate our accomplishments. In fact, it is a universal human characteristic to want to be acknowledged and treasured by others, and this is needed throughout life.

Beginning in childhood, we seek and need the approval of our parents or caregivers to build and reinforce our self-esteem. If a child recites the alphabet and looks to his or her parents to obtain acknowledgment of the accomplishment, the child needs to hear from his or her parent "Good job!" or the equivalent. If the child does well in school, having a parent acknowledge this and offer praise helps solidify the child's sense of self and self-concept. If a child is in a dance recital, a sporting event, or some other kind of contest or public presentation, the parent needs to be there to see the event and to appreciate the achievement. This helps the child feel good about him- or herself, as the child knows that he or she is worthwhile and that someone else has taken notice.

The same need for recognition continues throughout adulthood, whether this entails approval from a supervisor for a job well done, appreciation and respect from one's children, or knowing that one is valued by one's spouse and friends. Even the acknowledgment from a dinner guest that the meal we prepared was delicious makes us feel good that our effort was noticed.

Even people who have achieved some measure of distinction enjoy ongoing recognition. For example, let's assume that the chief executive officer (CEO) of a large corporation enters a room of employees who are mostly strangers but is recognized by other employees who have met him or her and acknowledge his or her presence. This makes the CEO feel special and helps augment his or her self-esteem. The local politician who is invited to address a community function and who receives special attention on his or her arrival is appreciative of the recognition, and this in turn augments his or her self-esteem. The scientist who writes an article that receives some public recognition and praise is appreciative of the acknowledgment.

In fact, recognition and appreciation are so important that numerous rituals have been created in society to give people respect and acknowledgment. Birthday celebrations, Father's Day and Mother's Day, Grandparents Day, Boss Appreciation Day, and Administrative Professionals' Day have all been established as forums to extend our gratitude to and show appreciation of others. Employee of the Month, Salesperson of the Year, the Academy Awards, the Grammy Awqrds, music video awards, country music singing awards, beauty pageants, the numerous magazines that declare who are the sexiest men and women in the world, the most valuable player awards in all professional sports, or being chosen as an all-star in many sports are all designed for the same purpose. So are the surveys that are completed in middle school and high school that determine who students consider the most attractive, the person with the best personality, the cutest couple, the person with the best sense of humor, or the one most likely to succeed. It should also be noted that no one is completely immune to the feedback we hear from others, whether positive or negative. Even someone with the healthiest self-esteem will begin to question his or her worth if consistent negative feedback is received.

RECOGNITION'S BEST FRIEND

If there is one proven way to attain recognition from others, it is being featured in the media. Media exposure can catapult a person from nobody to somebody almost overnight when his or her story hits the news and is watched by thousands of viewers. Certainly, if a person has accomplished something of value, over time and even without the power of mass media, this can become known by others, and eventually greater success and recognition can occur. However, if that same person's accomplishment can be placed in the media's spotlight, recognition and success can take place much more rapidly. A great example is when a book makes Oprah Winfrey's book club, as this typically results in the skyrocketing of book sales and instant appreciation and respect for the author. During and shortly after the 2008 Summer Olympics, when Michael Phelps won eight medals, he was suddenly a celebrity, and there was an incredible interest taken in his life. I am not taking anything away from this superlative athletic achievement, but it demonstrates how, when placed in the spotlight of the media, people can be catapulted to stardom. In fact, people often hire publicists to highlight their achievements, because if the spotlight can shine on them, the potential for success will be enhanced.

Even without significant accomplishment, being featured in the media can lead to public recognition, which can often lead to further opportunity and success if not some celebrity status. How appearing in the media and being placed inside the box known as television can lead to some achievement can be clearly seen in what occurred with the individuals involved in the O. J. Simpson trial, which was made into a huge media spectacle. In this regard, many of the characters involved in this trial achieved ministardom simply due to being in the news. Kato Kaelin, who testified at the trial, became a radio talk show host. The prosecutors, the defense attorneys, the police and detectives involved, Simpson's former girlfriend, and his niece all negotiated book deals, and his former girlfriend and one juror posed nude for *Playboy* magazine. In addition, two other defense attorneys negotiated a deal with CBS television to develop a series based on their lives. [1]

Even criminals can appear in the media and achieve celebrity status: Timothy McVeigh, who was convicted of killing 168 people at the Alfred P. Murrah Federal Building in Oklahoma City, appeared on the cover of *Newsweek* and was interviewed on *60 Minutes*. As Andy Warhol stated, "Nowadays if you're a crook you're still considered up there. You can write books, go on TV, give interviews—you're a big celebrity and nobody even looks down on you because you're a crook." [2]

In the creation of a celebrity, the importance of simply being well known can be seen in the celebrity status of television and movie actors and actresses as opposed to writers and directors. The brains and creative geniuses behind the scenes—the writers and the directors—do not receive due credit and rarely obtain celebrity status because they work out of the eye of the camera. Because it is the faces of the actors and actresses that we see, it is they who are elevated to celebrity status even though it is the writers and directors who give them the lines that we, the viewers, appreciate. Writers and directors should actually get more (if not at least equal) credit, as when the writers go on strike, the production of all television shows, including late-night talk shows, generally comes to a halt. Without good writing, actors and actresses don't have much to offer in the entertainment realm. Without good writing, they have nothing to enact, no characters to become, and little entertainment value.

In fact, as watching news has become entertainment and newscasters achieve public recognition, they too have obtained some celebrity status albeit on a smaller scale. Whether it is Katie Couric, Barbara Walters, Diane Sawyer, or George Stephanopoulos who is reporting the news, each has a small following. Wolf Blitzer, the news reporter who covered the first Gulf War in Kuwait, became a minicelebrity and a household name. Who leaves what station and what station they are going to next has become big news that is reported in the news. Even weatherpeople have become hot items and junior celebrities themselves. While weatherpeople and newscasters may never have the star appeal of actors and actresses, as they appear in the media to entertain us and have become widely known, we naturally become invested and interested in them. The same is true with individuals who play professional sports. The more frequently they appear in the media, the more their celebrity status increases.

As simply appearing in the media can give a person wide recognition along with some fame, which we all desire, *we, in turn, seek this ourselves.* In 1912, Anna Steese Richardson, a writer of *McClure's* magazine, wrote an article about filmitis, a disease that attacked the brain.[3] Under the spell of watching a movie, some people would begin to think that they could act just as well as the people they saw in the movies. Next, they began to think that it would be wrong not to share their talents with the public, and, finally, they became so delirious that they would spend all of their life savings to go to Hollywood to pursue a career in acting. While the article was designed to be humorous, in fact, between 1910 and 1930, thousands of individuals traveled to Hollywood to pursue their dreams of wealth and fame, and, reportedly, over 100 women came to Hollywood each week. Shelters needed to be set up to house these aspiring actresses, and others slept in the streets. When Hollywood became so overwhelmed by the numbers of people seeking acting careers, the film industry engaged in scare tactics to discourage others from coming. Articles were written that warned of the dangers of trying to break into the movies, and to dissuade people from pursuing an acting career in Hollywood, announcements were posted in newspapers coast to coast that underscored the slim possibility of a newcomer succeeding in the film industry.[4]

While the chance and hope to achieve recognition in a public way began a little over 100 years ago when people first flooded Hollywood hoping to get discovered and to become stars, today we no longer need to travel to achieve this dream. With the influx and proliferation of the media and the development of broadcasting venues that did not exist even just a short time ago, it is easier for people to achieve recognition (if not celebrity-hood) by receiving attention in the media.

How appealing it is to be seen in a public way, even for a brief period of time, can be seen by viewing *The Today Show*. People arrive from all parts of the country to congregate in the early morning hours around Rockefeller Center in the effort to be close to the action with the hope of being seen on national television. When the camera peers in their direction, frantic hand waving and jockeying for position instantly occurs, and I am sure that they have told all of their friends and family that they will be in New York, standing outside on *The Today Show*, and to look for them. Even if a person is interviewed by a newscaster about a car accident and was told that the story will be on the six o'clock news, you can be sure that all of their friends will be notified with the hope that their friends will turn on their televisions to see them in the limelight.

I certainly have fallen into the allure of being on television. When I wrote my first book, as well as other opportunities I have had to be interviewed on television and the radio, I always let all my friends and family know. I remember how excited I was when I was first contacted about appearing on a morning news show to be interviewed about my book. I couldn't wait to tell all my friends to be sure to tune in and see me on television. Apart from any other of my accomplishments, being featured and seen by many people in the media felt like a sign that I was special and that I had made it, as being highlighted in the media provides public recognition and validation.

Appearing on a reality television show is another way to get recognition, and with more and more reality television shows being created, there is more and more opportunity. Many websites allow a person to apply to be on a particular reality show. All you need to do is read about the show and write an e-mail inquiry about what makes you think you should be on the show, and if you are lucky, you may get chosen. In addition, as being on the television screen brings public recognition, in some cases this can lead to further success. Anyone with an extroverted personality, a propensity for drama, and a little luck now has the chance to become a star. There are also shows that explicitly give people the chance to show a particular skill with the chance of becoming famous and achieving stardom. Perhaps the first was *American Idol*, where people display their singing ability, and this paved the way for a multitude of copycat shows with a similar format. Other shows offer opportunities for people to exhibit their skills dancing, modeling, or cooking, all with the chance of achieving recognition and, with luck, fame.

Social media has grown in popularity and scope, and venues such as Facebook, Twitter, and Instagram can be used to achieve some kind of recognition right from your fingertips. Writing blogs or informational pieces on the Internet, or blogging, is another way to obtain a following. With all of these venues, a person can develop an audience by posting pictures, essays, and comments, and over time others may take notice, which is a way to obtain some kind of wider and more public acknowledgment. People can also get some recognition by simply taking a picture of their face and sending it around the circuit on a social media site, or what is called a "selfie." While taking pictures of oneself and posting them first began in the early 2000s, doing this has gained popularity over time, and in 2012, *Time* magazine noted that of the top 10 buzzwords of the year, "selfie" was number three.[5] In fact, in November 2013, the *Oxford English Dictionary* declared "selfie" the word of the year.[6]

Yet another way to obtain recognition is through YouTube, where a person can create an opportunity to get well known and become a celebrity by making a video. Users can find instructions on everything from what cameras to use, what microphones are best, what to name it, and what kinds of videos get the most hits (most viewings). There are also articles on how to promote your video using YouTube in an effort to ensure that after making and posting your video, it has the best chance to be viewed. In some cases, it can even go "viral," that is, picked up rapidly through the Web. While it doesn't happen to everyone, many people have become celebrities through YouTube.

Truly, launching an entertainment career over the Web has become a new platform. *USA Today* reported that Hollywood's top talent agencies, such as UTA, Endeavor, and Creative Artists Agency, have begun to look online to these videos to find new talent instead of just scouting comedy clubs and obscure movies.[7] And YouTube is just one very well known website; people have created and are developing their own websites to showcase their own and others' videos, and there are hundreds of these. One website, www.videomenu.com, lists over 100, and www.reelseo.com/list-video-sharing-websites lists over 300.

Some individuals make up publicity stunts for the purpose of getting their names and faces in the news. Take, for example, the couple from Colorado who fabricated a story that their son was inside a flying saucer type of balloon and drifted away inside of it. On closer scrutiny, the couple admitted that this was a complete hoax in an effort to pitch some kind of reality television show.[8] Another example is the couple who crashed President Barack Obama's state dinner in November 2009 honoring the Indian prime minister, Manmohan Singh. They, too, were aspiring reality television stars and did this with the hope of getting on the *Real Housewives of DC* show.[9]

It can also be argued that the craving for and seeking of attention is, at least in part, what fuels some individuals to commit heinous crimes. The appeal for recognition can be so all-consuming that it no longer matters to the person committing the crime that his or her act is despicable and that notoriety is what will be recorded in the annals of history. Being known and having a name that people know may be an element of the motivation.[10]

Another venue that affords some people recognition is the public airing of a tragic, real-life story on network television. People who appear on *The Jerry Springer Show*, *Hoarders*, *Intervention*, and *Dr. Phil* (and even *Oprah* when it was still running) fall in this category. Why would a person face a sister who is having sex with her husband, confront her boyfriend's wife, fight with his or her family, or reveal his or her most embarrassing and deepest and darkest secrets on national television? It is the overpowering compulsion to achieve some kind of public recognition and to feel like a *somebody*, a "star," and to obtain notoriety.

Some children attend summer camps where they are groomed to be the next big celebrity. Created by the producers of *American Idol*, FremantleMedia, and 19 Entertainment, Idol Camp, which first began in Northfield, Massachusetts, in 2007, charged around $2,900 to allow 700 or so 12- to 15-year-old celebrity wannabes to live there for 10 days to obtain performing arts training along with some more mundane camp activities, such as swimming and other sports. While there is no guarantee of becoming a real celebrity, that parents are willing to shell out about $300 a day demonstrates how becoming a star has become such a force in our society. [11]

THE DESIRE FOR RECOGNITION AND FAME

As has been written, "As long as there have been humans, there has always been fame. It is a human weakness. No other kind of living creature knows anything about fame, not even the peacock, who certainly craves attention but lacks the brain to know why." [12] Why do we crave to be known, and why is this so appealing? It is because being recognized and appreciated by others counters our feelings of inferiority and reinforces the belief that we are special, that we have value. Being known and acknowledged by others and knowing that others have an interest in us indicates that we matter and are special. A personality dimension that has been identified as relevant to a desire for fame is a sense of psychological vulnerability that consists of being unsure of oneself, having low self-esteem, feeling ignored, and having a poor body image. [13] The incessant desire to achieve fame and recognition is a way to feel good about ourselves, as this can counter this feeling.

On a still grander scale, the desire for recognition and fame can also be due to our feelings of insignificance and the realization that we are no different than any other animals that inhabit the earth. Just like any other animal, when we die, we are simply *food for worms*.[14] Ernest Becker suggests that our entire culture and all human achievements are designed to overcome our feelings of inferiority and insignificance that stem from our anxiety about our own death. To cope with this fear, which is at the core of our existence, we remain desirous of accomplishing something that matters as proof of our specialness and unique qualities. Achieving something grand helps counter any deep-seated feelings of inferiority while ensuring ourselves that we will be remembered and thought about from now to eternity. For this reason, kings, queens, warriors, and political figures all had busts and statues created and paintings drawn of them to ensure that their names would live forever. This practice continues to this day when heads of state routinely get pictures painted of themselves for public viewing.

Perhaps the quintessential way to cope with the fear of death is the attainment of fame and notoriety. Leo Braudy, in his book *The Frenzy of the Renown: Fame and Its History*, has noted that fame can help liberate a person from "powerless anonymity," which makes fame so alluring.[15] It has been written that "a morbid craving for fame" can help quell underlying death anxiety and the feeling that we truly do not matter.[16] In a psychological case review of 83 individuals who attacked or threatened a prominent public figure, the goal to achieve notoriety was offered as most important.[17] To be known, even for a despicable event, is a way to be remembered long after one dies. Other scientists have also demonstrated that when individuals are reminded of their death, their interest in and desire for fame increase.[18] While there can certainly be some drawbacks to fame and fortune, specifically the invasion of privacy and the destabilization of interpersonal relationships, in a study of celebrities, all stated that fame was worth the drawbacks.[19]

While an interest in fame is part of being human and has always existed, it is possible that there is an enhanced desire for public recognition now as the result of having such an array of opportunities available to us, such as YouTube, game show entertainment, appearing on a reality television show, or being able to tell your tragic story in front of a national audience. It has been stated that our desire for recognition that is a part of our nature is particularly sensitive to the "mode and extent of communications within a society."[20] The growth of the media machine has enhanced people's ability to achieve quick recognition, and for some this has become a central motif. As noted by Gretchen Voss in *The Boston Globe*, who quoted Neal Gabler, "Electronic media offer so many venues for kids to achieve some degree of fame or notoriety."[21] Whether the person has talent does not matter; the issue remains how to best achieve recognition and engineer a way into the limelight. With the universal need for validation and recognition by others, such venues have tremendous allure. It is like putting the forbidden fruit in front of someone's face. If the appeal is so great, it will not be resisted.

It is also possible that there is an enhanced interest in becoming famous because in today's society, there is less opportunity to get our needs met through meaningful work, an important source of self-esteem and recognition. In addition, with so many people inhabiting the world, how do we feel special? Desperate times demand desperate measures, and when it is harder to feel special about oneself, going for public recognition can become a way to achieve a sense of value and importance.

In support of the idea that becoming famous is an increasingly important motif, there was a study conducted in 2006 that looked at four groups of individuals: those who were born from 1981 to 1988, 1966 to 1980, and 1946 to 1965 and those born prior to 1946.[22] The researchers found that the youngest group placed the most emphasis on being famous as a lifetime goal than did the other groups of individuals. Specifically, about 50 percent rated becoming famous as their most important or second most important goal. While the reason or reasons for this are not clear, as people may simply value different things at different stages of life, the youngest generation's greater exposure to electronic media venues that allow opportunities to become famous may be a relevant factor. The increasing importance of fame in today's society can also be seen in another study that conducted a content analysis of the two most popular television shows geared to 9- to 11-year-olds once a decade during the course of 50 years beginning in 1967 and ending in 2007. Among the central characters in these shows, of 16 values, such as financial success, self-acceptance, benevolence, and the wish to be physically fit, to name just some, the desire for fame was the most important value in 2007, whereas in every other decade, wanting to be famous was fifteenth out of 16.[23]

THE CONNECTION TO CELEBRITY OBSESSION

So it is clear that we have a desire to be known and to be recognized by others. However, we need to establish the reason for our obsession with people in the entertainment industry. As reviewed in chapter 5, we have always created idols and have the tendency to place certain people on pedestals, which is an age-old phenomenon that goes back to the beginning of time. We also seem most attracted to the people who best epitomize the ideals of our heroes. For example, a young doctor may wish to follow in the footsteps of the more senior or esteemed physician, an artist will take an interest in a fellow sculptor whose work he or she most admires, a debut author of fiction will look with reverence at the esteemed novelist who has honed his or her craft to perfection, or a rookie football player will look up to the star of his team as he hopes to match his success. It is natural to take an interest in someone who shares our personal interests and values and who has attained some degree of success in his or her respective field.

Today, however, our heroes are seldom the philanthropists, inventors, surgeons, or others who do admirable things for humankind; rather, they are the celluloid figures about whom we know little to nothing except how they present in front of a camera when entertaining us. This idealization has occurred because in our society now, for many people, a priority and determination is to become known and to achieve public recognition. As a result, *we take an interest in and tend to idolize and focus on those people who have accomplished this. How or why they have achieved this is really quite secondary if not completely irrelevant. We worship those individuals who have succeeded at becoming well known because this is what we want for ourselves.*

In support of this concept, a study conducted in 2007 interviewed a group of adolescents to determine their interest in celebrities and who they gossiped about.[24] The study concluded that they focused on high-profile celebrities who were famous and known by larger audiences and consequently considered to be more prestigious. They were also very interested in the clothes they wore and their "glitter and glamour." While the authors interpreted this to mean that young people paid close attention to celebrities as a way to learn how to be successful, I believe that this interpretation is lacking. The interest these young people had in their famous celebrities had nothing to do with the strategies their heroes used to achieve fame, which was acting or playing a sport. Rather, it rested solely on the fact that they were famous. If these celebrities were to lose their stardom, their vested interest in them would likely erode as well. Their interest in them was predicated largely on the fact that they are famous.

Wide recognition and notoriety are the reasons that movie actors and actresses are so much bigger celebrities than are individuals who act in live theater, even though they may be equally talented if not more so. Actors of live theater do not have the luxury of retakes, and with no room for error, they must perform correctly at every performance. In the moviemaking business, scenes can be shot dozens and dozens of times, and there are many ways to make a scene particularly engaging. Movie actors and actresses are bigger celebrities because they have the benefit of the big screen and therefore appear larger than life. They are also portrayed on billboards and throughout mass media, and as a result they are more well known and thus have greater celebrity appeal. The same is true with television actors and actresses, newscasters, and those involved in sporting events who appear on television, including commentators. Their faces are known, much more so than are those of theater actors and actresses, and notoriety fosters idolization. That simple dimension gives a person power, prestige, and fame. Had Jack Nicholson, Tom Cruise, Angelina Jolie, or Cameron Diaz, to name just four, chosen to work in live theater, they never would have become household names and never would have achieved celebrity status. In today's world, fame depends on the media, as without this, notoriety is not possible. While fame has always existed, "when people lived in caves, every cave had someone famous in it. But that was as far as his, or her, fame went. There was no way of transmitting it except to write on the cave wall."[25]

Even many reality television stars have accomplished some celebrity status, and their life stories appear in many magazines. The news still occasionally focuses on the tax problems of Richard Hatch, who won the first American *Survivor* series. These individuals are ordinary people who have become well known, and *simply for that reason*, they have an appeal, and people are interested in their lives.

What is also true is that, compared to actors and actresses who work in the theater, television and movie actors and actresses also make much more money, as do many other entertainers, such as professional athletes and rock musicians. Money has always meant power and prestige, and this is no different here. With money, one can live lavishly, and in our society that goes a long way in establishing admiration. We undoubtedly are a money-obsessed society, and the extravagant sums of money that those who entertain us in the movies and on television make also helps fuel our admiration of them.

Money, however, is not the sole reason for celebrity obsession. If that were the case, the richest and most powerful CEOs worldwide—who are the wealthiest people in the world—would be at the center of our omnipotent adulation, and they are not. Our obsession with those in the entertainment field is multidimensional and involves other indicators, such as wide recognition, beauty, and that they spend their lives entertaining us. Rich CEOs generally don't have all of those traits: they typically are not gorgeous or young, most do not have facial recognition, and they are usually not particularly entertaining. The combination is needed to fuel our obsession. In fact, I would venture that you can rate a person's star power by measuring how attractive he or she is, including his or her age, how much he or she entertains us, how well known he or she is, and the degree to which he or she utilizes the media to be in the news. Think about people in the news and how many of these features they possess and then think of their overall star power.

WHAT ABOUT POLITICIANS?

While there are exceptions, most politicians, while they are known throughout the land and are also generally wealthy, are not typically seen as celebrities, and there are a number of factors that explain this. To begin, most of them aren't particularly attractive, and that, in and of itself, will hurt your celebrity status. It was Jay Leno who said that politics was show business for ugly people. Good looks matter tremendously, and if you are attractive, this will help. A case in point is Sarah Palin. She is more of a celebrity than most other female politicians who have done enormously more in the realm of politics, at least in part as a result of her physical attractiveness as well as her natural facility in front of a camera.

Politics also is lacking in drama, at least most of the time, an important factor in sustaining public interest. Politicians are writing and reviewing bills, meeting with constituents, voting on issues, debating issues, talking with others to generate support for their ideas, and attending meetings. It is no wonder that celebrity-hood isn't usually within their reach. This kind of stuff doesn't just create a great story line and isn't particularly entertaining.

On the other hand, when running for office, politicians are more celebrity-like, and this is because when campaigning, there is much more drama, conflict, and intensity, and this is entertainment. This grabs our attention, giving them greater celebrity appeal, and it all leads up to a climax on Election Day. The public is also first getting to know the candidates, their personalities, and what they are like, and this also creates interest. Furthermore, when an election is important, it creates even greater drama, and this helps increase the person's celebrity status. During the campaign, the media is involved, and this can make a debate seem like an important sporting event. In fact, after the debate, there is always the postdebate analysis, with newscasters commenting on who won, who lost, and why, just like the postgame analysis of a big football or basketball game.

However, once the debates and elections are over, it is back to business and politics as usual, and down goes the celebrity status. However, if the country faces a national emergency, a politician will again attain first-line billing, and interest about the person is again generated. Since drama creates interest, the politician who is again thrust back into the limelight can achieve the public status of a celebrity.

We also tend to focus on the external, and this is the reason that politicians who first enter the scene can achieve some measure of celebrity. They are also surrounded by the media, which by itself can generate attention and lead to being a celebrity. We also hear sound bites and hyperbole from new political figures who may feel the need to appeal to a majority of the voters in order to get elected—and that is good drama. Nonetheless, once politicians get elected, they must talk more about the details of their plans, acts, bills, and ideas and put these initiatives into action. No longer does the politician's popularity depend on what he or she says; rather, the proof is in what he or she does, and all too often the actions fail to measure up to what was said during the campaign. This explains the inevitable drop in the celebrity status of many politicians.

What would happen if politicians could keep the media around them and use the media fully after the election was over? Some have been able to maintain celebrity status and high popularity as a result of their innate theatrical skills and ability to generate good feeling when in front of the camera. Perhaps the best example of this was Ronald Reagan, who was a trained actor. He was supremely skilled at this, a man who "was an accomplished presidential performer"[26] and who was able to "sell good vibes."[27] When Reagan appeared in the media, he generated confidence no matter what crisis was going on in the world. It has even been suggested that he set the stage for future politicians, setting an example of how to present in front of the electorate.[28]

In summary, recognition and attention from others is a great way to feel good about one's life—the need and desire have always been there. Through hard work and talent, people often can obtain this. However, with the reach and power of the media in today's society, the ability to obtain recognition and notice without necessarily having to do the hard work has changed the landscape. Today, one guaranteed way to augment and solidify one's internal sense of self is simply to go for the recognition regardless of what is actually done to gain this. Rather than moving to Hollywood as would-be starlets did during 1910–1930, the media machine has given people the increased opportunity to rapidly achieve recognition and notoriety via YouTube, through other social media sites, or by appearing on some kind of reality television show— the new way to self-esteem and even wealth.

As we idolize those we want to be like, we in turn idolize those in the media who have achieved fame and notoriety, whether this is a movie or television actor, newscaster, athlete, singer, or reality television star. Add to that the money they make and, for many, their attractiveness, and we have individuals to idolize. All of these people represent and embody our ideal selves, as they have the things we all desire. Our obsessive preoccupation with those who are well known is because *they got what we want*.

14

VOYEURISM EXPLOITED

Some degree of novelty must be one of the materials in almost every instrument which works upon the mind; and curiosity blends itself, more or less, with all our pleasures. —Edmund Burke

The first and simplest emotion which we discover in the human mind, is curiosity. —Edmund Burke

Most people know more about their congressman via smear campaigns than they know about their own neighbor via conversations, and a lot of people know more about Britney Spears via tabloids than they know about their own congressman via voting booklets. Does anyone else see the problem here? —Brock Fiant

Closely related to our necessity for entertainment is our need for novelty and basic curiosity. We crave stimulation and knowing what is going on around us, and we cannot refrain from looking at disasters or accidents. In fact, we are drawn to being downright nosy, as it is built into our genetic predisposition. On some level, we must all be voyeurs, as knowing on what is going surrounding us has survival value. For example, being aware that a flood is heading our way will enable us to be prepared, or knowing that a dangerous individual has escaped from a prison in our area will help us take the necessary steps to avoid disaster. Knowing what cars or airlines are safest, what food products are con-

taminated, and that there has been a strange person seen in our neighborhood are things that we want to know about and automatically grab
our attention.

However, even apart from its survival value, for many of us the
satisfaction of our voyeurism can serve as a form of distraction and
amusement, and those working in the media field realized that our
prurience could be completely exploited for financial gain. This had its
beginnings in the 1830s with the creation of the "penny press," or newspapers that cost only one penny, whereas others generally cost six cents.
What separated the penny press from other newspapers, however, was
more than just the cost. The real differences were the target audience,
which for the penny press was the working class as opposed to a wealthy
and professional audience, as well as the content of the penny press,
which featured human interest stories as opposed to opinion pieces.
Human interest stories offered more entertainment value than did
more traditional newspapers, as, rather than news per se, it satiated our
voyeurism by focusing on the sufferings and misfortunes of people in
society. For example, in 1835, when *The Herald* was first published,
during the first two weeks of its publication, it featured three murders,
three suicides, the deaths of five people in a fire, a man who accidental-
ly blew his head off, a guillotine execution in France, and a riot in
Philadelphia.[1] People's interest in these kinds of stories can be seen in
the sheer number of copies these kinds of newspapers sold compared to
more traditional newspapers. In New York City, all 11 daily newspapers
in 1833 had a total circulation of 26,500. Two years later, the circulation
of just the penny newspapers was estimated to be 44,000.[2]

What also gave these kinds of newspapers (if not all newspapers)
assistance was the invention of the telegraph. With the telegraph, news
from thousands of miles away could be shared across the land. In addition, great amounts of information could be acquired, whether or not it
had any significance to a person's life. News of fires, floods, killings, or
other tragedies spread everywhere; it was news for the sake of news as
opposed to having true relevance for its readers. In fact, in *Walden*,
Henry David Thoreau perhaps foresaw the future when he wrote, "We

are in great haste to construct a magnetic telegraph from Maine to Texas; but Maine and Texas, it may be, have nothing important to communicate. . . . We are eager to tunnel under the Atlantic and bring the old world some weeks nearer to the new; but perchance the first news that will leak through into the broad flapping American ear will be that Princess Adelaide has the whooping cough."[3]

While we no longer have the penny press, the tradition of news focusing on sensational and shocking human interest stories continues to this day through tabloids, which are similar but, in addition to the written word, also contain pictures, which have a more visceral impact. Even more traditional newspapers write about such topics, as these kinds of stories capture our attention and are needed to help sell the newspapers. James Gordon Bennett, who was the main force behind *The Herald*, knew who his readers were and stated that they "were more ready to seek six columns of the details of a brutal murder, or the testimony of a divorce case, or the trial of a divine improprieties of conduct, than the same amount of words poured forth by the genius of the noblest author of the times."[4] While this was stated in the mid-1800s, this insight is true to this day.

As technology grew, our voyeurism continued and continues to be satiated via news shows that incessantly focus on misery, scandal, and tragedy. Whatever the event of the day, whether big or small, all of the news stations cover it. Whether a car accident, a fire, a money-laundering scandal, a drunk-driving arrest, or a troubled teenager bringing a knife to school, these life events are featured on prime-time news stations and are seen over and over again. In fact, with big events, people can become glued to the television, being almost unable to turn away.

With the further proliferation of the media through a variety of television shows, the fulfilling of our voyeurism has been exploited even further. While there are many examples, some of the most overt and obvious shows that completely demonstrate how the titillation of our voyeurism can be made into entertainment are *The Jerry Springer Show*, *Hoarders*, and *Intervention*. Even *Dr. Phil* has regressed to the level of almost complete voyeurism. In these shows, viewers obtain exposure to other people's private, troubled lives. That some people choose to be on these shows is another matter completely, and the reasons for this were reviewed in the previous chapter. The point here is that the fulfillment of our voyeurism through such shows has become a way to be entertained, albeit in a less formal way, than is simply watching a movie or a professionally produced weekly sitcom. We need a life story to satisfy our prurience, which has become a peculiar form of amusement. Right from *The Jerry Springer Show* website, these are the kinds of people the show is looking for:

- Is there someone you hate with all of your heart? Do you want to confront them on our show?
- Are you sleeping with a married man and want to confront his wife on our show?
- Are you ashamed of something you did and want to come clean on our show?
- Are you a prostitute and want to reveal it to your spouse/family?
- Are you suspicious your man is cheating with a close friend or relative and you're ready to confront them?
- Have you ever paid a prostitute for sex?
- Are you a transsexual with a shocking story?
- Do you have a crazy ex that won't stay out of your new relationship? Or are you the crazy ex?

If there was ever any doubt that we are a voyeuristic species, the fact that people want to watch these stories puts closure on this question.

So we see that peering into the lives of others, or being the viewer of "life stories," has long been a major motif in society. In fact, it can be argued that we no longer need well-thought-out writing or sophisticated moviemaking to be entertained; instead, we can simply focus on the events and the people around us that can give us this same entertainment fix. Truth is not only stranger than fiction; truth is as good as fiction, and it is much less expensive to produce. With good storytelling, sensational pictures, and a less-than-typical tale, our curiosity can be aroused, and we can become interested in most anybody, at least for a short period of time.

One great example of this was the fascination with Jon and Kate Gosselin and their family. For those who do not know, Jon and Kate Gosselin had a television show called *Jon and Kate Plus 8*, and their claim to fame was that they were the parents of eight children. These are everyday people who didn't do anything of particular value or achievement, excluding being the parents of eight young children. That this could be a watched television show and that the paparazzi follow their lives clearly demonstrates the unbridled intensity of our voyeurism. Since first having a show, they eventually decided to get a divorce, resulting in much interest regarding who is the better parent or the worse parent and who is going out with whom. As a result of the divorce, Jon was cut from the show, and the show was renamed *Kate Plus 8*, which was finally canceled after 150 episodes. And then there is the show *Keeping Up with the Kardashians*, which has been on television since 2007 and is now in its ninth season despite a petition that was signed by 180,049 people asking the *E!* network to remove the shows from its programming.[5]

THE CONNECTION TO CELEBRITY OBSESSION

While interest in these kind of reality television shows may be a mixed bag, the truth of the matter is that these individuals became famous celebrities not because of any particular talent but because they were placed on a television show, giving them public recognition. As was reviewed in the previous chapter, in our media-obsessed society, simply becoming known creates interest in whoever is featured, even if they are rather ordinary souls without any particular talent or noteworthy achievement. However, when people are *already* a known entity and there is *already* interest surrounding them, such as the present state of affairs among those who work in the entertainment field or our current celebrities, *our voyeuristic interest and wanting to learn more about their life stories is even greater*. News stations, late-night television, and magazines and shows that exclusively follow the lives of celebrities enhance and intensify our voyeuristic interests and have created yet another reason to be interested in their lives. Whether it is the O. J. Simpson trial; the Anna Nicole Smith tragedy; the challenges of Tiger Woods, Michael Jackson, and Charlie Sheen; Michael Vick's conviction of animal abuse; Ray Rice's assault on his wife; or the divorces, marriages, and babies of our celebrities, the covering of these events provides us with a form of amusement. Certainly, for many of these people, their real-life, off-screen stories have gotten more publicity (or at least equal coverage) than anything they have done in their careers. Their actual lives fulfill our voyeurism, and the focus on them has simply added fuel to our obsession with them. What is also true is that those who are already known can use the media to further augment interest in themselves by, for example, hiring publicity agents. Even if the media coverage is negative, the exposure can heighten our interest, as it taps into our voyeurism.

Actors and actresses who act in movies as opposed to those who perform onstage easily grab our attention. As already discussed, their role as entertainers, in and of itself, has a powerful ability to take hold of our minds. However, because such individuals change roles and personas from movie to movie, we can't and don't ever really get to know them, and as a result they remain, in large part, an enigma and more like an illusion. We see snippets of them, whereas actors who act in live theater are much more real. Theater actors are actually seen as opposed to appearing as a celluloid image, and this is another reason why we are less interested in them. The more we see and can know a person, the less voyeuristic interest we have in him or her; the less we know, the more we fantasize, and the greater interest we have. What we can't have we want, and what we can have we don't want as much. This is an absolutely perfect scenario to fuel our inherent voyeurism and our passion to learn who they are and what they are really like.

This inability to truly know certain people and how this increases our desire to learn about them can be seen in three music stars: Madonna, Lady Gaga, and Michael Jackson. Madonna changes her appearance, as did Michael Jackson when he was still alive. Lady Gaga, too, dresses outrageously, and one never knows how she will next appear and what she will look like. As a result, they cannot be as known as others who usually appear pretty much the same. I do not know whether Madonna's or Lady Gaga's constantly changing appearance or Michael Jackson's, before his untimely death, was a conscious decision on their parts. Regardless, I believe that this only adds to their enigmatic qualities and helps make them even bigger celebrities. What is also clear is that continually changing one's external appearance, especially when dress is outrageous, helps a person stand out and be unique. In turn, in our voyeuristic society, this ensures that the eye of the camera does not drift too far away or for too long a period of time.

Our prurient tendencies have only been heightened by the unlimited access to information that is now available to all of us. Today, a person can sit down at his or her computer and find out at least some information about almost any celebrity. Add to this magazines and newspapers, and you have an excess of information and an almost unlimited means to find out tidbits of information about a favorite star. This easy access to information adds fuel to our voyeurism and strengthens this attribute.

How our voyeurism has been impacted as a result of this easy access to information, largely through the Internet, is similar to how the Internet has impacted some of our other characteristics. For example, our addiction to pornography has increased due to its easy availability on the Internet.[6, 7] That is, some individuals have a vulnerability to get completely captivated by pornography but never did so in the past, as it was more difficult to do. While they might buy some magazines or watch some videos, they never got heavily engrossed in pornography. Enter the Internet, which is available 24 hours a day, seven days a week, and is fairly cheap as well as anonymous, and a sexual addiction could develop. Furthermore, while such a person might never seek out a prostitute, the Internet makes this much easier and can lead a person to take that step.

The same is true with gambling. With the Internet, it is much easier to gamble, and for some this easy access to gambling can lead to a gambling problem.[8, 9] State-sponsored gambling through the lottery can also tap in to a latent vulnerability to gamble and result in problematic gambling.[10] The point is that we are all subject to influences in our environment, and these forces interact with our internal attributes and can either augment or decrease these basic tendencies. Through multiple pathways, we are inundated with news about celebrities, and given our tendency to be voyeurs and our interest in other people's lives, ready access to this information has further intensified our fascination with such people.

FILLING THE VOID

As reviewed in chapter 3, we love to be around other people, we congregate together, and we need other people to survive and exist. However, as also noted, we live an increasingly isolated existence. In greater numbers, we tend to live alone, we live farther away from our families, we are a more mobile society, and there are fewer opportunities for socialization. Despite this, our need for intimacy and closeness has not atrophied. Years ago, when there was more social interaction with people in one's immediate surroundings, people would spend their free time socializing with each other. Local dances took place, get-togethers would be held, people would gather at the local tavern or store, and there was a social fabric and connection within one's local community. These kinds of activities, while they still take place within certain segments of society, are less common, and overall people are less connected to others in their local living area. Even when attended, it is often the norm not to even know others who are at the event. In fact, when communities become gentrified and neighborhoods break up, there is an outcry that the cohesive fabric of the community is being destroyed, but change continues to take place.

As a result of our greater social isolation and difficulty meeting others, the growth of dating sites (e.g., www.match.com, www.eharmony.

com, www.friendfinder.com, and www.matchmaker.com) has increased. There are literally hundreds of such sites, and while some of these are clearly meant for sexual encounters, others are legitimate sites to help a person find someone to truly connect with on a longer-term basis. Venues such as Facebook and even LinkedIn help foster and reestablish relationships with others with whom we have lost contact due to geographic moves or other reasons. There is a downside, however. Researchers have found that with the popularity of these social network sites and the rise in the use of the Internet, people living in the United States report that they are spending less time with family members. Twenty-eight percent of those interviewed in 2008 reported spending less time with members in their family households, or almost three times the number of people who reported this in 2006. The time spent on family socializing dropped during this time, from an average of 26 hours per month to about 18 hours, a 30 percent drop. There was also a 40 percent increase in reports of occasionally feeling ignored by family members due to their Internet use.[11] So, while electronic relationships may help counter our isolation, it may also lead, at least in part, to greater isolation and withdrawal from family members.

Even if using the computer creates isolation from family members, we nonetheless attempt to get our need for social connection met through the Internet and the thousands of chat rooms and online activities that exist. Another mechanism is through television, where a person can click on a channel and instantly have a visitor (if not many visitors) in one's home. Television provides us with people who talk to us and with social contact to mollify our isolation. Better yet is when over weeks, months, or years, we have gotten to know these people. It could be a newscaster, a talk show host, or an actor or actress in some sitcom. They fill our social void and become a part of our lives, and this fuels our attraction to them. It has been suggested that during postwar America, when families moved to the suburbs, families that appeared on television helped counter social isolation and gave a person a community of friends.[12] Especially for those on television who appear every day, attachments to them can feel personal. In a study of the reactions of viewers following the end of a popular television show, it was found that individuals who had established strong attachments to the characters experienced breakup distress.[13] In addition, those who can be added to this list of "friends" are people we have simply gotten to know by reading or hearing about their life stories through television, magazines, websites, and newspapers. In fact, we are on a first-name basis with many of these people, and this suggests true closeness and intimacy. To name some, these include Angelina Jolie, Brad Pitt, David Letterman, and Jay Leno. Do we really know these people? Certainly not, but we delude ourselves into thinking that we do.

As previously noted, why we develop such strong connections to these people is because our brain isn't designed to tell the difference between real relationships and those we have with people we have gotten to know through a variety of different media venues. Images get confused with reality, and we can begin to believe that we truly know these images. As aptly stated, "We see them in our bedrooms, we hear their voices when we dine: If this hypothesis is correct, how are we not to perceive them as our kin, our friends, or even our rivals? As a result, we automatically seek information about their physical health, about changes in their relative standing, and above all about their sexual relationships."[14] Other researchers have noted that when we are regularly inundated with news about celebrities, our brains make us believe (albeit falsely) that these people are part of our social networks.[15]

So what appears and who is featured in the media is our new social connector, the glue that helps hold us together in an increasingly isolated society, and the people in media become important because they give us a common frame of reference. It really doesn't matter who the focus is on, as this changes from day to day. Their life stories give us a common anchor, and this information has become a universal fabric in society that binds us together, unifies us as a group, and functions to fill a void we have in our social circle. Even without our greater isolation, we have an interest in "life stories" due to our voyeurism; however, add our isolation to the mix, and our interest increases exponentially.

Some psychologists who have studied this phenomenon refer to the relationships people have with celebrities as parasocial relationships.[16] Or, using slightly different language, our interactions with and investment in people we really do not know can be called artificial social relations.[17] These are one-sided relationships where one person (the fan) may know a great deal about the celebrity (or at least what the celebrity or media source wants the fan to know, whether true or not) but where the celebrity knows nothing about the fan. In these kinds of relationships, a person can have a desire to learn more about one person, the celebrity, and is able to achieve this through reading about the person, joining a fan club, purchasing pictures, or, if lucky enough, actually meeting the person. The celebrity knows nothing of this other person or even that the person exists—truly, a completely one-sided relationship. In extreme cases, this can become a true obsession that can include stalking.

Researchers have fairly recently been looking at the possible connection between loneliness and interest in celebrities. While more study is needed, some research has supported the hypothesis that our obsession with celebrities may be related to our isolation. One study found that older adults had a greater interest in the lives of celebrities than younger adults, and it was hypothesized that this helped fill the losses in their real-life social networks.[18] Another study showed that people turn to watching television when feeling lonely and that when watching television, they felt less lonely.[19] It was further suggested that the development of parasocial relationships with television characters can help people achieve a sense of belonging. Essentially, parasocial relationships are better than no relationships, and being able to fill our need for social relationships through these mechanisms is a part of the puzzle. Even if people aren't particularly lonely, information and stories about celebrities have become a piece of our social fabric and further help explain our fascination with them. As we have a need to belong and feel connected and celebrity news dominates the media, knowing about them helps us feel a part of society. Whereas in the past people might have a need to know what was happening where they lived and with the

people in their immediate social circles, with the wide-ranging proliferation of the media our social sphere has expanded, and people's interest now extends to the people who live around the world. Furthermore,
for some who have a need to be in the "in crowd," having a relationship
with them, even if it is parasocial, helps them feel that they have such
status and that they are a part of their world. This can be achieved by
reading about them, learning about them on television, seeing an Instagram of them, or, better yet, following their day-to-day lives on Twitter.
While people know that they will likely never become a celebrity, at
least knowing what is going on with such people helps them feel as
though they are a part of their world. It is the closest that they will come
to stardom, and it is certainly better than nothing.

WHAT HELPS FUEL OUR VOYEURISM?

While voyeurism is built in to our genetic makeup, one thing that fuels
our extreme interest in the lives of our celebrities is the vicarious iden-
tification with their good fortune. When good things happen to people
we care about, we in turn experience happiness. For example, when our
favorite team wins the Super Bowl or World Series, we in turn obtain
similar joy. The boundaries between our own identity and those of our
city's sports teams get blurred. We are as happy as they are and equally
celebrate the victory. When our favorite team wins, we gleefully ex-
claim, "We won!" Or if our favorite singer or musician wins a Grammy
award or our favorite actor or actress wins an Oscar, it can give us joy as
well. I have spoken to people who read celebrity magazines, and I often
hear that they do this because they obtain vicarious pleasure in learning
about these individuals' lives and what they do. For some, when reading
about celebrities, people fantasize and place themselves in the situations that they are reading about. They imagine that the good fortune
and lives that these celebrities have can be their own, and this can at
least temporarily make them feel better and raise their own self-esteem.
In fact, it can be argued that the distance between ordinariness and
celebrity-hood has shrunk with the multiple venues now available to

everyone to achieve at least some kind of fame, even if short term. As a result, it is easier to fantasize that other people's good fortunes can be one's own, and this can help enhance the interest.

Celebrities also have high popularity, and, for some, knowing what takes place in the lives of the most popular people in the world and feeling a part of this can enhance their own self-regard. Some research supports the idea that for people with low self-esteem, even writing about their favorite celebrity can actually increase their own sense of worth, at least temporarily.[20] It is like they feel that they have a close relationship with this person, and thinking about this individual augments their own pride and self-confidence. It has also been suggested that we are most likely to mimic individuals who have high status in society and who are most successful as an evolutionary adaptive strategy.[21] That is, we copy people who have attained high status in an effort to achieve this as well.[22] As celebrities are held in such high regard, we will naturally focus on and be interested in their lives and be exquisitely attuned to gossip about them, as we want to learn about and emulate their strategies for success,[23] whether this consists of going to places they visit, wearing the clothes they wear, or buying the merchandise they endorse or even purchasing their own product lines. So, our voyeuristic interest in the lives of celebrities can help us feel better about our own lives and even provide us with strategies for life enhancement and success going forward.

On the flip side, however, it is also true that learning about the wonderful things that occur to others can make us feel worse about our own lives, particularly if we do not feel that we will be able to attain those ourselves. Everything in this world is relative, and comparing ourselves to others is a natural part of life and helps us rate our own lives. Seeing what the Joneses are doing and keeping up with them is a common societal motif. If so-and-so has purchased a new car, then for many of us, we may want to do the same to continue to feel good about our own status and position in life. And if we cannot afford to do this, we in turn can feel bad. If Jenny gets her nails done every week, Erika may want to as well, but if Erika can't afford this, this can diminish how she feels about her own life.

In support of this, in a meta-analytic study that looked at over 75 studies that assessed the relationship between media exposure that depicted the thin-ideal body type and body dissatisfaction, it was found that exposure to these kinds of images was related to body image concerns among women.[24] It has also been found that among college women, viewing magazine images that depict thin women increased body dissatisfaction, negative mood states, and eating disorder symptoms and decreased self-esteem.[25] Viewing thin and attractive women automatically made these women feel worse about their own body image due to our natural inclination to compare ourselves to others. Because they were not as thin and did not feel as attractive, it diminished their self-esteem. It has also been found that the more frequently fifth- through twelfth-grade school-age girls read magazines who show beautiful and thin models, the more likely it was that they wanted to diet and exercise, as they felt worse about their own body image. In fact, an association was found between the frequency of reading women's magazines and having actually gone on a diet or begun an exercise program.[26]

Similar findings have also been found among boys and men. In a study that examined the impact of viewing muscular and attractive as opposed to average-looking singers in music video clips, it was found that the boys who saw the muscular singers reported poorer upper-body satisfaction, lower satisfaction with their appearance, lower happiness, and more depressive feelings than the boys who viewed the clips depicting singers of average appearance.[27] It has been found that when male college students viewed television commercials that depicted muscular men, this led to a decrease in their own muscle satisfaction as well as their overall physical appearance.[28] In a similar study, when college-age men were exposed to magazine images of muscular men or neutral images, it was found that the men who viewed muscular images reported significantly lower body esteem than men who viewed the neutral images.[29] It has also been found that men who viewed *Playboy* and *Penthouse* were more likely to find their own girlfriends less sexually attractive.[30] So, for some, a voyeuristic interest in others who have it better than they do may decrease their self-esteem and self-concept, as they will likely never be able to measure up to them with regard to lifestyle and attractiveness. As a result, people can end up feeling inadequate about their own lives.

The other component that fuels the incessant desire to know about our celebrities, one that I believe is even more important than learning about their good fortune, is learning about their misfortunes, as this can help us feel better about our own lives. Downward social comparison[31] is a theory that suggests that when people compare themselves to others who are less fortunate than they are, this can help them feel more positive about their own lives. Consequently, discovering and learning that our highly esteemed celebrities, who seem to have it all, also experience significant hardships helps many of us feel more positive about our own lives. Despite all of their fame and money, they are not immune to the darker side of life, they experience the same misfortunes that everyone else does, and this can provide vicarious pleasure, as it helps people feel better about their own life situation. In interviewing the readers of celebrity news, it was reported that "the misery of others made them to feel better about their own lives."[32] It has also been suggested that celebrity gossip brings celebrities down to earth and demonstrates that "that they were not better than we and in some cases worse."[33]

It is apparent that big news is generated when positive events happen to a celebrity. However, when negative events occur, it is generally even bigger news. Tiger Woods's infidelity and the subsequent stress this placed on him and his marriage dominated the news, and this was bigger news than any of his wins, his marriage, or the birth of his children. Britney Spears's breakdown also took over the airwaves and received more coverage than anything else she has ever done. The same is true regarding Paris Hilton's arrest and confinement, Lindsay Lohan's drug and legal problems, and Charlie Sheen's meltdown. An ugly divorce trumps a marriage in terms of readership appeal by a long shot. In this regard, it was reported that the ratings on *Jon and Kate* went up as their relationship went down. As they spoke about their divorce, more people watched.

A review of the headlines on the covers of 20 *Us Weekly* magazine issues over the course of several months in 2009 demonstrates this point. There were just two issues in which the headlines seemed to relay positive news, including some weddings, a couple moving in together, Brad Pitt and Angelina Jolie trying for baby number seven, and some recent love stories. The other 18 covered negative events, including obesity and diet problems, numerous extramarital affairs or allegations of adultery, romantic and marital breakups, fighting between couples, domestic violence, child abuse, psychological stress and problems, and rumors of plastic surgery.

Farrah Fawcett epitomizes the relationship between being a celebrity and tragedy. After all, she was the television star in just one season of *Charlie's Angels* and acted in just a few films along with appearing in some smaller stints on other television shows. The events that fueled her celebrity status were essentially the adversity and calamities in her life—her disoriented 1997 *David Letterman* interview, her naked appearances in *Playboy*, her extreme cosmetic surgery, her alleged assault by boyfriend James Orr, her on-and-off-again relationship with Ryan O'Neal, her son's alleged drug problems, and her premature death—all of this kept society interested in her life and helped enhance her status as a celebrity.

Support for this idea comes from a study that looked at the relationship between self-esteem and reading about celebrity news. It was hypothesized that high consumption of celebrity gossip, particularly in blogs, which tend to be more negative than other forms of celebrity news media, would be negatively correlated with self-esteem. That is, those who read a lot of this kind of gossip would have lower self-esteem because reading about negative gossip is an effort to augment poor self-esteem. It was also hypothesized that as people read negative information about celebrities, they would tend to feel superior to the celebrities. In fact, these hypotheses were supported, leading to the conclusion that one aspect of reading negative news about celebrities is to feel more positive about one's own life. [34]

So we see that reading about others' hardship, misery, and tragedy helps us feel better about our own lives. We are essentially saying that if they have problems, then perhaps our lives aren't so bad after all. A follow-up thought is that we don't even want their fame and money. As these people are our current icons and provide us with a common ground, having them to talk about, learning about their challenging life stories, and gauging our lives against theirs helps foster society's obsession with them. We compare ourselves to them, and particularly when their lives are filled with significant tribulation, it helps us feel more satisfied about our own lives.

In summary, our voyeurism and need for novelty, coupled with how this has been exploited and exacerbated by mass media, can further help explain our fascination with those in the business of entertaining us. Their actual life stories, which captivate our interest, have been made into amusement and entertainment, further heightening our interest in them. Our more isolated and alienated existence also contributes to our obsession with them, as they feel like our friends. They have entered and become a part of our extended social network, and they broaden the "social and moral community in which we live."[35] This allows "the pleasure of extending your family by including the stars."[36] Vicariously basking in our celebrities' glory and, even more important, deriving pleasure from their falls and adversities are additional components that fuel our voyeuristic interest in them. Even though the relationships we have with our current celebrities are parasocial and not real, they nevertheless are extremely powerful.

EPILOGUE

If only the sun-drenched celebrities are being noticed and worshiped, then our children are going to have a tough time seeing the value in the shadows, where the thinkers, probers, and scientists are keeping society together. —Rita Dove

In a world where celebrity equals talent, and where make-believe is called reality, it is most important to have real love, truth and stability in your life. —Bernie Brillstein

When I was a kid, we had to rely on our imaginations for entertainment. —Terry Brooks

In this book, I have tried to make sense of our obsession with individuals and the media that entertain us, whether this concerns people who appear in the movies and on television, musicians, professional athletes, and even those who simply appear frequently in the media. We truly do not know these individuals, yet they continue to fascinate us and are objects of our adoration. As a psychologist, I find this peculiarity to be intriguing. For certain, one reason I wrote this book was to share my understanding with others who may also find this perplexing and who want to make sense of this phenomenon. Here, let me summarize all of the vectors that have come together that have resulted in this obsession.

The entertainment machine, with its ingenuity and power to keep us amused, has capitalized on our humanness. Our need and lust for entertainment along with our basic voyeuristic tendencies, our love of beauty, our need for people, and our propensity to create idols are the targets of this spell. While the entertainment machine has become increasingly sophisticated and refined over the years—and amazingly entertaining—it has also been able to grab our attention because in our current social climate, we have a lot of time for leisure, we are more isolated and lonelier than in the past, and we are hungry to find pleasure and fulfillment through consumption. These secondary factors have made us even more susceptible to being captivated by this enchantment.

Essentially, the entertainment machine has given us a quick fix and easy way to feel good and has even provided us with people with whom we can have relationships, albeit parasocial ones. The real-life stories of our celebrities can provide us with even more entertainment, and learning about their tragedies can help us feel better about our own lives. As heroin, cocaine, or alcohol can capture our brains because we are vulnerable to addiction, our brains have been captured by the entertainment machine, which we rely on for pleasure and fulfillment. The entertainment machine has further intensified our need to be entertained, as due to habituation and tolerance, we need greater stimuli and entertainment to achieve pleasure. While alcohol, cocaine, heroin, gambling, sex, and food are all used to excess by many people to help them feel good, we may add watching entertainment to the list of yet another addictive activity. We have become addicted to this medium to experience pleasure. *That is, we have come to rely on being entertained to feel good.*

Now, in reason and moderation, there is nothing wrong with being entertained, just like there is nothing wrong with occasional drinking or gambling. We all need entertainment and a way to get outside of our usual routines and states of being. However, what I am saying is that we have literally become *strung out* on the entertainment machine to obtain pleasure and to feel good about our lot in life. Furthermore, as we have become addicted to this medium, we no longer do the harder work of finding other ways to entertain ourselves and to feel good about our lives, just like the individual who is addicted to alcohol or gambling no longer works to find other sources of pleasure that do not include continued alcohol use or gambling. Our constricted focus to obtain pleasure in the world has become centered on being entertained. Our addictive vulnerability is the icing on the cake that seals and solidifies the obsession.

The entertainment machine has also made actors and actresses, in particular, intriguing and compelling due to fantastic storytelling and story writing, as well as focusing on their real-life stories in the media, satisfying our voyeurism and providing us with vicarious gratification. The general good looks of many of the people featured in these venues, in conjunction with our obsession with people's external presentation, also fuel our interest. These people or celluloid images make us feel good, and as we are an idol-creating species, we, of course, will become enamored with those who give us this pleasure. Our brains also have difficulty distinguishing between real people and images of people, and this only enhances the obsession. As we are addicted to being entertained, by extension we have become addicted to and obsessed with those who do the entertaining.

Furthermore—and every bit as important—due to mass communication and the proliferation and power of the media, these people, as well as athletes, sportscasters, musicians, newscasters, reality television stars, and others who appear in the media for any reason, have become larger-than-life figures because they have obtained wide-reaching recognition. They have become the most popular people in society, and we want to be a part of their lives. In fact, I almost don't know which is more important: what they do before the camera or the fact that they have become so well known and have recognition. Regardless, they are idolized both because the entertainment machine has helped make them so interesting and because of the power of the media, and they have *achieved recognition and notoriety, and in today's culture that goes very far.* While the need for recognition has always existed, it is now a driving force and a goal in and of itself. The numerous media venues that now exist, that offer the chance and possibility to attain instant fame and "success," titillate and have likely expanded our desire for fame. As the allure of appearing in the media is so great, this has become a more central motif in our culture. *In turn, we have become obsessed with those who have become famous and achieved recognition because we are attracted to others who exemplify and embody what we want for ourselves.* The riches they have due to being in an industry that has become so valued simply adds to their allure, and we have people to idolize and adore.

Finally, such people also help fill the void in our increasingly isolated existence. In some ways, our social network involves and revolves around them as they provide us with a common language. We can talk with each other and bond about the entertainment we have seen, the entertainment we want to see, and our shared knowledge of the lives of these people. In our isolated and entertainment-focused existence, the universal language and fabric in society has become our obsessional preoccupation with those in the entertainment arena. We have incorporated them into our social networks, and they have become assimilated into our lives.

For those of you who are not obsessed with celebrities or even with entertainment but who decided to read this book because you find this phenomenon perplexing (if not sometimes irritating) and wanted to broaden your understanding of this spectacle, I hope that I have helped you achieve a greater awareness of what has spawned this. A comprehension of this spectacle has enabled me to see our celebrity culture through a different lens, and I have found myself more detached from the array of celebrity news that appears in the media. Whereas I used to get annoyed by it, I am now more amused by it than anything else. I also have a greater compassion for those who are obsessed with celebrities as well as those who are consumed with becoming famous. Perhaps understanding this phenomenon will enable you, too, to have the same type of empathy. In addition, if society's infatuation with such people used to sometimes annoy you, appreciating the various elements that have caused this wonder may help you disengage from it and see it for what it is: the hijacking of the susceptible brain of a vulnerable person.

In contrast, some of you may have decided to read this book because you are infatuated with celebrities and wanted to achieve an understanding as to what is responsible for this. I hope that you can now see the variety of forces that cause you to be so enamored with entertainment and those who work in the entertainment field. As you can see, there are a multitude of reasons that are involved, and the reasons for one may be different than for another. For some, your obsession with celebrities may be an effort to alleviate your social isolation, whereas for others, it may be a way to forget about your own life and immerse yourself in a life that you wish you had. It is also possible that you are exquisitely sensitive and vulnerable to the influence of the media and its ability to capture your interest, just like some people are acutely sensitive to the pleasurable effects of drugs, alcohol, gambling, or food. It can even be—and likely is—a combination of various elements.

Whatever the reasons, your obsession with celebrities fulfills one or more needs within you, and you can certainly continue on the same path and stay immersed in the lives of society's icons. On the other hand, by recognizing how your obsession with celebrities satisfies you, you may think about attempting to get your needs met in other ways that you may eventually find to be even more fulfilling. For example, if social isolation is paramount and fuels your obsession, perhaps finding ways to connect with others and developing real relationships will enable you to achieve greater overall life satisfaction instead of coping with your loneliness by having parasocial relationships. Or if focusing on celebrities is a way to feel better about your own life either by fantasizing that their lives can be yours or, conversely, by learning about their problems, perhaps placing efforts on improving your life will, over time, result in greater life satisfaction. If celebrity news seems to grab your attention like alcohol or drugs does for others, by being mindful of this, catching yourself, and making efforts to avoid this kind of stimulation, you may learn to occupy your mind with other activities that ultimately will provide you with greater joy and fulfillment. My bias, for certain, is that it would behoove you to understand what fuels your celebrity obsession and to do the harder work of finding other ways to meet those needs instead of reading about and focusing on the lives of those who you do not know and never will know. I certainly believe that real, authentic relationships are better than parasocial ones. I also think that there are more rewarding things to do with one's life than voyeuristically learning and reading about the lives of individuals who entertain us. The decision, however, to change your interest in and preoccupation with celebrities is a choice that only you can make.

IS THERE A WAY OUT?

Apart from shedding light on how and why celebrity obsession exists, I am also worried about this phenomenon, as I believe it is a negative trend in our society. That we are obsessed with individuals whom we do not know—and, in fact, some of these people aren't necessarily people to fawn over—is a concern. It would likely be more beneficial to society if people were more interested in real heroes who did important things for society, whether or not they appeared in the media's eye, and if people tried to emulate those individuals. It would also be better if people had a greater interest in other ventures and activities rather than in placing so much energy on being entertained and on wanting to learn about those who do the entertaining. Another purpose for writing this book is to get people to wake up, to look at themselves, and to see this spectacle through a different lens and from another perspective.

Society's obsession with those in the entertainment field as well as with those who have for a variety of reasons become known is well established. Yet at the same time, I wonder if there is a way to move beyond this. While this is a tall order, as this state of affairs is multiply determined and has much to do simply with who we are, let me share a few thoughts. Perhaps this societal fixation can at least be tempered.

Clearly, the entertainment machine is committed to keeping our focus and attention. Television, movies, magazines, and sporting events are big businesses, and many people have a powerful and vested interest in making the enormous sums of money that they do. These industries do not want anything to be changed, as making millions of dollars is something that they want to continue to do. As the car industry wants to keep people buying cars and the clothing industry wants to keep us buying new clothes, the entertainment industry wants to keep everyone obsessed with entertainment and entertainers. So catalysts for change will never happen there. Instead, it must begin elsewhere, and the most obvious and important place is within the family.

To begin, parents should talk with and educate their children about the power of the media. While young children will always idolize certain figures (and initially this may be important to help shore up an identity when children grow older), parents can gently speak with their children and explain that these larger-than-life figures are, in fact, human like everyone else and that they, too, have their faults and liabilities. While they may be good at acting, singing, or playing a particular sport and while these attributes are commendable, there are many other less publicized and less marketed attributes that are also admirable, such as being a good person, caring about others, and doing something positive for society, to name just a few. Parents can acknowledge what a great athlete, musician, or actor so and so is, but they can also mention, if they exist, the other things they do that are noteworthy. For example, many celebrities make positive contributions to society either by volunteering themselves for causes that are of interest to them or through their generous philanthropy. These can be highlighted and mentioned, as can their other more widely known accomplishments and attributes. Parents can also help their children appreciate other individuals who have traits that may be more suitable for admiration than how a person presents in front of a camera or what he or she does on the playing field.

Often, when a television show or movie is watched and a particular actor or actress gets admired, what is really admirable is the character the actor or actress is enacting and what that character did. For example, Sally Fields enacted the story of Norma Rae, Ben Kingsley enacted the character of Mahatma Gandhi, Russell Crowe played the role of

Jeffrey Wigand, or some actor enacted the role of some fictitious person who was involved in something particularly worthy. As we tend to confuse the actor or actress with the character he or she is playing, we idolize Ben Kingsley instead of Mahatma Gandhi, Sally Fields as opposed to Norma Rae, or Russell Crowe instead of Jeffrey Wigand.

The point is that when children are captivated with something they watch, parents should have a conversation with them about what it is that enthralled them so much. Rather than having children simply focus on the actor or actress and how marvelous he or she is, parents can talk with their children to discover what it was that so impressed their children. Is it the cause the actor took up in the story? Was it because of the inner fortitude the actor portrayed? Maybe it was the dedication the person showed or the love and compassion he or she showed toward someone or how he or she stood up for what he or she believed in. Perhaps it was because the person learned something about him- or herself and was able to change and become a better individual. Whatever the reason, parents should help their children get past the surface and see and appreciate in a deeper way what they are so enamored with and what they admire. The qualities they so much respect could be qualities that they could internalize and emulate, and these could be made a focus of discussion as opposed to how awesome the actor was in a particular film. Parents can help nurture and foster traits in their children that they admire instead of simply allowing them to idolize those who portray those attributes.

In movies and television shows, actors and actresses are often heroes, as that creates great entertainment. They take up a cause, they do something heroic for another person, or they take on evil. Encourage your children (and yourself as well) to be a hero. There are many ways to do this, maybe not as dramatically as saving the world, but lesser ways do exist. Helping out at a shelter or at a nursing care home, cleaning up a park or a beach, or assisting a person who is in need are all ways.

In truth, there is ample research that demonstrates that volunteering and doing positive things for others and society can increase a person's self-esteem, well-being, and mental health.[1, 2] Volunteering can also have a positive impact on a person's physical health and can even lead to increased longevity.[3, 4] Even doing little things for others can lead to greater happiness, such as helping out a friend or visiting an elderly relative.[5] I am reminded of what President John F. Kennedy said: "Ask not what your country can do for you but what you can do for your country." Again, embracing this can be positive for society but can also be a mechanism to enhance one's own self-esteem.

Efforts can also be made to enhance children's creativity and other interests instead of placing them in front of a television set or having them view another type of entertainment. While there is a place to watch a good movie or television program, children should be encouraged to do more with their lives than this. If your child thinks acting is something that he or she wants to do, then assist him or her in taking up acting. If singing or playing sports is an interest, then help him or her achieve that goal. If a child has an interest in science, help foster, strengthen, and develop that. This will help the child obtain fulfillment in ways that can enhance his or her self-esteem and self-concept.

The amount of time that we as a society spend being entertained, largely by watching television, is huge and leads to many health problems. To combat this, parents can make efforts to limit the amount of television their children watch, and this will help not only decrease their preoccupation with entertainers but also force them to do other things with their lives. Accomplishing this demands that parents may need to watch less television and do other things with their own time. Parents are the most important role models for their children, and that cannot be forgotten. If parents don't want their children to drink alcohol excessively, then they shouldn't drink excessively themselves. If they don't want their children to lie, then they shouldn't lie themselves. Likewise, if they want their children to do other, more productive things with their time, then they must do so as well.

What if there were no television? Instead of sitting back and watching the tube to fill up the void, what would people do? They certainly wouldn't sit around and do absolutely nothing. They would find other things to do, and I imagine that these would be more productive activities than passively sitting around watching television. More parents could consider experimenting with turning off the television, even for limited periods of time, and helping their children and themselves find other constructive activities to do with their time.

Parents can also help their children develop real relationships with others, and, unfortunately, this is often harder to accomplish, as we live more isolated and alienated lives. Instead of allowing children to develop parasocial relationships with entertainers, encourage their social natures. Help them get involved in social events and things that they enjoy, whether this includes clubs at school, involvement in sports, or other group activities. This is solid parenting advice in general, but it can also help mitigate youths' propensity to become too preoccupied with our current entertainers. A real relationship beats a parasocial one by a long shot.

Our enchantment with those who are pretty and attractive will never change, and in today's fast-paced, industrialized, highly mobile, consumer-driven society, our focus on external appearance has only been intensified. Those who present well and are attractive clearly have an advantage. Parents, though, can help their children look beyond this and appreciate that there is much more to a person than attractiveness. Regardless of physical appearance, parents can ask their children what the person is like. Is the person friendly, caring or self-centered, honest, or generous? Such a discussion can help children see that there is much more to a person than simply external appearance, which has relevance to our preoccupation with celluloid images. At least there can be a greater appreciation of the full range of elements that make up a person rather than a more limited focus on a person's external presentation.

Finally, while everyone has a need for recognition, there presently seems to be a greater focus on this, as rapid recognition can be achieved through the proliferation of the media. Anything that gains the attention of the spotlight can be viewed as "success," and individuals seek this instead of doing the harder work of making more meaningful contributions to society. More and more individuals today are obsessed with becoming famous, and how fame is achieved is less important than

simply getting it. If parents see that their children are unduly concerned with becoming famous, they should talk with their children
about this and try to clarify what truly matters in the world. Parents can
engage their children in what kinds of values are most important and
help them develop these principles. In a similar vein, if parents notice
that their children are enamored with those who are well known, regardless of their accomplishments, parents can have a discussion with
them about this. It could be suggested that there is more to life than
simply becoming well known. It is to be hoped that honest and frank
discussions about this subject can at least have some impact on modify-
ing this trend in our society.

Apart from what takes place in the family, a school curriculum that
focuses on media literacy is another important mechanism that can and
is being used to help children maneuver and navigate what they are
exposed to in the media. Media literacy teaches people how to access,
analyze, evaluate, and produce media. It can help individuals more fully
understand and appreciate the nature of mass media, the techniques it
uses, and the impact of these techniques on our thinking. By making
youth more media literate, youth can become less susceptible to media's influence on them and be made more critical thinkers. As we are
constantly surrounded by the influence of mass media, media literacy is
a critical life skill.

To address this, a number of universities have established programs
that focus on issues of media literacy, conducting research, education,
and professional development on such issues. Resources have been developed that educators can use to help their students more fully appreciate the power of the media and be more critical viewers of media in its
many forms. Relevant to our obsession with celebrities, Renee Hobbs,
the founder and director of the Media Education Lab at the University
of Rhode Island, developed an 18-session media literacy curriculum
designed for students from kindergarten through twelfth grade. The
final session focuses specifically on our culture of celebrity and helps
students more critically evaluate this in our society. Some exercises
include viewing some famous figures and having a discussion about the

similarities and differences between celebrities and heroes. Students also engage in an activity in which they make a student into a celebrity by creating story about the person along with a photo. Students are helped to better appreciate how the media can create a celebrity and how what they read and see may not necessarily be true. So, in addition to work that can be done within the family, schools offering this and other kinds of media literacy education can also be used to help moderate our celebrity-worshipping culture.

SUMMARY

To feel fulfilled in life, people must have positive relationships with others and be engaged in life and should feel that their life has some purpose and meaning. Erik Erikson was a psychologist who developed a theory of developmental stages that individuals progress through during the course of their lives.[6] According to Erikson, within each stage, we are faced with a critical task that we more or less either master or remain stuck in. For example, the first stage of life is trust or mistrust. Either the world comes to be seen as a trusting place, or, if parenting was deficient or the person experienced other kinds of traumas, the world can be seen as unfriendly and untrusting. If trust has not been attained, then future interactions with others in the world will be tainted by mistrust. As the person ages and moves on to the next stage, this basic sense of mistrust stays with the individual and can color his or her future perception and sense of the world. This can also affect mastery of each subsequent developmental task.

Erikson conceptualized the last stage in life as one of either integrity or despair. If a person experiences integrity, this is because the person can look back on and feel content with and happy about what he or she has accomplished and experienced during the course of his or her life. With integrity, people feel fulfilled, and, often, a part of this is feeling like they have made a contribution to life. On the other hand, with despair, a person looks back on life and experiences a lack of fulfillment and purpose. While there are many elements that determine whether a person experiences integrity or despair, a component of this often relates to whether the person feels that he or she has in some way contributed to life, to others, and to the betterment of society. These do not need to be great and noble causes, though they could be. They can be smaller things that, nonetheless, had a positive impact on others. Providing children with a good life, being a good wife or husband, caring for an ill relative, being a good friend to others, being an ethical businessperson, engaging in fair and equitable relationships with others, or taking an interest in or volunteering for a cause are just a handful of ways.

An important question is whether celebrity worship and the obsession with entertainment gives people this kind of contentment or inner peace. That is, does the preoccupation and fascination with such figures lead to true positive emotions? Does life satisfaction result from a fanatical preoccupation with the lives of such individuals or with the entertainment we have seen? When we are approaching the end of our lives and reflecting on what we have experienced, what things will stand out, and what will be important to remember? Will it be what we knew about some celebrity or what movies, television program, or sporting event we watched, or might it be something else? That is a question that behooves all of us to ponder and answer for ourselves. You need to be sure that you do not miss out on the best things in life.

NOTES

INTRODUCTION

1. Daniel Boorstin, *The Image* (New York: Vintage Books, 1961), 57.
2. Lacey Rose, "The most expensive celebrity photos," *Forbes*, July 18, 2007, www.forbes.com/2007/07/17/celebrities-photojournalism-magazines-biz-media- cx_lr_0718celebphotos.html.
3. Boorstin, *The Image*.
4. Frank Newport, David Moore, and Lydia Saad, "Most admired men and women: 1948–1998: Fascinating parade of personalities voted most admired over last half century." Gallup News Service, December 13, 1999, www.gallup.com/poll/1678/Most-Admired-Man-Woman.aspx.
5. Jake Halpern, *Fame Junkies* (Boston: Houghton Mifflin, 2007).

I. ENTERTAINMENT AND NOVELTY

1. Michael Levy, "Listening to our clients: The prevention of relapse," *Journal of Psychoactive Drugs* 40, no. 2 (June 2008): 167–72.
2. Timothy D. Wilson, David A. Reinhard, Erin C. Westgate, Daniel T. Gilbert, Nicole Ellerbeck, Cheryl Hahn, Casey L. Brown, and Adi Shaked, "Just think: The challenges of the disengaged mind," *Science* 345, no. 6192 (July 2014): 75–77.

3. A. C. Nielsen, "A2/M2 Three Screen Report, 1st Quarter, 2009," www.nielsen.com/content/dam/corporate/us/en/newswire/uploads/2009/05/nielsen_threescreenreport_q109.pdf

4. *USA Today*, "*USA Today* college football coach salaries: Football bowl subdivision coaches, 2006–2014," www.usatoday.com/story/sports/2014/10/03/college-football-coach-salaries/16634823.

5. Jena McGregor, "Tackling college football coaches' high pay," *Washington Post*, November 7, 2014, www.washingtonpost.com/blogs/on-leadership/wp/2013/11/07/tackling-college-football-coaches-high-pay.

6. Steve Berkowitz, Jodi Upton, and Erik Brady, "Most NCAA Division 1 athletic departments take subsidies," *USA Today*, July 1, 2013, www.usatoday.com/story/sports/college/2013/05/07/ncaa-finances-subsidies/2142443.

7. Carmel Houston-Price and Satsuki Nakai, "Distinguishing novelty and familiarity effects in infant preference procedures," *Infant and Child Development* 13, no. 4 (December 2004): 341–48; Susan A. Rose, Allen W. Gottfried, Patricia Melloy-Carminar, and Wagner H. Bridger, "Familiarity and novelty preferences in infant recognition memory: Implications for information processing," *Developmental Psychology* 18, no. 5 (September 1982): 704–13.

8. Ivan Sechenov, *Reflexes of the Brain* (Cambridge, MA: MIT Press, 1965).

9. Michael E. Behen, Emily Helder, Robert Rothermel, Katherine Solomon, and Harry T. Chugani, "Incidence of specific absolute neurocognitive impairment in globally intact children with histories of early severe deprivation," *Child Neuropsychology* 14, no. 2 (2008): 453–69.

10. J. D. Salinger, *The Catcher in the Rye* (New York: Bantam, 1951).

11. *Boston Globe*, "Rubbernecking: Put a screen on it," August 22, 2011, www.boston.com/bostonglobe/editorial_opinion/editorials/articles/2011/08/22/rubbernecking_put_a_sheet_on_it.

12. Edward B. Blanchard, Eric Kuhn, Dianna L. Rowell, Edward J. Hickling, David Wittrock, Rebecca L. Rogers, Michelle R. Johnson, and Debra C. Steckler, "Studies of the vicarious traumatization of college students by the September 11th attacks: Effects of proximity, exposure, and connectedness," *Behavior Research and Therapy* 42 (2004): 191–205.

2. THE IRRESISTIBILITY OF BEAUTY

1. Nancy Etcoff, *Survival of the Prettiest: The Science of Beauty* (New York: Doubleday, 1999).

2. ABC News Staff, "100 million dieters: The weight loss industry by the numbers," May 8, 2012, http://abcnews.go.com/Health/100-million-dieters-20-billion-weight-loss"industry/story?id=16297197.

3. Nancy Signorelli, "A content analysis: Reflections of girls in the media. A study of television shows and commercials, movies, music videos, and teen magazine articles and ads. An executive summary," Henry J. Kaiser Family Foundation and Children Now, April 1997.

4. Jessica Bennett, "Generation diva: How our obsession with beauty is changing our kids," *Newsweek*, March 30, 1999.

5. American Society for Aesthetic and Plastic Surgery, "Cosmetic surgery national data bank," www.surgery.org/sites/default/files/Stats2013_4.pdf.

6. Associated Press, "Miss Plastic Hungary 2009 (photos): A pageant for surgically enhanced beauties," March 18, 2010, www.huffingtonpost.com/2009/10/09/miss-plastic-hungary-2009_n_316181.html.

7. Mirror.co.uk, "'Winning is my only chance to be normal': The beauty pageant where the top prize is plastic surgery," April 27, 2012, www.mirror.co.uk/news/real-life-stories/miss-cosmetic-surgery-2012-the-beauty-807928.

8. Rinah Yamamoto, Dan Ariely, Won Chi, Daniel D. Langleben, and Igor Elman, "Gender differences in the motivational processing of babies are determined by their facial attractiveness," *PLoS One* 4, no. 6 (2009): e6042, doi:10.1371/journal.pone.0006042.

9. Judith H. Langlois, Jean M. Ritter, Rita J. Casey, and Douglas B. Sawin, "Infant attractiveness predicts maternal behaviors and attitudes," *Developmental Psychology* 31, no. 3 (May 1995): 464–72.

10. Judith H. Langlois, Lori A. Roggman, Rita J. Casey, Jean M. Ritter, Loretta A. Rieser-Danneer, and Vivian Y. Jenkins, "Infant preferences for attractive faces: Rudiments of a stereotype," *Developmental Psychology* 23, no. 3 (May 1987): 363–89.

11. Judith H. Langlois, Jita M. Ritter, Lori A. Roggman, and Lesley S. Vaughn, "Facial diversity and infant preferences for attractive faces," *Developmental Psychology* 27, no. 1 (1991): 79–84.

12. Pamela Kanealy, Neil Frude, and William Shaw, "Influence of children's physical attractiveness on teacher expectations," *Journal of Social Psychology* 128, no. 3 (1988): 373–83.

13. Michael B. Ross and John Salvia, "Attractiveness as a biasing factor in teacher judgments," *American Journal of Mental Deficiency* 80, no. 1 (July 1975): 96–98.

14. J. Richard Udry and Bruce K. Eckland, "Benefits of being attractive: Differential payoffs for men and women," *Psychological Reports* 54, no. 1 (February 1984): 47–56.

15. Glen H. Elder Jr., "Appearance and education on marriage mobility," *American Sociological Review* 34, no. 4 (August 1969): 519–33.

16. David Wilson, "Helping behavior and physical attractiveness," *Journal of Social Psychology* 104, no. 2 (April 1978): 313–14.

17. Peter L. Benson, Stuart A. Karabenick, and Richard M. Lerner, "Pretty pleases: The effects of physical attractiveness, race, and sex on receiving help." *Journal of Experimental Social Psychology* 12, no. 5 (September 1976): 409–15.

18. Michael Cunningham, "Measuring the physical in physical attractiveness: Quasi-experiments on the sociobiology of female facial beauty," *Journal of Personality and Social Psychology* 50, no. 5 (May 1986): 925–35.

19. *Forbes*, "The world's most powerful celebrities," June 30, 2014, www.forbes.com/profile/gisele-bundchen.

20. Malcolm Gladwell, *Blink* (New York: Little, Brown, 2005).

21. Joe McGinness, *The Selling of the President* (New York: Penguin, 1988).

22. Irene H. Frieze, Josephine E. Olson, and Deborah C. Good, "Perceived and actual discrimination in the salaries of male and female managers," *Journal of Applied Social Psychology* 20, no. 1 (January 1990): 46–67.

23. Timothy A. Judge and Daniel M. Cable, "The effect of physical height on workplace success and income: Preliminary test of a theoretical model." *Journal of Applied Psychology* 89, no. 3 (June 2004): 426–41.

24. Paul J. Lavrakas, "Female preference for male physiques," *Journal of Research in Personality* 9, no. 4 (December 1975): 324–34.

25. David M. Buss, *The Evolution of Desire*, rev. ed. (New York: Basic Books, 2003).

26. John M. Townsend and Gary D. Levy, "Effect of potential partners' costume and physical attractiveness on sexuality and partner selection," *Jour-*

nal of Psychology: Interdisciplinary and Applied 124, no. 4 (July 1990): 371–89.

27. John M. Townsend and Gary D. Levy, "Effect of potential partners' physical attractiveness and socioeconomic status on sexuality and partner selection," *Archives of Sexual Behavior* 19, no. 2 (April 1990): 149–64.

3. SOCIABILITY

1. John Bowlby, *Attachment*, 2nd ed. (New York: Basic Books, 1983).

2. Harry Harlow and Robert Zimmerman, "The development of affective responses in infant monkeys," *Proceedings of the American Philosophical Society* 102, no. 5 (1958): 501–9.

3. Gary Griffin and Harry Harlow, "Effects of three months of total social separation on adjustment and learning in the rhesus monkey," *Child Development* 37, no. 3 (1966): 533–47.

4. Bill Seay and Harry Harlow, "Maternal separation in the rhesus monkey," *Journal of Nervous and Mental Disease* 140, no. 6 (1965): 434–41.

5. Merriam-Webster, www.merriam-webster.com/dictionary/gossip.

6. Charlotte J. S. De Backer, Mark Nelissen, Patrick Vyncke, Johan Braeckman, and Francis T. McAndrew, "Celebrities: From teachers to friends. A test of two hypotheses on the adaptiveness of celebrity gossip," *Human Nature* 18 (2007): 334–54.

7. Robin I. M. Dunbar, "Gossip in evolutionary perspective," *Review of General Psychology* 8, no. 2 (2004): 100–110.

8. Dunbar, "Gossip in evolutionary perspective."

9. De Backer et al., "Celebrities."

10. John L. Shelton and Raymond S. Sanders, "Mental health intervention in a campus homicide," *Journal of the American College Health Association* 21, no. 4 (April 1973): 346–50.

11. Dunbar, "Gossip in evolutionary perspective."

12. Erik Erickson, *Childhood and Society* (New York: Norton, 1950).

13. Abraham Maslow, *Motivation and Personality* (New York: Harper and Row, 1954).

14. Roy F. Baumeister, Lauren E. Brewer, Dianne M. Tice, and Jean M. Twenge, "Thwarting the need to belong: Understanding the interpersonal and

inner effects of social exclusion," *Social and Personality Psychology Compass* 1, no. 1 (November 2007): 506–20.

15. Kipling D. Williams and Steve A. Nida, "Ostracism: Consequences and coping," *Current Directions in Psychological Science* 20, no. 2 (2011): 71–75.

16. Geoff MacDonald and Mark R. Leary, "Why does social exclusion hurt? The relationship between social and physical pain," *Psychological Bulletin* 131, no. 2 (2005): 202–23.

4. AN ADDICTIVE VULNERABILITY

1. National Institute on Drug Abuse, *The Science of Drug Abuse and Addiction: The Basics*, 2014, www.drugabuse.gov/publications/media-guide/science-drug-abuse-addiction-basics.

2. National Institute on Drug Abuse, *Drugs, Brains, and Behavior: The Science of Addiction*, NIH Publication No. 14-5605, July 2014, www.drugabuse.gov/sites/default/files/soa_2014.pdf.

3. Luis C. Maas, Scott E. Lukas, Marc J. Kaufman, Roger D. Weiss, Sarah L. Daniels, Veronica W. Rogers, Thellea J. Kukes, and Perry F. Rendsaw, "Functional magnetic resonance imaging of human brain activation during cue-induced cocaine craving," *American Journal of Psychiatry* 155 no. 1 (January 1998): 124–26.

4. Gaetano Di Chiara and Assunta Imperato, "Drugs abused by humans preferentially increase synaptic dopamine concentrations in the mesolimbic system of freely moving rats," *Proceedings of the National Academy of Sciences* 85 no. 14 (1988): 5274–78.

5. Dennis F. Fiorino and Anthony G. Phillips, "Facilitation of sexual behavior and enhanced dopamine efflux in the nucleus accumbens of male rats after D-amphetamine behavioral sensitization," *Journal of Neuroscience* 19 no. 1 (1999): 456–63.

6. Gaetano Di Chiara, Gianluigi Tanda, Cristina Cadoni, Elio Acquas, Valentina Bassareo, and Ezio Carboni, "Homologies and differences in the action of drugs of abuse and a conventional reinforcer (food) on dopamine transmission: An interpretive framework of the mechanism of drug dependence," *Advances in Pharmacology* 42 (1997): 983–87.

7. National Institute on Drug Abuse, *Drugs, Brains, and Behavior*.

8. Donald W. Goodwin, "Alcoholism and heredity," *Archives of General Psychiatry* 36, no. 1 (1979): 57–61.

9. Marc A. Schuckit, Donald W. Goodwin, and George Winokur, "A study of alcoholism in half siblings," *American Journal of Psychiatry* 128, no. 9 (March 1972): 1132–36.

10. Marc A. Schuckit, "Reactions to alcohol in sons of alcoholics and controls," *Alcoholism: Clinical and Experimental Research* 12, no. 4 (August 1988): 465–70.

11. Marc A. Schuckit, Tom L. Smith, and Jelger Kalmijn, "The search for genes contributing to the low level of response to alcohol: Patterns of findings across studies," *Alcoholism: Clinical and Experimental Research* 28, no. 10 (October 2004): 1449–58.

12. Ming T. Tsuang, Michael J. Lyons, Joanne M. Meyer, Thomas Doyle, Seth A. Eisen, Jack Goldberg, William True, Nong Lin, Rosemary Toomey, and Lindon Eaves, "Co-occurrence of abuse of different drugs in men: The role of drug-specific and shared vulnerabilities," *Archives of General Psychiatry* 55 (1998): 967–72.

13. Kenneth Kendler and Carol Prescott, "Cannabis use, abuse, and dependence in a population-based sample of female twins," *American Journal of Psychiatry* 155, no. 8 (1998): 1016–22.

14. Kenneth Kendler and Carol Prescott, "Cocaine use, abuse, and dependence in a population," *British Journal of Psychiatry* 173 (1998): 345–50.

15. National Institute on Drug Abuse, *Drugs, Brains, and Behavior.*

16. Edward Khantzian, "The self-medication hypothesis of addictive disorders: Focus on heroin and cocaine dependence," *American Journal of Psychiatry* 142, no. 11 (1985): 1259–64.

17. Substance Abuse and Mental Health Services Administration, Results from the 2012 National Survey on Drug Use and Health: Mental Health Findings , NSDUH Series H-47, HHS Publication No. (SMA) 13-4805 (Rockville, MD: Substance Abuse and Mental Health Services Administration, 2013).

18. National Institute on Drug Abuse, *Comorbidity: Addiction and Mental Illnesses*, NIH Publication No. 10-5771 (Washington, DC: U.S. Department of Health and Human Services, December 2008, rev. September 2010).

19. Ashley J. Gearhardt, Sonja Yokum, Patrick T. Orr, Eric Stice, William R. Corbin, and Kelly D. Brownell, "Neural correlates of food addiction," *Archives of General Psychiatry* 68, no. 8 (2011): 808–16.

20. Nicole M. Avena, Pedro Rada, and Bartley G. Hoebel, "Evidence for sugar addiction: Behavioral and neurochemical effects of intermittent, excessive sugar intake," *Neuroscience and Biobehavioral Reviews* 32, no. 1 (2008): 20–39.

21. Goodarz Danaei, Eric L. Ding, Dariush Mozaffarian, Ben Taylor, Jurgen Rehm, Christopher J. L. Murray, and Majid Ezzati, "The preventable causes of death in the United States: Comparative risk assessment of dietary, lifestyle, and metabolic risk factors," *PLoS Medicine* 6, no. 4 (2009): e1000058. doi:10.1371/journal.pmed.1000058.

5. OUR NEED FOR IDOLS

1. Independent PR Source, "Neil Armstrong signed check earns record-setting $27,350 at auction," July 16, 2009, www.auctioncentralnews.com/index.php/auctions/auction-results/1159-neil-armstrong-signed-check-makes-27350-after-all-night-bidding-war?format=pdf.

2. Associated Press, "Lennon's white 'Abbey Road' suit sells for $46K," January 3, 2011, www.today.com/id/40887379/ns/today-today_entertainment/t/lennons-white-abbey-road-suit-sells-k/#.VIy2m4znbIV.

3. Wenn, "Hendrix guitar fetches $190,000 at auction," February 17, 2005, www.contactmusic.com/news-article/hendrix-guitar-fetches-190000-at-auction.

4. Christine Lagorio, "Marilyn Monroe auction nets $150K," Associated Press, June 5, 2005, www.cbsnews.com/news/marilyn-monroe-auction-nets-150k.

5. Virginia Bohlin, "Antiques and collectibles," *Boston Globe*, December 9, 2012, www.bostonglobe.com/lifestyle/travel/2012/12/09/antiques-collectibles/QCzAJB5jzaRPvdNSdG4JWP/story.html.

6. Lacey Rose, "The most expensive celebrity photos," *Forbes*, July 18, 2007, www.forbes.com/2007/07/17/celebrities-photojournalism-magazines-biz-media- cx_lr_0718celebphotos.html.

7. Charles Darwin, *On the Origin of Species by Means of Natural Selection, or the Preservation of Favoured Races in the Struggle for Life* (London: Murray, 1859).

8. Ernest Becker, *The Denial of Death* (New York: Free Press, 1973).

9. Becker, *The Denial of Death*, 26.

10. Scott Mayerowitz, "Capt. Chesley 'Sully' Sullenberger auctions captain's hat," December 11, 2009, http://abcnews.go.com/Travel/BusinessTraveler/capt-chesley-sully-sullenberger-auctions-captains-hat/story?id=9311875.

11. Mayerowitz, "Capt. Chesley 'Sully' Sullenberger auctions captain's hat."

6. SELF-ESTEEM

1. Donald W. Winnicott, *The Maturational Process and the Facilitative Environment* (New York: International Universities Press , 1965).

2. Alfred Adler, *The Individual Psychology of Alfred Adler* (New York: Basic Books, 1956).

3. Heinz Kohut, *The Analysis of the Self: A Systemic Approach to the Psychoanalytic Treatment of Narcissistic Personality Disorders* (Chicago: University of Chicago Press, 1971).

4. Abraham Maslow, "A theory of human motivation," *Psychological Review* 50, no. 4 (July 1943): 370–96.

5. Abraham Maslow, *Motivation and Personality* (New York: Harper and Row, 1954).

6. Ernest Becker, *The Denial of Death* (New York: Free Press, 1973).

7. John E. Mack and Steven L. Ablon, eds., *The Development and Sustaining of Self-Esteem in Childhood* (New York: International Universities Press, 1983), xiii.

8. Mack and Ablon, *The Development and Sustaining of Self-Esteem in Childhood*, 9.

9. Jean M. Twenge and W. Keith Campbell, *The Narcissism Epidemic: Living in the Age of Entitlement* (New York: Free Press, 2009).

10. Polly Young-Eisendrath, *The Self-Esteem Trap: Raising Confident and Compassionate Children in an Age of Self-Importance* (New York: Little, Brown, 2008).

11. Dan Kindlon, *Too Much of a Good Thing* (New York: Hyperion, 2003).

7. ALIENATION AND ISOLATION

1. Frank Hobbs and Nicole Stoops, *Demographic Trends in the 20th Century: Census 2000 Special Reports*, CENSR-4 (Washington, DC: U.S. Government Printing Office, 2002).

2. Hobbs and Stoops, *Demographic Trends in the 20th Century*.

3. David K. Ihrke and Carol S. Faber, *Geographical Mobility: 2005 to 2010. Population Characteristics*, P20-567 (Washington, DC: U.S. Department of Commerce, Economics and Statistics Administration, U.S. Census Bureau, December 2012), www.census.gov/prod/2012pubs/p20-567.pdf.

4. James H. Kunstler, *The Geography of Nowhere: The Rise and Decline of America's Manmade Landscape* (New York: Simon and Schuster, 1993).

5. J. Eric Oliver, "Mental life and the metropolis in suburban America. The psychological correlates of metropolitan place characteristics," *Urban Affairs Review* 39, no. 2 (2003): 228–53, doi:10.1177/1078087403254445.

6. Congress of the New Urbanism, "Charter of the New Urbanism," www.cnu.org/charter.

7. Disaster Center, *United States Crime Rates 1960–2013*, www.disastercenter.com/crime/uscrime.htm.

8. Centers for Disease Control, "Rates of homicide, suicide, and firearm-related death among children—26 industrialized countries," *Morbidity and Mortality Weekly Report* 46, no. 05 (February 7, 1997): 101–5, www.cdc.gov/mmwr/preview/mmwrhtml/00046149.htm.

9. Melonie Heron, "Deaths: Leading causes for 2010," *National Vital Statistics Reports* 62, no. 6 (December 20, 2013), www.cdc.gov/nchs/data/nvsr/nvsr62/nvsr62_06.pdf.

10. Erin G. Richardson and David Hemenway, "Homicide, suicide and unintentional firearm fatality: Comparing the United States with other high-income countries," *Journal of Trauma* 70, no. 1 (2011): 238–43.

11. Joseph F. Sheley and James D. Wright, *Gun Acquisition and Possession in Selected Juvenile Samples*, Research in Brief (Washington, DC: U.S. Department of Justice, National Institute of Justice, Office of Juvenile Justice and Delinquency Prevention, 1993), www.ncjrs.gov/App/publications/abstract.aspx?ID=145326.

12. Federal Bureau of Investigation, *Uniform Crime Reports, Crimes in the United States 2012*, www.fbi.gov/about-us/cjis/ucr/crime-in-the-u.s/2012/

crime-in-the-u.s.-2012/tables/1tabledatadecoverviewpdf/ta-
ble_1_crime_in_the_united_states_by_volume_and_rate_per_100000_inhabit
ants_1993-2012.xls.

13. Julie C. Lumeng, Danielle Appugliese, Howard J. Cabral, Robert H.
Bradley, and Barry Zuckerman, " Neighborhood safety and overweight status
in children," *Archives of Pediatric and Adolescent Medicine* 160, no. 1 (2006):
25–31.

14. Robert D. Putnam, *Bowling Alone: The Collapse and Revival of
American Community* (New York: Simon and Schuster, 2000).

8. WHAT MAKES US FEEL GOOD?

1. Eli Zaretsky, *Capitalism, the Family, and Personal Life* (New York:
Harper Colophon Books, 1976).

2. William James, *The Principles of Psychology* (New York: Holt, 1890).

3. Thomas Dublin, "Women, work, and protest in the early Lowell mills:
'The oppressing hand of avarice would enslave us,'" *Labor History* 16, no. 1
(Winter 1975): 99–116.

4. Steven F. Hipple, "Self-employment in the United States: An update,"
Monthly Labor Review, July 2004.

5. Steven F. Hipple, "Self-employment in the United States," *Monthly
Labor Review*, September 2010.

6. Zaretsky, *Capitalism, the Family, and Personal Life*, 61.

7. Jurgen Kuczynski, *The Rise of the Working Class* (New York: McGraw-
Hill, 1967). 115.

8. Edward Filene, *Successful Living in the Machine Age World* (New York:
Thomas Y. Crowell, 1931), 143.

9. Filene, *Successful Living in the Machine Age World*, 274.

10. Zaretsky, *Capitalism, the Family, and Personal Life*, 68.

11. Union of Concerned Scientists, "World scientists' warning to humanity,"
1992, www.ucsusa.org/about/1992-world-scientists.html#.VEPlZMJOXIU.

12. U.S. Bureau of Labor Statistics, *Historical Statistics of the United States
1789 – 1945* (Washington, DC: U.S. Bureau of Labor Statistics, 1949),
www2.census.gov/prod2/statcomp/documents/HistoricalStatisticsoftheUnited-
States1789-1945.pdf.

13. Guillaume Vandenbroucke, "Trends in hours: The U.S. from 1900 to 1950," *Journal of Economic Dynamics and Control* 33, no. 1 (January 2009): 237–49.

14. U.S. Bureau of Labor Statistics, "Average weekly hours and overtime of all employees on private nonfarm payrolls by industry sector, seasonally adjusted," Economic News Release, March 6, 2015, Table B-2, www.bls.gov/news.release/empsit.t18.htm.

15. Lynn E. McCutcheon, John Maltby, James Houran, and Diane D. Ashe, *Celebrity Worshipers: Inside the Minds of Stargazers* (Baltimore: PublishAmerica, 2004), 54.

16. Jean M. Twenge and W. Keith Campbell, *The Narcissism Epidemic. Living in the Age of Entitlement* (New York: Free Press, 2009).

17. Ian D. Wyatt and Daniel E. Hecker, "Occupational changes in the 20th century," *Monthly Labor Review*, March 2006, 35–57.

18. Samantha Barbas, *Movie Crazy* (New York: Palgrave Macmillan, 2001), 36.

19. Lary May, *Screening Out the Past: The Birth of Mass Culture and the Motion Picture Industry* (Chicago: University of Chicago Press, 1983).

20. Dale Carnegie, *How to Make Friends and Influence People* (New York: Simon and Schuster, 1936).

21. www.dalecarnegie.com/events/how_to_communicate_with_diplomacy_and_tact.

22. Cecil B. Hartley, *The Gentlemen's Book of Etiquette, and Manual of Politeness: Being a Complete Guide for a Gentleman's Conduct in All His Relations towards Society . . . from the Best French, English, and American Authorities* (Boston: DeWolfe, Fiske and Co., 1873).

23. George W. Hervey, *The Principles of Courtesy: With Hints and Observations on Manners and Habits* (New York: Harper and Brothers, 1856).

24. George S. Weaver, *Hopes and Helps for the Young of Both Sexes: Relating to the Formation of Character, Choice of Avocation, Health, Amusement, Music, Conversation, Cultivation of Intellect, Moral Sentiment, Social Affection, Courtship, and Marriage* (New York: Fowlers and Wells, 1854).

25. Joan Jacobs Brumberg, *The Body Project: An Intimate History of American Girls* (New York: Vintage, 1998), xxi.

9. MASS MEDIA

1. Daniel Boorstin, *The Image* (New York: Vintage Books, 1961), 48.

2. Boorstin, *The Image*.

3. U.S. Census Bureau, "Measuring America," February 3, 2014, www.census.gov/hhes/computer/files/2012/Computer_Use_Infographic_FINAL.pd.

4. Kaiser Family Foundation, "Generation M2: Media in the lives of 8–18-year olds," January 20, 2010, www.kff.org/entmedia/mh012010pkg.cfm.

5. Marcella Nunez-Smith, Elizabeth E. Wolf, Helen M. Huang, Ezekiel J. Emanuel, and Cary P. Gross, "Media and child and adolescent health: A systematic review," 2008, http://ipsdweb.ipsd.org/uploads/IPPC/CSM%20Media%20Health%20Report.pdf.

6. Gina M. Wingood, Ralph J. DiClemente, Jay M. Bernhardt, Kathy Harrington, Susan L. Davies, Alyssa Robillard, and Edward W. Hook III, "A prospective study of exposure to rap music videos and African American female adolescents' prospective health," *American Journal of Public Health* 93, no. 3 (March 2003): 437–39.

7. Rutger C. M. E. Engels, Roel Hermans, Rick B. van Baaren, Tom Hollenstein, and Sandra M. Bot, "Alcohol portrayal on television affects actual drinking behavior," *Alcohol and Alcoholism* 44, no. 3 (2009): 244–49.

8. Jean Kilbourne, "'The more you subtract, the more you add'; Cutting girls down to size," in *Psychology and Consumer Culture*, ed. Tim Kasser and Allen D. Kanner, 251–70 (Washington, DC: American Psychological Association, 2004).

9. Allison E. Field, Lillian Cheung, Anne M. Wolf, David B. Herzog, Steven L. Gortmaker, and Graham A. Colditz, "Exposure to the mass media and weight concerns among girls," *Pediatrics* 103, no. 3 (March 1999): 36–41.

10. Marsha L. Richens, "Social comparison and idealized images of advertising," *Journal of Consumer Research* 18, no. 1 (1991): 71–83; Deborah Then, "Women's magazines: Messages they convey about looks, men, and careers," paper presented at the 100th annual meeting of the American Psychological Association, Washington, DC, August 2002.

11. Jeannine Stein, "Why girls as young as 9 fear fat and go on diets to lose weight," *Los Angeles Times*, October 29, 1986, http://articles.latimes.com/1986-10-29/news/vw-7933_1_eating-disorders; Cindy Rodriguez, "Even in middle school, girls are thinking thin," *Boston Globe*, November 27, 1998.

12. Kristen Harrison and Bradley J. Bond, "Ideal-body print media and preadolescent boys' drive for muscularity," paper presented at the 104th annual meeting of the American Psychological Association, New Orleans, August 2006.

13. Kristen Harrison and Bradley J. Bond, "Gaming magazines and the drive for muscularity in preadolescent boys: A longitudinal examination," *Body Image* 4 (2007): 269–77.

14. Brad J. Bushman and Craig A. Anderson, "Media violence and the American public: Scientific facts versus media misinformation." *American Psychologist* 56, no. 6/7 (June/July 2001): 477–89.

15. Stuart Elliott, "Madison Avenue's chief seer," *New York Times*, March 22, 2009.

16. James B. Twitchell, *Adcult USA: The Triumph of Advertising in American Culture* (New York: Columbia University Press, 1996).

17. Colman McCarthy, "In thingdom, laying waste our powers," *Washington Post*, November 11, 1990.

18. Sut Jhally, *Advertising and the End of the World* (motion picture) (Northampton, MA: Media Education Foundation, 1998).

19. Margaret Mead, speech given at Richdale Community College, Richdale, TX, 1977.

20. Alex Konrad, "Even with record prices, expect a $10 million Super Bowl ad soon," *Forbes*, February 2, 2013.

21. Paul M. Fischer, Meyer P. Schwartz, John W. Richards Jr., Adam O. Goldstein, and Tina H. Rojas, "Brand logo recognition by children aged 3 to 6 years: Mickey Mouse and Old Joe the Camel," *Journal of the American Medical Association* 266, no. 22 (December 1991): 3145–48.

22. Stuart Elliott, "The media business: Advertising—Camel's success and controversy," *New York Times*, December 12, 1991.

23. *Mangini v. R. J. Reynolds Tobacco Co.*, 7 Cal. 4th 1057, 1073–74 (1994), http://legacy.library.ucsf.edu/tid/dyf53a00; Patrick J. Coughlin and Frank Janacek Jr., "A review of R. J. Reynolds' internal documents produced in Mangini vs. R. J. Reynolds Tobacco Company, Civil Number 939359: The case that rid California and the American landscape of 'Joe Camel,'" 1997, http://legacy.library.ucsf.edu/research/doc_research_mangini.jsp.

24. Public Health Cigarette Smoking Act of 1969. www.gpo.gov/fdsys/pkg/STATUTE-84/pdf/STATUTE-84-Pg87-2.pdf.

25. Michael Gormley, "Top magazines agree to keep tobacco ads from school copies," Associated Press, June 20, 2005.

26. Duff Wilson, "Senate approves tight regulation over cigarettes," *New York Times*, June 12, 2009.

27. Cheryl D. Fryar, Margaret P. Carroll, and Cynthia L. Ogden, "Prevalence of obesity among children and adolescents: United States, trends 1963–1965 through 2009–2010," *NCHS Health E-Stat* (Washington, DC: Centers for Disease Control and Prevention, September 2012), www.cdc.gov/nchs/data/hestat/obesity_child_09_10/obesity_child_09_10.pdf.

28. Julie C. Lumeng, Danielle Appugliese, Howard J. Cabral, Robert H. Bradley, and Barry Zuckerman, "Neighborhood safety and overweight status in children," *Archives of Pediatric and Adolescent Medicine* 160, no. 1 (2006): 25–31.

29. Institute of Medicine, "Overview of the IOM report on food marketing to youth: Threat or opportunity," December 2005, www.iom.edu/~/media/Files/Report%20Files/2005/Food-Marketing-to-Children-and-Youth-Threat-or-Opportunity/KFMOverviewfinal2906.pdf.

30. OpenSecrets.org, "Money web," www.opensecrets.org/PRES08/money-web.php?cycle=2008.

31. Jerusha B. Detweiler, Brian T. Bedell, Peter Salovey, Emily Pronin, and Alexander Rothman, "Message framing and sunscreen use: Gain framed messages motivate beachgoers," *Health Psychology* 18 (March 1999): 189–96.

32. Ad Council, www.adcouncil.org/Our-Campaigns/The-Classics/Wildfire-Prevention.

33. Ad Council, www.adcouncil.org/Our-Campaigns/The-Classics/Pollution-Keep-America-Beautiful-Iron- Eyes-Cody.

34. Ad Council, www.adcouncil.org/Our-Campaigns/The-Classics/United-Negro-College-Fund.

35. Advertising Educational Foundation, www.aef.com/exhibits/social_responsibility/ad_council/2367.

36. Ad Council, www.adcouncil.org/Our-Campaigns/The-Classics/Drunk-Driving-Prevention.

10. ENTERTAINMENT ADDICTION

1. Neil Postman, *Amusing Ourselves to Death* (New York: Penguin Books, 1985).

2. Neal Gabler, *Life: The Movie* (New York: Vintage Books, 1998).

3. Daniel J. Czitrom, *Media and the American Mind: From Morse to McLuhan* (Chapel Hill: University of North Carolina Press, 1982).

4. Gabler, *Life*, 50–51.

5. Steven B. Karch, *A Brief History of Cocaine*, 2nd ed. (Boca Raton, FL: CRC Press, 2005).

6. Hugo Munsterberg, *The Photoplay: A Psychology Study* (New York: D. Appleton and Company, 1916), 220.

7. Moving Picture World, "How the cinematographer works and some of his difficulties," May 18, 1907, http://ia601200.us.archive.org/15/items/MPW01-1907-05/MPW01-1907-05.pdf. 165.

8. Walter Lippmann, "Blazing Publicity," in *Vanity Fair: A Cavalcade of the 1920s and 1930s*, ed. Cleveland Amory and Frederic Bradlee (New York: Viking Press, 1960), 122.

9. Edward J. Epstein, "Dumb money—The madness of movie advertising," *Slate Online Magazine*, June 6, 2005, www.slate.com/id/2120335.

10. A. C. Nielsen, "Americans watching more TV than ever; Web and mobile video up too," May 20, 2009, http://blog.nielsen.com/nielsenwire/online_mobile/americans-watching-more-tv-than-ever.

11. Norman Herr, "Television and health," 2007, www.csun.edu/science/health/docs/tv&health.html.

12. Fred W. Danner, "A national longitudinal study of the association between hours of TV viewing and the trajectory of BMI growth among US children," *Journal of Pediatric Psychology* 33, no. 10 (2008): 1100–1107.

13. Julie C. Lumeng, Sahand Rahnama Danielle Appugliese, Niko Kaciroti, and Robert H. Bradley, "Television exposure and overweight risk in preschoolers," *Archives of Pediatrics and Adolescent Medicine* 160, no. 4 (2006): 417–22.

14. Leonard H. Epstein, James N. Roemmich, Jodi L. Robinson, Rocco A. Paluch, Dana D. Winiewicz, Janene H. Fuerch, and Thomas N. Robinson, "A randomized trial of the effects of reducing television viewing and computer use on body mass index in young children," *Archives of Pediatrics and Adolescent Medicine* 162, no. 3 (2008): 239–45.

15. Thomas N. Robinson, "Reducing children's television viewing to prevent obesity: A randomized controlled trial," *Journal of the American Medical Association* 282, no. 16 (1999): 1561–67.

16. Kristi R. Jenkins and Nancy H. Flutz, "The relationship of older adults' activities and body mass index," *Journal of Aging and Health* 20, no. 2 (2008): 217–34.

17. John P. Robinson and Steve Martin, "What do happy people do?," *Social Indicators Research* 89, no. 3 (2008): 565–71.

18. David Satcher, *Physical Activity and Health: A Report of the Surgeon General* (Atlanta: U.S. Department of Health and Human Services, Centers for Disease Control and Prevention, 1996).

19. Charles Winick, "The functions of television: Life without the big box," in *Television as a Social Issue*, ed. Stuart Oskamp, 217–37 (Newbury Park, CA: Sage, 1988).

20. Winick, "The functions of television."

21. Keith Reed, "Fenway suites are even more luxurious," *Boston Globe*, April 9, 2007, www.boston.com/business/articles/2007/04/09/fenway_suites_are_even_more_luxurious.

22. Baseball Almanac, "Babe Ruth salary draws," original article in *Sporting News*, April 1932, www.baseball-almanac.com/tsn/babe_ruth_salary.shtml.

23. Associated Press, "MLB average salary is $3.39M," December 18, 2013, http://espn.go.com/mlb/story/_/id/10158314/mlb-average-salary-54-percent-339-million.

24. Gabler, *Life*, 17.

11. ENTERTAINMENT AS LIFE FULFILLMENT

1. David Myers, "The secret to happiness: Look inside at what actually gives you joy, and the good life may be closer than you think," *Yes!*, June 18, 2004.

2. Neal Gabler, *Life: The Movie* (New York: Vintage Books, 1998), 70.

3. Adam Leipzig, "The Sundance odds get even longer," *New York Times*, January 16, 2005.

4. U.S. Bureau of Labor Statistics, "American time use survey: Charts from the American time use survey," September 30, 2014, www.bls.gov/tus/charts/home.htm.

5. U.S. Bureau of Labor Statistics, "Volunteering in the United States, 2013," February 25, 2013, www.bls.gov/news.release/volun.nr0.htm.

6. Robert D. Putnam, *Bowling Alone: The Collapse and Revival of American Community* (New York: Simon and Schuster, 2000), 113–14.

7. Jean M. Twenge, Stacey M. Campbell, Brian J. Hoffman, and Charles E. Lance, "Generational differences in work values: Leisure and extrinsic values increasing, social and intrinsic values decreasing," *Journal of Management* 36, no. 5 (2010): 1117–42.

8. Gabler, *Life*, 9.

9. Associated Press, "Nobel laureate laments cultural impact of Internet: Vargas Llosa says it limits thinking," December 7, 2010, www.boston.com/news/world/europe/articles/2010/12/07/nobel_laureate_laments_cultural_impact_of_internet.

10. Robert Schickel, *Intimate Strangers: The Celebrity of Culture* (Garden City, NY: Doubleday, 1985), 135.

11. Kiku Adatto, "Sound bite democracy: Network evening news presidential campaign coverage, 1968 and 1988," Research Paper R-2 (Cambridge: Joan Shorenstein Barone Center, Harvard University, June 1990), 11.

12. Joan Didion, "Insider Baseball," *New York Review of Books*, October 27, 1988.

13. Kurt Anderson, "Entertainer-in-chief," *The New Yorker*, February 16, 1998.

14. Lou Cannon, *President Reagan: The Role of a Lifetime* (New York: Simon and Schuster, 1991), 51.

15. National Park Service, "The Lincoln-Douglas debates of 1858," www.nps.gov/liho/historyculture/debates.htm.

16. Lincoln Institute, "Speech at Peoria, October 16, 1854," www.mrlincolnandfreedom.org/inside.asp?ID=11&subjectID=2.

12. TRANSFORMATION AND OBSESSION

1. Neil Harris, *Humbug: The Art of P. T. Barnum* (Chicago: University of Chicago Press, 1973).

2. *New York Herald*, "Mademoiselle Jenny Lind," September 16, 1850, http://chnm.gmu.edu/lostmuseum/lm/164.

3. Harris, *Humbug*, 113.

4. Roberta Pearson, *Eloquent Gestures* (Berkeley: University of California Press, 1992).

5. Samantha Barbas, *Movie Crazy* (New York: Palgrave Macmillan, 2001).

6. Barbas, *Movie Crazy*, 15–16.

7. Barbas, *Movie Crazy*, 30.

8. Charles Carter, "Letter writing lunacy," *Picture Play*, November 1920, 3.

9. Tom Gunning, *D. W. Griffith and the Origins of the American Narrative Film* (Chicago: University of Illinois Press, 1991).

10. Clive James, *Fame in the 20th Century* (New York: Random House, 1993), 30.

11. Richard Schickel, *Intimate Strangers: The Celebrity of Culture* (Garden City, NY: Doubleday, 1985), 35–36.

12. Warren I. Susman, *Culture as History: The Transformation of American Society in the Twentieth Century* (New York: Pantheon, 1984).

13. Museum of Broadcast Communications, "Marcus Welby, MD. U.S. medical drama," www.museum.tv/eotv/marcuswelby.htm.

14. Charlotte J. S. De Backer, Mark Nelissen, Patrick Vyncke, Johan Braeckman, and Francis T. McAndrew, "Celebrities: From teachers to friends. A test of two hypotheses on the adaptiveness of celebrity gossip," *Human Nature* 18 (2007): 334–54.

15. James, *Fame in the 20th Century*, 33.

16. Neil Postman, *Amusing Ourselves to Death* (New York: Penguin Books, 1985), 100–101.

17. Christopher Olivola and Alexander Todorov, "The look of a winner," *Scientific American*, May 9, 2009, www.scientificamerican.com/article/the-look-of-a-winner.

18. Christopher Olivola and Alexander Todorov, "Elected in 100 milliseconds: Appearance-based trait inferences and voting," *Journal of Nonverbal Behavior* 34, no. 2 (June 2010): 83–110.

19. Anthony C. Little, Robert P. Burriss, Benedict C. Jones, and S. Craig Roberts, "Facial appearance affects voting decisions," *Evolution and Human Behavior* 28, no. 1 (January 2007): 18–27.

20. Anthony C. Little, S. Craig Roberts, Benedict C. Jones, and Lisa M. DeBruine, "The perception of attractiveness and trustworthiness in male faces affects hypothetical voting decisions differently in wartime and peacetime sce-

narios," *Quarterly Journal of Experimental Psychology* 65, no. 10 (October 2012): 2018–32, http://dx.doi.org/10.1080/17470218.2012.677048.

21. Joan Y. Chiao, Nicholas E. Bowman, and Harleen Gill, "The political gender gap: Gender bias in facial inferences that predict voting behavior," *PLoS One* 3, no. 10 (October 31, 2008): e3666. doi:10.1371/journal.pone.0003666.

13. THEY GOT WHAT I WANT

1. Timothy Egan, "After Simpson trial, inquiries and deals," *New York Times*, October 6, 1995.

2. Andy Warhol, *The Philosophy of Andy Warhol (From A to B and Back Again)* (New York: Harcourt Brace Jovanovich, 1975), 85.

3. Anna Steese Richardson, "Filmitis: The modern malady," *McClure's*, January 1916.

4. Samantha Barbas, *Movie Crazy* (New York: Palgrave Macmillan, 2001).

5. Katy Steinmetz, "Top 10 buzzwords," *Time*, December 4, 2013, http://newsfeed.time.com/2013/12/04/pop-culture-and-social-media/slide/top-10-buzzwords.

6. Oxford Dictionaries, "Oxford Dictionaries word of the year in 2013 is selfie," http://blog.oxforddictionaries.com/2013/11/word-of-the-year-2013-winner.

7. Marco R. Della Cava, "Searching the Web for the next big thing!," *USA Today*, May 30–June 1, 2008, http://www.bregentertainmentmarketing.blogspot.com/2008/06/searching-web-for-next-big-thing.html.

8. Brian Stelter, "Calling story of boy and balloon a hoax, sheriff seeks felony charges," *New York Times*, October 18, 2009, www.nytimes.com/2009/10/19/us/19balloon.html.

9. Helene Cooper and Brian Stelter, "Obamas' uninvited guests prompt an inquiry," *New York Times*, November 26, 2009.

10. Robert J. Morton and Mark A. Hillts, eds., *Serial Murder: Multi-Disciplinary Perspectives for Investigators* (Washington, DC: Behavioral Analysis Unit, National Center for the Analysis of Violence, Federal Bureau of Investigation U.S. Department of Justice, July 2008), www.fbi.gov/stats-services/publications/serial-murder/serial-murder-july-2008-pdf.

11. Associated Press, "'American Idol' goes to summer camp," *USA Today*, February 23, 2007, http://usatoday30.usatoday.com/life/music/news/2007-02-23-idol-camp_x.htm.

12. Clive James, *Fame in the 20th Century* (New York: Random House, 1993).

13. John Maltby, Liz Day, David Giles, Ralphael Gillett, Marianne Quick, Honey Langcaster-James, and P. Alex Linley, "Implicit theories of a desire for fame," *British Journal of Psychology* 99, no. 2 (May 2008): 279–92.

14. Ernest Becker, *The Denial of Death* (New York: Free Press, 1973), 26.

15. Leo Braudy, *The Frenzy of the Renown: Fame and Its History*, 2nd ed. (New York: Vintage, 1997), 7.

16. David R. Loy, "The nonduality of life and death: A Buddhist view of repression," *Philosophy East and West* 40, no. 2 (April 1990): 151–74.

17. Robert A. Fein and Brian Vossekuil, "Preventing attacks on public officials and public figures: A secret service perspective," in *The Psychology of Stalking: Clinical and Forensic Perspectives*, ed. J. Reid Meloy, 175–91 (San Diego, CA: Academic Press, 1998).

18. Jeff Greenberg, Spee Kosloff, Sheldon Solomon, Florette Cohen, and Mark Landau, "Toward understanding the fame game: The effect of mortality salience on the appeal of fame." *Self and Identity* 9, no. 1 (2010): 1–18.

19. Donna Rockwell and David C. Giles, "Being a celebrity: A phenomenology of fame," *Journal of Phenomenological Psychology* 40, no. 2 (2009): 178–210.

20. Braudy, *The Frenzy of Renown*, 587.

21. Gretchen Voss, "Desperately seeking stardom," *Boston Globe*, June 17, 2007, www.boston.com/news/globe/magazine/articles/2007/06/17/desperately_seeking_stardom/?page=full.

22. Pew Research Center, *How Young People View Their Lives, Futures, and Politics: A Portrait of "Generation X"* (Washington, DC: Pew Research Center for the People and the Press, January 9, 2007), http://pewsocialtrends.org/files/2010/10/300.pdf.

23. Yalda T. Uhls and Patricia M. Greenfield, "The rise of fame: An historical content analysis," *Cyberpsychology: Journal of Psychosocial Research on Cyberspace* 5, no. 1, article 1 (2011), www.cyberpsychology.eu/view.php?cisloclanku=2011061601.

24. Charlotte J. S. De Backer, Mark Nelissen, Patrick Vyncke, Johan Braeckman, and Francis T. McAndrew, "Celebrities: From teachers to friends.

A test of two hypotheses on the adaptiveness of celebrity gossip," *Human Nature* 18 (2007): 334–54.

25. James, *Fame in the 20th Century*, 15.

26. Lou Cannon, *President Reagan: The Role of a Lifetime* (New York: Simon and Schuster, 1991), 50–51.

27. Neal Gabler, *Life: The Movie* (New York: Vintage Books, 1998), 109.

28. Gabler, *Life*, 112.

14. VOYEURISM EXPLOITED

1. James L. Crouthamel, *Bennett's New York Herald and the Rise of the Popular Press* (Syracuse, NY: Syracuse University Press, 1989), 25.

2. Michael Schudson, *Discovering the News: A Social History of American Newspapers* (New York: Basic Books, 1978), 18.

3. Henry David Thoreau, *Walden* (Boston: Houghton Mifflin, 1957), 36.

4. Isaac C. Pray, *Memoirs of James Gordon Bennett and His Times by a Journalist* (New York: Stringer and Townsend, 1855), 255.

5. Stephanie Marcus, "Why people like the Kardashians: People aspire to be them or to befriend them says E! president," *Huffington Post*, December 30, 2011, www.huffingtonpost.com/2011/12/30/why-people-like-the-kardash-ians-people-aspire-to-be-them-or-befriend-them-e-president-suzanne-kolb-_n_1176250.html.

6. Kimberly S. Young, "Internet addiction: A new clinical phenomenon and its consequences," *American Behavioral Scientist* 48, no. 4 (2004): 402–15.

7. Al Cooper, "Sexuality and the internet: Surfing into the new millennium," *Cyberpsychology and Behavior* 1, no. 2 (Summer 1998): 187–93, doi:10.1089/cpb.1998.1.187.

8. Mark Griffiths, "Internet gambling: Issues, concerns, and recommendations," *Cyberpsychology and Behavior* 6, no. 6 (2003): 557–68, doi:10.1089/109493103322725333.

9. Sally M. Gainsbury, Alex Russell, Nerilee Hing, Robert Wood, Dan I. Lubman, and Alex Blaszczynski, "The prevalence and determinants of problem gambling in Australia: Assessing the impact of interactive gambling and new technologies," *Psychology of Addictive Behaviors* 28, no. 3 (September 2014): 769–79.

10. Valerie C. Lorenz, "State lotteries and compulsive gambling," *Journal of Gambling Studies* 6, no. 4 (Winter 1990): 383–96.

11. Justin Pierce, "Family time decreasing with Internet use," University of Southern California, Annenberg School for Communication, Center for the Digital Future, June 16, 2009, http://mail-dog.com/pics/justkid/library/cdf_family_time.pdf.

12. Lynn Spigel, *Welcome to the Dreamhouse: Popular Media and Postwar Suburbs* (Durham, NC: Duke University Press, 2001).

13. Keren Eyal and Jonathan Cohen, "When good friends say goodbye: A parasocial breakup study," *Journal of Broadcasting and Electronic Media* 50, no. 3 (September 2006): 502–23.

14. Jerome Barkow, "Beneath new culture is old psychology: Gossip and social stratification," in *The Adaptive Mind: Evolutionary Psychology and the Generation of Culture*, ed. Jerome Barkow, Leda Cosmides, and John Tooby (Oxford: Oxford University Press, 1992), 629–30.

15. Charlotte J. S. De Backer, Mark Nelissen, Patrick Vyncke, Johan Braeckman, and Francis T. McAndrew, "Celebrities: From teachers to friends. A test of two hypotheses on the adaptiveness of celebrity gossip," *Human Nature* 18 (2007): 334–54.

16. Donald Horton and Richard R. Wahl, "Mass communication and para-social relationships: Observations on intimacy at a distance," *Psychiatry* 19, no. 3 (1956): 215–29.

17. John L. Caughey, "Artificial social relations in modern America," *American Quarterly* 30 (Spring 1978): 70–89.

18. De Backer et al., "Celebrities."

19. Jaye L. Derrick, Shira Gabriel, and Kurt Hugenberg, "Social surrogacy: How favored television programs provide the experience of belonging," *Journal of Experimental Social Psychology* 45, no. 2 (February 2009): 352–62.

20. Jaye L. Derrick, Shira Gabriel, and Brooke Tippin, "Parasocial relationships and self- discrepancies: Faux relationships have benefits for low self-esteem individuals," *Personal Relationships* 15, no. 2 (June 2008): 261–80.

21. Jerome Barkow, "Attention structure and the evolution of human psychological characteristics," in *The Social Structure of Attention*, ed. Michael R. A. Chance and Ray R. Larson, 203–20 (London: Wiley, 1989).

22. Joseph Henrich and Francisco J. Gil-White, "The evolution of prestige," *Evolution and Human Behavior* 22, no. 3 (May 2001): 165–96.

23. Robert Boyd and Peter J. Richerson, *Culture and the Evolutionary Process* (Chicago: University of Chicago Press, 1985).

24. Shelly Grabe, Monique L. Ward, and Janet S. Hyde, "The role of the media in body image concerns among women: A meta-analysis of experimental and correlational studies," *Psychological Bulletin* 134, no. 3 (May 2008): 460–76.

25. Nicole Hawkins, P. Scott Richards, H. Mac Granley, and David M. Stein, "The impact of exposure to the thin-ideal media image on women," *Eating Disorders* 12, no. 1 (2004): 35–50.

26. Alison E. Field, Lillian Cheung, Anne M. Wolf, David B. Herzog, Steven L. Gortmaker, and Graham A. Colditz, "Exposure to the mass media and weight concerns among girls," *Pediatrics* 103, no. 3 (March 1999): 36–41.

27. Kate E. Mulgrew, Diana Volcevski-Kostas, and Peter G. Rendell, "The effect of music video clips on adolescent boys' body image, mood, and schema activation," *Journal of Youth and Adolescence* 43, no. 1 (January 2014): 92–103.

28. Duane A. Hargreaves and Marika Tiggemann, "Muscular ideal media images and men's body image: Social comparison processing and individual vulnerability," *Psychology of Men and Masculinity* 12, no. 2 (April 2009): 109–19.

29. Cody L. Hobza and Aaron B. Rochlen, "Gender role conflict, drive for muscularity, and the impact of ideal media portrayals on men," *Psychology of Men and Masculinity* 10, no. 2 (April 2009): 120–30.

30. Victor C. Strasberger, "Adolescent sexuality and the media," *Pediatric Clinics of North America* 36, no. 3 (June 1989): 747–73.

31. Thomas A. Willis, "Downward comparison principles in social psychology," *Psychological Bulletin* 90, no. 2 (1981): 245–71.

32. Joke Hermes, "Media figures in identity construction," in *Rethinking the Media Audience: The New Agenda*, ed. Pertti Alasuutari (London: Sage, 1999), 80.

33. Neal Gabler, *Winchell* (New York: Vintage Books, 1994), xiii.

34. Namrata Mahajan, Jessica B. Clevering, and Dana C. Turcotte, "Celebrity gossip as a form of downward social comparison," paper presented at the American Psychological Association Conference, San Francisco, August 2007.

35. Graeme Turner, *Understanding Celebrity* (London: Sage, 2004), 115.

36. Joke Hermes, *Reading Women's Magazines: An Analysis of Everyday Media Use* (Cambridge: Polity Press, 1995), 124.

EPILOGUE

1. Carolyn Schwartz, Janice B. Meisenhelder, Yuncheng B. Ma, and George Reed, "Altruistic social interest behaviors are associated with better mental health," *Psychosomatic Medicine* 65, no. 5 (2003): 778–85.

2. Karl Pillemer, Thomas E. Fuller-Rowell, M. C. Reid, and Nancy M. Well, "Environmental volunteering and health outcomes over a 20-year period," *The Gerontologist* 50, no. 5 (October 2010): 594–602.

3. Stephanie Brown, Randolph M. Resse, Amiram D. Vonokur, and Dylan M. Smith, "Providing social support may be more beneficial than receiving it: Results from a prospective study of mortality," *Psychological Science* 14, no. 4 (July 2003): 320–27.

4. Morris A. Okun, Ellen W. Yeung, and Stephanie Brown, "Volunteering by older adults and risk of mortality: A meta-analysis," *Psychology and Aging* 28, no. 2 (2013): 564–77, http://dx.doi.org/10.1037/a0031519.

5. Sonja Lyubomirsky, Kennon M. Sheldon, and David Schkade, "Pursuing happiness: The architecture of sustainable change," Review of General Psychology 9, no. 2 (2005): 111–31.

6. Erik Erikson, *Childhood and Society* (New York: Norton, 1950).

REFERENCES

ABC News Staff. "100 million dieters, $20 billion: The weight loss industry by the numbers." May 8, 2012. http://abcnews.go.com/Health/100-million-dieters-20-billion-weight-loss"industry/story?id=16297197

A. C. Nielsen. "A2/M2 Three Screen Report, 1st Quarter, 2009." www.nielsen.com/content/dam/corporate/us/en/newswire/uploads/2009/05/nielsen_threescreenreport_q109.pdf

———. "Americans watching more TV than ever; Web and mobile video up too." May 20, 2009. http://blog.nielsen.com/nielsenwire/online_mobile/americans-watching-more-tv-than-ever

Ad Council. www.adcouncil.org/Our-Campaigns/The-Classics/Drunk-Driving-Prevention

———. http://www.adcouncil.org/Our-Campaigns/The-Classics/Pollution-Keep-America-Beautiful-Iron-Eyes-Cody

———..www.adcouncil.org/Our-Campaigns/The-Classics/United-Negro-College-Fund

———. www.adcouncil.org/Our-Campaigns/The-Classics/Wildfire-Prevention

Adatto, Kiku. "Sound bite democracy: Network evening news presidential campaign coverage, 1968 and 1988." Research Paper R-2. Cambridge, MA: Joan Shorenstein Barone Center, Harvard University, June 1990.

Adler, Alfred. *The Individual Psychology of Alfred Adler*. New York: Basic Books, 1956.

Advertising Educational Foundation. www.aef.com/exhibits/social_responsibility/ad_council/2367

American Society for Aesthetic and Plastic Surgery. "Cosmetic surgery national data bank." www.surgery.org/sites/default/files/Stats2013_4.pdf

Anderson, Kurt. "Entertainer-in-Chief." *The New Yorker*, February 16, 1998.

Associated Press. "'American Idol' goes to summer camp." *USA Today*, February 23, 2007. http://usatoday30.usatoday.com/life/music/news/2007-02-23-idol-camp_x.htm

———. "Lennon's white 'Abbey Road' suit sells for $46K." January 3, 2011. www.today.com/id/40887379/ns/today-today_entertainment/t/lennons-white-abbey-road-suit-sells-k/#.VIy2m4znbIV

———. "Miss Plastic Hungary 2009 (photos): A pageant for surgically enhanced beauties." March 18, 2010. www.huffingtonpost.com/2009/10/09/miss-plastic-hungary-2009_n_316181.html

————. "MLB average salary is $3.39M." December 18, 2013. http://espn.go.com/mlb/story/_/id/10158314/mlb-average-salary-54-percent-339-million

————. "Nobel laureate laments cultural impact of Internet: Vargas Llosa says it limits thinking." December 7, 2010. www.boston.com/news/world/europe/articles/2010/12/07/nobel_laureate_laments_cultural_impact_of_internet

Avena, Nicole M., Pedro Rada, and Bartley G. Hoebel. "Evidence for sugar addiction: Behavioral and neurochemical effects of intermittent, excessive sugar intake." *Neuroscience and Biobehavioral Reviews* 32, no. 1 (2008): 20–39.

Barbas, Samantha. *Movie Crazy*. New York: Palgrave Macmillan, 2001.

Barkow, Jerome. "Attention structure and the evolution of human psychological characteristics." In *The Social Structure of Attention*, edited by Michael R. A. Chance and Ray R. Larson, 203–20. London: Wiley, 1989.

————. "Beneath new culture is old psychology: Gossip and social stratification." In *The Adaptive Mind: Evolutionary Psychology and the Generation of Culture*, edited by Jerome Barkow, Leda Cosmides, and John Tooby, 627–37. Oxford: Oxford University Press, 1992.

Baseball Almanac. "Babe Ruth salary draws." Original article in *Sporting News*, April 1932. www.baseball-almanac.com/tsn/babe_ruth_salary.shtml

Baumeister, Roy F., Lauren E. Brewer, Dianne M. Tice, and Jean M. Twenge. "Thwarting the need to belong: Understanding the interpersonal and inner effects of social exclusion." *Social and Personality Psychology Compass* 1, no. 1 (November 2007): 506–20.

Becker, Ernest. *The Denial of Death*. New York: Free Press, 1973.

Behen, Michael E., Emily Helder, Robert Rothermel, Katherine Solomon, and Harry T. Chugani. "Incidence of specific absolute neurocognitive impairment in globally intact children with histories of early severe deprivation." *Child Neuropsychology* 14, no. 2 (2008): 453–69.

Bennett, Jessica. "Generation diva: How our obsession with beauty is changing our kids." *Newsweek*, March 30, 1999.

Benson, Peter L., Stuart A. Karabenick, and Richard M. Lerner. "Pretty pleases: The effects of physical attractiveness, race, and sex on receiving help." *Journal of Experimental Social Psychology* 12, no. 5 (September 1976): 409–15.

Berkowitz, Steve, Jodi Upton, and Erik Brady. "Most NCAA Division 1 athletic departments take subsidies." *USA Today*, July 1, 2013. www.usatoday.com/story/sports/college/2013/05/07/ncaa-finances-subsidies/2142443

Blanchard, Edward B., Eric Kuhn, Dianna L. Rowell, Edward J. Hickling, David Wittrock, Rebecca L. Rogers, Michelle R. Johnson, and Debra C. Steckler. "Studies of the vicarious traumatization of college students by the September 11th attacks: Effects of proximity, exposure, and connectedness." *Behavior Research and Therapy* 42 (2004): 191–205.

Bohlin, Virginia. "Antiques and collectibles." *Boston Globe*, December 9, 2012. www.bostonglobe.com/lifestyle/travel/2012/12/09/antiques-collectibles/QCzAJB5jzaRPvdNSdG4JWP/story.html

Boorstin, Daniel. *The Image*. New York: Vintage Books, 1961.

Boston Globe. "Rubbernecking: Put a screen on it." August 22, 2011. www.boston.com/bostonglobe/editorial_opinion/editorials/articles/2011/08/22/rubbernecking_put_a_sheet_on_it

Bowlby, John. *Attachment*. 2nd ed. New York: Basic Books, 1983.

Boyd, Robert, and Richerson, Peter J. *Culture and the Evolutionary Process*. Chicago: University of Chicago Press, 1985.

Braudy, Leo. *The Frenzy of the Renown: Fame and Its History.* 2nd ed. New York: Vintage, 1997.

Brown, Stephanie, Randolph M. Resse, Amiram D. Vonokur, and Dylan M. Smith. "Providing social support may be more beneficial than receiving it: Results from a prospective study of mortality." *Psychological Science* 14, no. 4 (July 2003): 320–27.

Brumberg, Joan Jacobs. *The Body Project: An Intimate History of American Girls.* New York: Vintage, 1998.

Bushman, Brad J., and Craig A. Anderson. "Media violence and the American public: Scientific facts versus media misinformation." *American Psychologist* 56, no. 6/7 (June/July 2001): 477–89.

Buss, David M. *The Evolution of Desire.* Rev. ed. New York: Basic Books, 2003.

Cannon, Lou. *President Reagan: The Role of a Lifetime.* New York: Simon and Schuster, 1991.

Carnegie, Dale. *How to Win Friends and Influence People.* New York: Simon and Schuster, 1936.

Carter, Charles. "Letter writing lunacy." *Picture Play*, November 1920.

Caughey, John L. "Artificial social relations in modern America." *American Quarterly* 30 (Spring 1978): 70–89.

Centers for Disease Control. "Rates of homicide, suicide, and firearm-related death among children—26 industrialized countries." *Morbidity and Mortality Weekly Report* 46, no. 05 (February 7, 1997): 101–5. www.cdc.gov/mmwr/preview/mmwrhtml/00046149.htm

Chiao, Joan Y., Nicholas E. Bowman, and Harleen Gill. "The political gender gap: Gender bias in facial inferences that predict voting behavior." *PLoS One* 3, no. 10 (October 31, 2008): e3666. doi:10.1371/journal.pone.0003666

Congress of the New Urbanism. "Charter of the New Urbanism." www.cnu.org/charter

Cooper, Al. "Sexuality and the internet: Surfing into the new millennium." *Cyberpsychology and Behavior* 1, no. 2 (Summer 1998): 187–93. doi:10.1089/cpb.1998.1.187

Cooper, Helene, and Brian Stelter. "Obamas' uninvited guests prompt an inquiry." *New York Times*, November 26, 2009. www.nytimes.com/2009/11/27/us/politics/27party.html

Coughlin, Patrick J., and Frank Janacek Jr. "A review of R. J. Reynolds' internal documents produced in Mangini vs. R. J. Reynolds Tobacco Company, Civil Number 939359: The case that rid California and the American landscape of 'Joe Camel.'" 1997. http://legacy.library.ucsf.edu/research/doc_research_mangini.jsp

Crouthamel, James L. *Bennett's New York Herald and the Rise of the Popular Press.* Syracuse, NY: Syracuse University Press, 1989.

Cunningham, Michael. "Measuring the physical in physical attractiveness: Quasi-experiments on the sociobiology of female facial beauty." *Journal of Personality and Social Psychology* 50, no. 5 (May 1986): 925–35.

Czitrom, Daniel J. *Media and the American Mind: From Morse to McLuhan.* Chapel Hill: University of North Carolina Press, 1982.

Danaei, Goodharz, Eric L. Ding, Dariush Mozaffarian, Ben Taylor, Jurgen Rehm, Christopher J. L. Murray, and Majid Ezzati. "The preventable causes of death in the United States: Comparative risk assessment of dietary, lifestyle, and metabolic risk factors." *PLoS Medicine* 6, no. 4 (2009): e1000058. doi:10.1371/journal.pmed.1000058

Danner, Fred W. "A national longitudinal study of the association between hours of TV viewing and the trajectory of BMI growth among US children." *Journal of Pediatric Psychology* 33, no. 10 (2008): 1100–1107.

Darwin, Charles. *On the Origin of Species by Means of Natural Selection, or the Preservation of Favoured Races in the Struggle for Life.* London: Murray, 1859.

De Backer, Charlotte J. S., Mark Nelissen, Patrick Vyncke, Johan Braeckman, and Francis T. McAndrew. "Celebrities: From teachers to friends. A test of two hypotheses on the adaptiveness of celebrity gossip." *Human Nature* 18 (2007): 334–54.

Della Cava, Marco R. "Searching the Web for the next big thing!" *USA Today*, May 30–June 1, 2008. http://bregentertainmentmarketing.blogspot.com/2008/06/searching-web-for-next-big-thing.html

Derrick, Jaye L., Shira Gabriel, and Kurt Hugenberg. "Social surrogacy: How favored television programs provide the experience of belonging." *Journal of Experimental Social Psychology* 45, no. 2 (February 2009): 352–62.

Derrick Jaye L., Shira Gabriel, and Brooke Tippin. "Parasocial relationships and self-discrepancies: Faux relationships have benefits for low self-esteem individuals." *Personal Relationships* 15, no. 2 (June 2008): 261–80.

Detweiler, Jerusha B., Brian T. Bedell, Peter Salovey, Emily Pronin, and Alexander Rothman. "Message framing and sunscreen use: Gain framed messages motivate beachgoers." *Health Psychology* 18 (March 1999): 189–96.

Di Chiara, Gaetano, and Imperato Assunta. "Drugs abused by humans preferentially increase synaptic dopamine concentrations in the mesolimbic system of freely moving rats." *Proceedings of the National Academy of Sciences* 85, no. 14 (1988): 5274–78.

Di Chiara, Gaetano, Gianluigi Tanda, Cristina Cadoni, Elio Acquas, Valentina Bassareo, and Ezio Carboni. "Homologies and differences in the action of drugs of abuse and a conventional reinforcer (food) on dopamine transmission: An interpretive framework of the mechanism of drug dependence." *Advances in Pharmacology* 42 (1997): 983–87.

Didion, Joan. "Insider Baseball." *New York Review of Books*, October 27, 1988.

Disaster Center. *United States Crime Rates 1960–2013*. www.disastercenter.com/crime/us-crime.htm

Dublin, Thomas. "Women, work, and protest in the early Lowell mills: 'The oppressing hand of avarice would enslave us.'" *Labor History* 16, no. 1 (Winter 1975): 99–116.

Dunbar, Robin I. M. "Gossip in evolutionary perspective." *Review of General Psychology* 8, no. 2 (2004): 100–110.

Egan, Timothy. "After Simpson trial, inquiries and deals." *New York Times*, October 6, 1995.

Elder, Glen H., Jr. "Appearance and education on marriage mobility." *American Sociological Review* 34, no. 4 (August 1969): 519–33.

Elliott, Stuart. "Madison Avenue's chief seer." *New York Times,* March 22, 2009.

———. "The media business: Advertising—Camel's success and controversy." *New York Times*, December 12, 1991.

Engels, Rutger C. M. E., Roel Hermans, Rick B. van Baaren, Tom Hollenstein, and Sandra M. Bot. "Alcohol portrayal on television affects actual drinking behavior." *Alcohol and Alcoholism* 44, no. 3 (2009): 244–49.

Epstein, Edward J. "Dumb money—The madness of movie advertising." *Slate Online Magazine*, June 6, 2005. www.slate.com/id/2120335

Epstein, Leonard H., James N. Roemmich, Jodi L. Robinson, Rocco A. Paluch, Dana D. Winiewicz, Janene H. Fuerch, and Thomas N. Robinson. "A randomized trial of the effects of reducing television viewing and computer use on body mass index in young children." *Archives of Pediatrics and Adolescent Medicine* 162, no. 3 (2008): 239–45.

Erikson, Erik. *Childhood and Society*. New York: Norton, 1950.

Etcoff, Nancy. *Survival of the Prettiest: The Science of Beauty*. New York: Doubleday, 1999.

Eyal, Keren, and Jonathan Cohen. "When good friends say goodbye: A parasocial breakup study." *Journal of Broadcasting and Electronic Media* 50, no. 3 (September 2006): 502–23.

Federal Bureau of Investigation. *Uniform Crime Reports, Crimes in the United States 2012.* www.fbi.gov/about-us/cjis/ucr/crime-in-the-u.s/2012/crime-in-the-u.s.-2012/tables/1tabledatadecoverviewpdf/table_1_crime_in_the_united_states_by_volume_and_rate_per_100000_inhabitants_1993-2012.xls

Fein, Robert A., and Bryan Vossekuil. "Preventing attacks on public officials and public figures: A secret service perspective." In *The Psychology of Stalking: Clinical and Forensic Perspectives,* edited by J. Reid Meloy, 175–91. San Diego, CA: Academic Press, 1998.

Field, Allison E., Lillian Cheung, Anne M. Wolf, David B. Herzog, Steven L. Gortmaker, and Graham A. Colditz. "Exposure to the mass media and weight concerns among girls." *Pediatrics* 103, no. 3 (March 1999): 36–41.

Filene, Edward. *Successful Living in the Machine Age World.* New York: Thomas Y. Crowell, 1931.

Fiorino, Dennis F., and Anthony G. Phillips. "Facilitation of sexual behavior and enhanced dopamine efflux in the nucleus accumbens of male rats after D-amphetamine behavioral sensitization." *Journal of Neuroscience* 19, no. 1 (1999): 456–63.

Fischer, Paul M., Meyer P. Schwartz, John W. Richards Jr., Adam O. Goldstein, and Tina H. Rojas. "Brand logo recognition by children aged 3 to 6 years: Mickey Mouse and Old Joe the Camel." *Journal of the American Medical Association* 266, no. 22 (December 1991): 3145–48.

Forbes. "The world's most powerful celebrities." June 30, 2014. www.forbes.com/celebrities/list/#tab:overall

Frieze, Irene H., Josephine E. Olson, and Deborah C. Good. "Perceived and actual discrimination in the salaries of male and female managers." *Journal of Applied Social Psychology* 20, no. 1 (January 1990): 46–67

Fryar, Cheryl D., Margaret P. Carroll, and Cynthia L. Ogden. "Prevalence of obesity among children and adolescents: United States, trends 1963–1965 through 2009–2010." *NCHS Health E-Stat.* Washington, DC: Centers for Disease Control and Prevention, September 2012). www.cdc.gov/nchs/data/hestat/obesity_child_09_10/obesity_child_09_10.pdf

Gabler, Neal. *Life: The Movie.* New York: Vintage Books, 1998.

———. *Winchell.* New York: Vintage Books, 1994.

Gainsbury, Sally M., Alex Russell, Nerilee Hing, Robert Wood, Dan I. Lubman, and Alex Blaszczynski. "The prevalence and determinants of problem gambling in Australia: Assessing the impact of interactive gambling and new technologies." *Psychology of Addictive Behaviors* 28, no. 3 (September 2014): 769–79.

Gearhardt, Ashley J., Sonja Yokum, Patrick T. Orr, Eric Stice, William R. Corbin, and Kelly D. Brownell. "Neural correlates of food addiction." *Archives of General Psychiatry* 68, no. 8 (2011): 808–16.

Gladwell, Malcolm. *Blink.* New York: Little, Brown and Company, 2005.

Goodwin, Donald W. "Alcoholism and heredity." *Archives of General Psychiatry* 36, no. 1 (1979): 57–61.

Gormley, Michael. "Top magazines agree to keep tobacco ads from school copies." Associated Press, June 20, 2005.

Grabe, Shelly, Monique L. Ward, and Janet S. Hyde. "The role of the media in body image concerns among women: A meta-analysis of experimental and correlational studies." *Psychological Bulletin* 134, no. 3 (May 2008): 460–76.

Greenberg, Jeff, Spee Kosloff, Sheldon Solomon, Florette Cohen, and Mark Landau. "Toward understanding the fame game: The effect of mortality salience on the appeal of fame." *Self and Identity* 9, no. 1 (2010): 1–18.

Griffin, Gary, and Harry Harlow. "Effects of three months of total social separation on adjustment and learning in the rhesus monkey." *Child Development* 37, no. 3 (1966): 533–47.

Griffiths, Mark, "Internet gambling: Issues, concerns, and recommendations." *Cyberpsychology and Behavior* 6, no. 6 (2003): 557–68. doi:10.1089/109493103322725333

Gunning, Tom. *D. W. Griffith and the Origins of the American Narrative Film*. Chicago: University of Illinois Press, 1991.

Halpern, Jake. *Fame Junkies*. Boston: Houghton Mifflin, 2007.

Hargreaves, Duane A., and Marika Tiggemann. "Muscular ideal media images and men's body image: Social comparison processing and individual vulnerability." *Psychology of Men and Masculinity* 12, no. 2 (April 2009): 109–19.

Harlow, Harry, and Robert Zimmerman. "The development of affective responses in infant monkeys." *Proceedings of the American Philosophical Society* 102, no. 5 (1958): 501–9.

Harris, Neil. *Humbug: The Art of P. T. Barnum*. Chicago: University of Chicago Press, 1973.

Harrison, Kristen, and Bradley J. Bond. "Gaming magazines and the drive for muscularity in preadolescent boys: A longitudinal examination." *Body Image* 4 (2007): 269–77.

———. "Ideal-body print media and preadolescent boys' drive for muscularity." Paper presented at the 104th annual meeting of the American Psychological Association, New Orleans, August 2006.

Hartley, Cecil B. *The Gentlemen's Book of Etiquette, and Manual of Politeness: Being a Complete Guide for a Gentleman's Conduct in All His Relations towards Society . . . from the Best French, English, and American Authorities*. Boston: DeWolfe, Fiske and Co., 1873.

Hawkins, Nicole, P. Scott Richards, H. Mac Granley, and David M. Stein. "The impact of exposure to the thin-ideal media image on women." *Eating Disorders* 12, no. 1 (2004): 35–50.

Henrich, Joseph, and Francisco J. Gil-White. "The evolution of prestige." *Evolution and Human Behavior* 22, no. 3 (May 2001): 165–96.

Hermes, Joke. "Media figures in identity construction." In *Rethinking the Media Audience: The New Agenda*, edited by Pertti Alasuutari, 69–85. London: Sage, 1999.

———. *Reading Women's Magazines: An Analysis of Everyday Media Use*. Cambridge: Polity Press, 1995.

Heron, Melonie. "Deaths: Leading causes for 2010." *National Vital Statistics Reports* 62, no. 6 (December 20, 2013). www.cdc.gov/nchs/data/nvsr/nvsr62/nvsr62_06.pdf

Herr, Norman. "Television and health." 2007. www.csun.edu/science/health/docs/tv&health.html

Hervey, George W. *The Principles of Courtesy: With Hints and Observations on Manners and Habits*. New York: Harper and Brothers, 1856.

Hipple, Steven F. "Self-employment in the United States: An update." *Monthly Labor Review*, July 2004.

———. "Self-employment in the United States." *Monthly Labor Review*, September 2010.

Hobbs, Frank, and Nicole Stoops. *Demographic Trends in the 20th Century: Census 2000 Special Reports*. CENSR-4. Washington, DC: U.S. Government Printing Office, 2002.

Hobza, Cody L., and Aaron B. Rochlen. "Gender role conflict, drive for muscularity, and the impact of ideal media portrayals on men." *Psychology of Men and Masculinity* 10, no. 2.

Horton, Donald, and Richard R. Wahl. "Mass communication and parasocial relationships: Observations on intimacy at a distance." *Psychiatry* 19, no. 3 (1956): 215–29.

Houston-Price, Carmel, and Satsuki Nakai. "Distinguishing novelty and familiarity effects in infant preference procedures." *Infant and Child Development* 13, no. 4 (December 2004): 341–48.

Ihrke, David K., and Carol S. Faber. *Geographical Mobility: 2005 to 2010. Population Characteristics.* P20-567. Washington, DC: U.S. Department of Commerce, Economics and Statistics Administration, U.S. Census Bureau, December 2012. www.census.gov/prod/2012pubs/p20-567.pdf

Independent PR Source. "Neil Armstrong signed check earns record-setting $27,350 at auction." July 16, 2009. www.auctioncentralnews.com/index.php/auctions/auction-results/1159-neil-armstrong-signed-check-makes-27350-after-all-night-bidding-war?format=pdf

Institute of Medicine. "Overview of the IOM report on food marketing to youth: Threat or opportunity." December 2005. www.iom.edu/~/media/Files/Report%20Files/2005/Food-Marketing-to-Children-and-Youth-Threat-or-Opportunity/KFMOverviewfinal2906.pdf

James, Clive. *Fame in the 20th Century.* New York: Random House, 1993.

James, William. *The Principles of Psychology.* New York: Holt, 1890.

Jenkins, Kristi R., and Nancy H. Fultz. "The relationship of older adults' activities and body mass index." *Journal of Aging and Health* 20, no. 2 (2008): 217–34.

Jhally, Sut. *Advertising and the End of the World* (motion picture). Northampton, MA: Media Education Foundation, 1998.

Judge, Timothy A., and Daniel M. Cable. "The effect of physical height on workplace success and income: Preliminary test of a theoretical model." *Journal of Applied Psychology* 89, no. 3 (June 2004):426–41.

Kaiser Family Foundation. "Generation M2: Media in the lives of 8–18-year olds." January 20, 2010. www.kff.org/entmedia/mh012010pkg.cfm

Kanealy, Pamela, Neil Frude, and William Shaw, "Influence of children's physical attractiveness on teacher expectations." *Journal of Social Psychology* 128, no. 3 (1988): 373–83.

Karch, Steven B. *A Brief History of Cocaine.* 2nd ed. Boca Raton, FL: CRC Press, 2005.

Kendler, Kenneth, and Carol Prescott. "Cocaine use, abuse, and dependence in a population." *British Journal of Psychiatry* 173 (1998): 345–50.

———. "Cannabis use, abuse, and dependence in a population-based sample of female twins." *American Journal of Psychiatry* 155, no. 8 (1998): 1016–22.

Khantzian, Edward. "The self-medication hypothesis of addictive disorders: focus on heroin and cocaine dependence." *American Journal of Psychiatry* 142, no. 11 (1985): 1259–64.

Kilbourne, Jean. "'The more you subtract, the more you add'; Cutting girls down to size." In *Psychology and Consumer Culture*, edited by Tim Kasser and Allen D. Kanner, 251–70. Washington, DC: American Psychological Association, 2004.

Kindlon, Dan. *Too Much of a Good Thing.* New York: Hyperion, 2003.

Kohut, Heinz. *The Analysis of the Self: A Systemic Approach to the Psychoanalytic Treatment of Narcissistic Personality Disorders.* Chicago: University of Chicago Press, 1971.

Konrad, Alex. "Even with record prices, expect a $10 million Super Bowl ad soon." *Forbes*, February 2, 2013.

Kuczynski, Jurgen. *The Rise of the Working Class.* New York: McGraw-Hill, 1967.

Kunstler, James H. *The Geography of Nowhere: The Rise and Decline of America's Manmade Landscape.* New York: Simon and Schuster, 1993.

Lagorio, Christine. "Marilyn Monroe auction nets $150K." Associated Press, June 5, 2005. www.cbsnews.com/news/marilyn-monroe-auction-nets-150k

Langlois, Judith H., Jean M. Ritter, Rita J. Casey, and Douglas B. Sawin. "Infant attractiveness predicts maternal behaviors and attitudes." *Developmental Psychology* 31, no. 3 (May 1995): 464–72.

Langlois, Judith H., Jita M. Ritter, Lori A. Roggman, and Lesley S. Vaughn. "Facial diversity and infant preferences for attractive faces." *Developmental Psychology* 27, no. 1 (1991): 79–84.

Langlois, Judith H., Lori A. Roggman, Rita J. Casey, Jean M. Ritter, Loretta A. Rieser-Danneer, and Vivian Y. Jenkins. "Infant preferences for attractive faces: Rudiments of a stereotype." *Developmental Psychology* 23, no. 3 (May 1987): 363–89.

Lavrakas, Paul J. "Female preference for male physiques." *Journal of Research in Personality* 9, no. 4 (December 1975): 324–34.

Leipzig, Adam. "The Sundance odds get even longer." *New York Times*, January 16, 2005.

Levy, Michael. "Listening to our clients: The prevention of relapse." *Journal of Psychoactive Drugs* 40, no. 2 (June 2008): 167–72.

Lincoln Institute. "Speech at Peoria, October 16, 1854." www.mrlincolnandfreedom.org/inside.asp?ID=11&subjectID=2

Lippmann, Walter. "Blazing Publicity." In *Vanity Fair: A Cavalcade of the 1920s and 1930s*, edited by Cleveland Amory and Frederic Bradlee. New York: Viking Press, 1960.

Little, Anthony C., Robert P. Burriss, Benedict C. Jones, and S. Craig Roberts. "Facial appearance affects voting decisions." *Evolution and Human Behavior* 28, no. 1 (January 2007): 18–27.

Little, Anthony C., S. Craig Roberts, Benedict C. Jones, and Lisa M. DeBruine. "The perception of attractiveness and trustworthiness in male faces affects hypothetical voting decisions differently in wartime and peacetime scenarios." *Quarterly Journal of Experimental Psychology* 65, no. 10 (October 2012): 2018–32. http://dx.doi.org/10.1080/17470218.2012.677048

Lorenz, Valerie C. "State lotteries and compulsive gambling." *Journal of Gambling Studies* 6, no. 4 (Winter 1990): 383–96.

Loy, David R. "The nonduality of life and death: A Buddhist view of repression." *Philosophy East and West* 40, no. 2 (April 1990): 151–74.

Lumeng, Julie C., Danielle Appugliese, Howard J. Cabral, Robert H. Bradley, and Barry Zuckerman. "Neighborhood safety and overweight status in children." *Archives of Pediatric and Adolescent Medicine* 160, no. 1 (2006): 25–31.

Lumeng, Julie C., Sahand Rahnama, Danielle Appugliese, Niko Kaciroti, and Robert H. Bradley. "Television exposure and overweight risk in preschoolers." *Archives of Pediatrics and Adolescent Medicine* 160, no. 4 (2006): 417–22.

Lyubomirsky, Sonja, Kennon M. Sheldon, and David Schkade. "Pursuing happiness: The architecture of sustainable change." *Review of General Psychology* 9, no. 2 (2005): 111–31.

Maas, Luis C., Scott E. Lukas, Marc J. Kaufman, Roger D. Weiss, Sarah L. Daniels, Veronica W. Rogers, Thellea J. Kukes, and Perry F. Rendsaw. "Functional magnetic resonance imaging of human brain activation during cue-induced cocaine craving." *American Journal of Psychiatry* 155 no. 1 (January 1998): 124–26.

MacDonald, Geoff, and Mark R. Leary. "Why does social exclusion hurt? The relationship between social and physical pain." *Psychological Bulletin* 131, no. 2 (2005): 202–23.

Mack, John E., and Steven L. Ablon, eds. *The Development and Sustaining of Self-Esteem in Childhood.* New York: International Universities Press, 1983.

Mahajan, Namrata, Jessica B. Clevering, and Dana C. Turcotte. "Celebrity gossip as a form of downward social comparison." Paper presented at the American Psychological Association Conference, San Francisco, August 2007.

Maltby, John, Liz Day, David Giles, Ralphael Gillett, Marianne Quick, Honey Langcaster-James, and P. Alex Linley. "Implicit theories of a desire for fame." *British Journal of Psychology* 99, no. 2 (May 2008): 279–92.

Mangini v. R. J. Reynolds Tobacco Co., 7 Cal. 4th 1057, 1073–74 (1994).http://legacy.library.ucsf.edu/tid/dyf53a00

Marcus, Stephanie. "Why people like the Kardashians: People aspire to be them or to befriend them says E! president." *Huffington Post*, December 30, 2011. www.huffingtonpost.com/2011/12/30/why-people-like-the-kardashians-people-aspire-to-be-them-or-befriend-them-e-president-suzanne-kolb-_n_1176250.html

Maslow, Abraham. "A theory of human motivation." *Psychological Review* 50, no. 4 (July 1943): 370–96.

———. *Motivation and Personality*. New York: Harper and Row, 1954.

May, Lary. *Screening Out the Past: The Birth of Mass Culture and the Motion Picture Industry*. Chicago: University of Chicago Press, 1983.

Mayerowitz, Scott. "Capt. Chesley 'Sully' Sullenberger auctions captain's hat." December 11, 2009. http://abcnews.go.com/Travel/BusinessTraveler/capt-chesley-sully-sullenberger-auctions-captains-hat/story?id=9311875

McCarthy, Colman. "In thingdom, laying waste our powers." *Washington Post*, November 11, 1990.

McCutcheon, Lynn E., John Maltby, James Houran, and Diane D. Ashe. *Celebrity Worshipers: Inside the Minds of Stargazers*. Baltimore: PublishAmerica, 2004.

McGinness, Joe. *The Selling of the President*. New York: Penguin, 1988.

McGregor, Jena. "Tackling college football coaches' high pay." *Washington Post*, November 7, 2014. www.washingtonpost.com/blogs/on-leadership/wp/2013/11/07/tackling-college-football-coaches-high-pay

Mead, Margaret. Speech given at Richdale Community College, Richdale, TX, 1977.

Merriam-Webster. www.merriam-webster.com/dictionary/gossip

Mirror.co.uk. "'Winning is my only chance to be normal': The beauty pageant where the top prize is plastic surgery." April 27, 2012. www.mirror.co.uk/news/real-life-stories/miss-cosmetic-surgery-2012-the-beauty-807928

Morton, Robert J., and Hilts, Mark A., eds. *Serial Murder: Multi-Disciplinary Perspectives for Investigators*. Washington, DC: Behavioral Analysis Unit, National Center for the Analysis of Violence, Federal Bureau of Investigation, U.S. Department of Justice, July 2008). www.fbi.gov/stats-services/publications/serial-murder/serial-murder-july-2008-pdf

Moving Picture World. "How the cinematographer works and some of his difficulties." May 18, 1907. http://ia601200.us.archive.org/15/items/MPW01-1907-05/MPW01-1907-05.pdf

Mulgrew, Kate E., Diana Volcevski-Kostas, and Peter G. Rendell. "The effect of music video clips on adolescent boys' body image, mood, and schema activation." *Journal of Youth and Adolescence* 43, no. 1 (January 2014): 92–103.

Munsterberg, Hugo. *The Photoplay: A Psychology Study*. New York: D. Appleton and Company, 1916.

Museum of Broadcast Communications. "Marcus Welby, MD. U.S. medical drama." www.museum.tv/eotv/marcuswelby.htm

Myers, David. "The secret to happiness: Look inside at what actually gives you joy, and the good life may be closer than you think." *Yes!*, June 18, 2004.

National Institute on Drug Abuse. *Comorbidity: Addiction and Mental Illnesses*. NIH Publication No. 10-5771. Washington, DC: U.S. Department of Health and Human Services, December 2008, rev. September 2010.

————. *Drugs, Brains, and Behavior: The Science of Addiction*. NIH Publication No. 14-5605. July 2014. www.drugabuse.gov/sites/default/files/soa_2014.pdf

————. *The Science of Drug Abuse and Addiction: The Basics*. Updated 2014. www.drugabuse.gov/publications/media-guide/science-drug-abuse-addiction-basics

National Park Service. "The Lincoln-Douglas debates of 1858." www.nps.gov/liho/historyculture/debates.htm

Newport, Frank, David Moore, and Lydia Saad. "Most admired men and women: 1948–1998: Fascinating parade of personalities voted most admired over last half century." Gallup News Service, December 13, 1999. www.gallup.com/poll/1678/Most-Admired-Man-Woman.aspx

New York Herald. "Mademoiselle Jenny Lind." September 16, 1850. http://chnm.gmu.edu/lostmuseum/lm/164

Nunez-Smith, Marcella, Elizabeth E. Wolf, Helen M. Huang, Ezekiel J. Emanuel, and Cary P. Gross. "Media and child and adolescent health: A systematic review." 2008. http://ipsdweb.ipsd.org/uploads/IPPC/CSM%20Media%20Health%20Report.pdf

Okun, Morris A., Ellen W. Yeung, and Stephanie Brown. "Volunteering by older adults and risk of mortality: A meta-analysis." *Psychology and Aging* 28, no. 2 (2013): 564–77.http://dx.doi.org/10.1037/a0031519

Oliver, J. Eric. "Mental life and the metropolis in suburban America. The psychological correlates of metropolitan place characteristics." *Urban Affairs Review* 39, no. 2 (2003): 228–53. doi:10.1177/1078087403254445

Olivola, Christopher, and Alexander Todorov. "Elected in 100 milliseconds: Appearance-based trait inferences and voting." *Journal of Nonverbal Behavior* 34, no. 2 (June 2010): 83–110.

————. "The look of a winner." *Scientific American*, May 9, 2009, www.scientificamerican.com/article/the-look-of-a-winner

OpenSecrets.org. "Money web." www.opensecrets.org/PRES08/moneyweb.php?cycle=2008

Oxford Dictionaries. "Oxford Dictionaries word of the year in 2013 is selfie." http://blog.oxforddictionaries.com/2013/11/word-of-the-year-2013-winner

Pearson, Roberta. *Eloquent Gestures*. Berkeley: University of California Press, 1992.

Pew Research Center. *How Young People View Their Lives, Futures, and Politics: A Portrait of "Generation X."* Washington, DC: Pew Research Center for the People and the Press, January 9, 2007. http://pewsocialtrends.org/files/2010/10/300.pdf

Pierce, Justin. "Family time decreasing with Internet use." University of Southern California, Annenberg School for Communication, Center for the Digital Future, June 16, 2009. http://mail-dog.com/pics/justkid/library/cdf_family_time.pdf

Pillemer, Karl, Thomas E. Fuller-Rowell, M. C. Reid, and Nancy M. Well. "Environmental volunteering and health outcomes over a 20-year period." *The Gerontologist* 50, no. 5 (October 2010): 594–602.

Postman, Neil. *Amusing Ourselves to Death*. New York: Penguin Books, 1985.

Pray, Isaac C. *Memoirs of James Gordon Bennett and His Times by a Journalist*. New York: Stringer and Townsend, 1855.

Public Health Cigarette Smoking Act of 1969. www.gpo.gov/fdsys/pkg/STATUTE-84/pdf/STATUTE-84-Pg87-2.pdf

Putnam, Robert D. *Bowling Alone: The Collapse and Revival of American Community*. New York: Simon and Schuster, 2000.

Reed, Keith. "Fenway suites are even more luxurious." *Boston Globe*, April 9, 2007. www.boston.com/business/articles/2007/04/09/fenway_suites_are_even_more_luxurious

Richardson, Anna Steese. "Filmitis: The modern malady." *McClure's*, January 1916.

Richardson, Erin G., and David Hemenway. "Homicide, suicide and unintentional firearm fatality: Comparing the United States with other high-income countries." *Journal of Trauma* 70, no. 1 (2011): 238–43.

Richins, Marsha L. "Social comparison and idealized images of advertising." *Journal of Consumer Research* 18, no. 1 (1991): 71–83.

Robinson, John P., and Steve Martin. "What do happy people do?" *Social Indicators Research* 89, no. 3 (2008): 565–71.

Robinson, Thomas N. "Reducing children's television viewing to prevent obesity: A randomized controlled trial." *Journal of the American Medical Association* 282, no. 16 (1999): 1561–67.

Rockwell, Donna, and David C. Giles. "Being a celebrity: A phenomenology of fame." *Journal of Phenomenological Psychology* 40, no. 2 (2009): 178–210.

Rodriguez, Cindy. "Even in middle school, girls are thinking thin." *Boston Globe*, November 27, 1998.

Rose, Lacey. "The most expensive celebrity photos." *Forbes*, July 18, 2007. www.forbes.com/2007/07/17/celebrities-photojournalism-magazines-biz-media-cx_lr_0718celebphotos.html

Rose, Susan A., Allen W. Gottfried, Patricia Melloy-Carminar, and Wagner H. Bridger. "Familiarity and novelty preferences in infant recognition memory: Implications for information processing." *Developmental Psychology* 18, no. 5 (September 1982): 704–13.

Ross, Michael B., and John Salvia. "Attractiveness as a biasing factor in teacher judgments." *American Journal of Mental Deficiency* 80, no. 1 (July 1975): 96–98.

Salinger, J. D. *The Catcher in the Rye*. New York: Bantam, 1951.

Satcher, David. *Physical Activity and Health: A Report of the Surgeon General*. Atlanta: U.S. Department of Health and Human Services, Centers for Disease Control and Prevention, 1996.

Schickel, Richard. *Intimate Strangers: The Celebrity of Culture*. Garden City, NY: Doubleday, 1985.

Schuckit, Marc A. "Reactions to alcohol in sons of alcoholics and controls." *Alcoholism: Clinical and Experimental Research* 12, no. 4 (August 1988): 465–70.

Schuckit, Marc A., Donald W. Goodwin, and George Winokur. "A study of alcoholism in half siblings." *American Journal of Psychiatry* 128, no. 9 (March 1972): 1132–36.

Schuckit, Marc A., Tom L. Smith, and Jelger Kalmijn. "The search for genes contributing to the low level of response to alcohol: Patterns of findings across studies." *Alcoholism: Clinical and Experimental Research* 28, no. 10 (October 2004): 1449–58.

Schudson, Michael. *Discovering the News: A Social History of American Newspapers*. New York: Basic Books, 1978.

Schwartz, Carolyn, Janice B. Meisenhelder, Yuncheng B. Ma, and George Reed. "Altruistic social interest behaviors are associated with better mental health." *Psychosomatic Medicine* 65, no. 5 (2003): 778–85.

Seay, Bill, and Harry Harlow. "Maternal separation in the rhesus monkey." *Journal of Nervous and Mental Disease* 140, no. 6 (1965): 434–41.

Sechenov, Ivan. *Reflexes of the Brain*. Cambridge, MA: MIT Press, 1965.

Sheley, Joseph F., and James D. Wright. *Gun Acquisition and Possession in Selected Juvenile Samples*. Research in Brief. Washington, DC: U.S. Department of Justice, National Institute of Justice, Office of Juvenile Justice and Delinquency Prevention, 1993. www.ncjrs.gov/App/publications/abstract.aspx?ID=145326

Shelton, John L., and Raymond S. Sanders. "Mental health intervention in a campus homicide." *Journal of the American College Health Association* 21, no. 4 (April 1973): 346–50.

Signorelli, Nancy. "A content analysis: Reflections of girls in the media. A study of television shows and commercials, movies, music videos, and teen magazine articles and ads. An executive summary." Henry J. Kaiser Family Foundation and Children Now, April 1997.

Spigel, Lynn. *Welcome to the Dreamhouse: Popular Media and Postwar Suburbs.* Durham, NC: Duke University Press, 2001.

Stein, Jeannine. "Why girls as young as 9 fear fat and go on diets to lose weight." *Los Angeles Times*, October 29, 1986. http://articles.latimes.com/1986-10-29/news/vw-7933_1_eating-disorders

Steinmetz, Katy. "Top 10 buzzwords." *Time*, December 4, 2013. http://newsfeed.time.com/2013/12/04/pop-culture-and-social-media/slide/top-10-buzzwords

Stelter, Brian. "Calling story of boy and balloon a hoax, sheriff seeks felony charges." *New York Times*, October 18, 2009. www.nytimes.com/2009/10/19/us/19balloon.html

Strasburger, Victor C. "Adolescent sexuality and the media." *Pediatric Clinics of North America* 36, no. 3 (June 1989): 747–73.

Substance Abuse and Mental Health Services Administration. Results from the 2012 National Survey on Drug Use and Health: Mental Health Findings . NSDUH Series H-47. HHS Publication No. (SMA) 13-4805. Rockville, MD: Substance Abuse and Mental Health Services Administration, 2013.

Susman, Warren I. *Culture as History: The Transformation of American Society in the Twentieth Century.* New York: Pantheon, 1984.

Then, Deborah. "Women's magazines: Messages they convey about looks, men, and careers." Paper presented at the 100th annual meeting of the American Psychological Association, Washington, DC, August 2002.

Thoreau, Henry David. *Walden.* Boston: Houghton Mifflin, 1957.

Townsend, John M., and Gary D. Levy. "Effect of potential partners' physical attractiveness and socioeconomic status on sexuality and partner selection." *Archives of Sexual Behavior* 19, no. 2 (April 1990): 149–64.

———. "Effect of potential partners' costume and physical attractiveness on sexuality and partner selection." *Journal of Psychology: Interdisciplinary and Applied* 124, no. 4 (July 1990): 371–89.

Tsuang, Ming T., Michael J. Lyons, Joanne M. Meyer, Thomas Doyle, Seth A. Eisen, Jack Goldberg, William True, Nong Lin, Rosemary Toomey, and Lindon Eaves. "Co-occurrence of abuse of different drugs in men: The role of drug-specific and shared vulnerabilities." *Archives of General Psychiatry* 55 (1998): 967–72.

Turner, Graeme. *Understanding Celebrity.* London: Sage, 2004.

Twenge, Jean M., and W. Keith Campbell. *The Narcissism Epidemic. Living in the Age of Entitlement.* New York: Free Press, 2009.

Twenge, Jean M., Stacey M. Campbell, Brian J. Hoffman, and Charles E. Lance. "Generational differences in work values: Leisure and extrinsic values increasing, social and intrinsic values decreasing." *Journal of Management* 36, no. 5 (2010): 1117–42.

Twitchell, James B. *Adcult USA: The Triumph of Advertising in American Culture.* New York: Columbia University Press, 1996.

Udry, J. Richard, and Bruce K. Eckland. "Benefits of being attractive: Differential payoffs for men and women." *Psychological Reports* 54, no. 1 (February 1984): 47–56.

Uhls, Yalda T., and Patricia M. Greenfield. "The rise of fame: An historical content analysis." *Cyberpsychology: Journal of Psychosocial Research on Cyberspace* 5, no. 1, article 1 (2011). www.cyberpsychology.eu/view.php?cisloclanku=2011061601

Union of Concerned Scientists. "World scientists' warning to humanity." 1992. www.ucsusa.org/about/1992-world-scientists.html#.VEPlZMJOXIU

U.S. Bureau of Labor Statistics. "American time use survey: Charts from the American time use survey." September 30, 2014. www.bls.gov/tus/charts/home.htm

———. "Average weekly hours and overtime of all employees on private nonfarm payrolls by industry sector, seasonally adjusted." Economic News Release. Table B-2. March 6, 2015. www.bls.gov/news.release/empsit.t18.htm

———. *Historical Statistics of the United States 1789–1945*. Washington, DC: U.S. Bureau of Labor Statistics, 1949. www2.census.gov/prod2/statcomp/documents/HistoricalStatis-ticsoftheUnitedStates1789-1945.pdf

———. "Volunteering in the United States, 2013." February 25, 2013. www.bls.gov/news.release/volun.nr0.htm

U.S. Census Bureau. "Measuring America." February 3, 2014. www.census.gov/hhes/com-puter/files/2012/Computer_Use_Infographic_FINAL.pdf

USA Today. "*USA Today* college football coach salaries: Football bowl subdivision coaches, 2006–2014." www.usatoday.com/story/sports/2014/10/03/college-football-coach-salaries/16634823

Vandenbroucke, Guillaume. "Trends in hours: The U.S. from 1900 to 1950." *Journal of Economic Dynamics and Control* 33, no. 1 (January 2009): 237–49.

Voss, Gretchen. "Desperately seeking stardom." *Boston Globe*, June 17, 2007. www.boston.com/news/globe/magazine/articles/2007/06/17/desperately_seeking_stardom/?page=full

Warhol, Andy. *The Philosophy of Andy Warhol (From A to B and Back Again)*. New York: Harcourt Brace Jovanovich, 1975.

Weaver, George S. *Hopes and Helps for the Young of Both Sexes: Relating to the Formation of Character, Choice of Avocation, Health, Amusement, Music, Conversation, Cultivation of Intellect, Moral Sentiment, Social Affection, Courtship, and Marriage*. New York: Fowlers and Wells, 1854.

Wenn. "Hendrix guitar fetches $190,000 at auction." February 17, 2005. www.contactmusic.com/news-article/hendrix-guitar-fetches-190000-at-auction

Williams, Kipling D., and Steve A. Nida. "Ostracism: Consequences and coping." *Current Directions in Psychological Science* 20, no. 2 (2011): 71–75.

Willis, Thomas A. "Downward comparison principles in social psychology." *Psychological Bulletin* 90, no. 2 (1981): 245–71.

Wilson, David. "Helping behavior and physical attractiveness." *Journal of Social Psychology* 104, no. 2 (April 1978): 313–14.

Wilson, Duff. "Senate approves tight regulation over cigarettes." *New York Times*, June 12, 2009.

Wilson, Timothy D., David A. Reinhard, Erin C. Westgate, Daniel T. Gilbert, Nicole Ellerbeck, Cheryl Hahn, Casey L. Brown, and Adi Shaked. "Just think: The challenges of the disengaged mind." *Science* 345, no. 6192 (July 2014): 75–77.

Wingood, Gina M., Ralph J. DiClemente, Jay M. Bernhardt, Kathy Harrington, Susan L. Davies, Alyssa Robillard, and Edward W. Hook III. "A prospective study of exposure to rap music videos and African American female adolescents' prospective health." *American Journal of Public Health* 93, no. 3 (March 2003): 437–39.

Winick, Charles. "The functions of television: Life without the big box." In *Television as a Social Issue*, edited by Stuart Oskamp, 217–37. Newbury Park, CA: Sage, 1988.

Winnicott, Donald W. *The Maturational Process and the Facilitative Environment*. New York: International Universities Press, 1965.

Wyatt, Ian D., and Daniel E. Hecker. "Occupational changes in the 20th century." *Monthly Labor Review*, March 2006, 35–57.

Yamamoto, Rinah, Dan Ariely, Won Chi, Daniel D. Langleben, and Igor Elman. "Gender differences in the motivational processing of babies are determined by their facial attractiveness." *PLoS One* 4, no. 6 (2009): e6042. doi:10.1371/journal.pone.0006042

Young, Kimberly S. "Internet addiction: A new clinical phenomenon and its consequences." *American Behavioral Scientist* 48, no. 4 (2004): 402–15.

Young-Eisendrath, Polly. *Raising Confident and Compassionate Children in an Age of Self-Importance.* New York: Little, Brown, 2008.

Zaretsky, Eli. *Capitalism, the Family, and Personal Life.* New York: Harper Colophon Books, 1976.

INDEX

ABOUT THE AUTHOR

Michael S. Levy, PhD, is a clinical psychologist who is the director of substance use services at the North Shore Medical Center in Salem, Massachusetts. He also maintains a private practice in psychotherapy in Andover, Massachusetts, and is a lecturer in psychiatry at Harvard Medical School. He has often been interviewed on radio and television. Levy has published numerous articles and book chapters, gives many lectures and workshops, and is the author of one previous book, *Take Control of Your Drinking . . . And You May Not Need to Quit*.